Images of Change

Edited by
Dennis William Magill
and
William Michelson

Editorial assistance by
James Mackenzie Russell

Canadian Scholars' Press Inc. Torónto 1999

Images of Change
edited by Dennis William Magill and William Michelson

First published in 1999 by
Canadian Scholars' Press Inc.
180 Bloor Street West, Ste. 1202
Toronto, Ontario
M5S 2V6

We acknowledge the financial support of the Government of Canada through the Book Publishing Industry Development Programme for our publishing activities.

Canadian Cataloguing in Publication Data

Main entry under title:

Images of change

Includes bibliographical references.
ISBN 1-55130-170-9

1. Clark, S. D. (Samuel Delbert), 1910– . 2. Sociology—Canada. I. Magill, Dennis William, 1939– . II. Michelson, William, 1940– . III. Russell, James Mackenzie, 1973– .

HM479.C52I42 1999 301'.092 C99-932457-8

Page layout by Brad Horning
Cover design by James Mackenzie Russell

To S.D. and Rosemary Clark

CONTRIBUTORS

Dennis William Magill, Department of Sociology, University of Toronto
Douglas F. Campbell, Department of Sociology, University of Toronto
David A. Nock, Department of Sociology, Lakehead University
Harry H. Hiller, Department of Sociology, University of Calgary
Carl Berger, Department of History, University of Toronto
Deborah Harrison, Department of Sociology, University of New Brunswick
Richard Helmes-Hayes, Department of Sociology, University of Waterloo
S.D. Clark, Professor Emeritus, Department of Sociology, University of Toronto

CONTENTS

Preface
Dennis William Magill and William Michelson ix

Introduction
Lorne Tepperman xv

Chapter One
Social Science Paradigms
Dennis William Magill 1

Chapter Two
S.D. Clark: "The Dean of Canadian Sociology"
Douglas F. Campbell 39

Chapter Three
'Crushing the Power of Finance':
The Socialist Prairie Roots of S.D. Clark
David Nock 89

Chapter Four
Research Biography and Disciplinary Development:
S.D. Clark and Canadian Sociology
Harry H. Hiller 115

Chapter Five
Reorientation: S.D. Clark
Carl Berger 137

Chapter Six
The Limits of Liberalism in Canadian Sociology:
Some Notes on S.D. Clark
Deborah Harrison 149

Chapter Seven
The Image of Inequality in S.D. Clark's Writings
on Pioneer Canadian Society
Richard C. Helmes-Hayes 175

Chapter Eight
The Study of Canadian Society
S.D. Clark 207

Chapter Nine
The Changing Image of Sociology in English-Speaking Canada
S.D. Clark 227

Appendix
Bibliography of S.D. Clark's Work
H.J. Hiller 241

PREFACE

It is certainly no exaggeration to say that Samuel Delbert Clark contributed significantly to the establishment of sociological research in Canada. Widely known as the "dean" of Canadian sociology, he taught sociology at the University of Toronto when few others were teaching the subject anywhere else in the country. He conducted a number of penetrating research projects on his native land and taught a generation of students who have since taught new generations of students across this nation and the world. He established and served as first Chair of the Department of Sociology at the University of Toronto which, as a consequence of his leadership and hiring practices, became a major setting and training ground for sociological research and teaching.

Clark served as President of both the Canadian Society for Sociology and Anthropology and the Royal Society of Canada. Since his formal retirement from the University of Toronto, he has continued to spread his knowledge. Born in 1910, S.D. Clark has advanced the development of sociology in Canada through most of the 20th century.

In this last year of the 1900s, the family and friends of S.D. Clark made a substantial contribution to establish the S.D. Clark Chair in Sociology at the University of Toronto, the first endowed chair in U of T's Department of Sociology. It enables members of the faculty to carry forward S.D. Clark's name and legacy in perpetuity and provides for the expansion of personnel and activities in the department. This Chair, in turn, is viewed as a signal honour accorded to its namesake, whose activities for so many years created departmental excellence, brought honour to the University of Toronto, and enriched the sociological examination of Canadian society.

This book is meant to accompany and complement the inauguration of the S.D. Clark Chair in Sociology. The President and Chancellor of the University of Toronto have already honoured Professor Clark on May 5, 1999, by means of a banquet in which he actively participated. Now, with this volume, we invite others who have not known Clark personally to understand and appreciate his impact upon the development of an academic discipline that plays such an important role in allowing us to understand who we are as Canadians. With this volume, we hope that the life's work of S.D. Clark will live beyond those who know S.D. Clark personally.

We decided in mid-July to embark on a project to edit a collection of essays written about Clark. Lorne Tepperman, the Department's Chair and a student of Clark, urged us to publish these papers as a book. His vision was that the book would be launched at the inaugural S.D. Clark lecture on October 29, 1999. We had busy schedules and were not sure we could meet a four-and-one-half month deadline. To meet this schedule, Professor Tepperman provided financial assistance so that we could employ James Russell for two months as an editorial assistant. Thank you, James, for your amazing organizational skills and assistance.

We have assembled in this volume some of the seminal writings by scholars who have examined and elaborated upon the work of S.D. Clark. Always appreciative, these writers are both positive and critical towards his work. Whether they agree or disagree with the directions or conclusions of his work, they unanimously view it as important. In the process, they show the intellectual and historical contexts in which S.D. Clark developed his approach and conducted his studies. They indicate his career paths. They detail the topics with which he dealt and the conclusions he reached.

The volume concludes with two chapters by Clark himself, reflecting different times and concerns. He is a scholar of many interests, and it is difficult—even in a collection of this size—to truly demonstrate the breadth of his inquiries. Nonetheless, this book attempts to make these apparent for all readers.

In addition to the papers written by Clark, this volume contains seven papers written about Clark. The first paper, by Dennis William Magill, identifies four social science paradigms that have emerged in English Canada:

Fabian, ecological, staple and frontier-social change. The first three had an intellectual influence on S.D. Clark; the fourth is Clark's own contribution to Canadian social science.

If Magill outlines the skeleton of Clark's approach, Douglas Campbell's paper provides, so to speak, the flesh and blood. The underlying assumptions of the frontier-social change paradigm are clearly specified and Campbell summarizes the ideas of The Clarkian Trilogy—*The Social Development of Canada, Church and Sect in Canada*, and *Movements of Political Protest in Canada*.

Both Magill and Campbell refer to the radicalism of the young Clark and in his paper, "Crushing the Power of Finance," David Nock specifically documents Clark's early democratic socialist ideology. Nock's position is that Clark's agrarian radicalism is implicit in his early writings, but that it wanes until the mid-1950s when it fades entirely from view.

Clark's bibliographer, Harry Hiller, is the author of the fourth essay. He places Clark's career within the disciplinary development of Canadian sociology. Hiller elaborates this analysis in his book *Society and Change: S.D. Clark and The Development of Canadian Sociology*. This book is recommended reading for any Clarkian scholar who is interested in the socio-historical influences on Clark's personal life and his research career.

Carl Berger's essay reinforces the fact that Clark made a major contribution to historical sociology. Berger observes that Clark's publications were rooted in the traditions of Harold Innis at a time when historians were disengaging themselves from this perspective.

Our sixth selection, by Deborah Harrison, explores a dichotomy in Clark's work, demonstrating that Clark was simultaneously the father of a collective Canadian sociology and an importer of the American individualist tradition.

Richard Helmes-Hayes' essay critically examines Clark's image and empirical descriptions of inequality on the Canadian pioneer frontier. His analysis leads him to conclude that Clark was a "romantic" who had an idealized view of the frontier. Clark's image, according to Helmes-Hayes, is rooted in a liberal individualist model of social structure. Thus, Clark's description of frontier life took on the character of celebration rather than just documentation; not entirely objective, it was an idealized version of what Clark would have liked to have been the case.

Clark's paper on the study of Canadian society is critical of human ecology, Marxism, and functionalism. Canadian society, he states, can only be examined from a historical perspective. Given this basic assumption, he presents his sociological view of social change.

The last article in this volume was published by Clark in 1979. He had witnessed the academic role of Canadian sociologists in the 1930s, '40s, '50s, '60s and '70s including the difficult period of 1968-1973. Those were troublesome years and they led to the stereotyping of sociology departments as centres of discord and disruption. But despite these conflicts, Clark noted that excellent work was being done in sociology at Canadian universities. It was his hope that, in time, such work would become recognized for what it was, and that sociology would again take its place as one of the accepted and well-regarded disciplines within the Canadian academic community and beyond.

We believe that time has proven him right. In the twenty years since Clark published his essay, sociology has become an integral part of the Canadian academic community. And it is safe to say that its role as a key social science discipline owes much to the research and legacy of Samuel Delbert Clark.

At the very least, S.D. Clark contributed to the development of sociological research on Canadian society if only because his own research mirrored the changing essence and challenges of that society itself. He did research on what worried him about his country. His work illuminated and helped in the understanding of situations into which few others had begun to delve. To study Clark's research is to study the ongoing development of Canadian society.

If this were not enough, S.D. Clark's research has other lessons to offer us today. He studied history, political science, economics and sociology, and he taught in departments that covered all of these subjects as well as anthropology. Although not an explicit advocate of interdisciplinarity, S.D. Clark is a truly interdisciplinary scholar. He draws on the considerations and materials of whatever is germane to his subject. His research and interpretations are not compromised by the limitations of disciplinary perspectives and research tools. This helps provide him with the well rounded, convincing interpretations he makes on many subjects.

Additionally, Clark draws on problematic situations in the real world as the basis for his work. He does not deal with theory for its own sake or with statistical elegance divorced from substantive meaning. His methods vary according to the subject matter. His research deals tangibly with the reality it examines. Though not generally considered to be a virtuoso with methodology, S.D. Clark gets to the heart of his research problems and conveys a far richer understanding than existed before.

Insofar as S.D. Clark's work has addressed the many contexts of Canadian life—political, socio-geographic, economic, social—he has given Canadians more knowledge of the world in which they live and how they might guide it more positively in the future. His sociological imagination exemplifies a genuine commitment to an enlightened public. Not only does this spirit of sociological endeavour distinguish Clark, but it is also a challenge to many others who profess the same field. Long may we heed his spirit and its virtues.

Dennis William Magill
Professor and Acting Chair,
Department of Sociology,
University of Toronto

William Michelson
S.D. Clark Chair of Sociology
and Associate Dean, Social Sciences,
University of Toronto

August, 1999

INTRODUCTION

It is awkward having to write the first words of a book that, as you will find out, provides a brief but comprehensive overview of the work of S.D. Clark. I could use this space to foreshadow what others will say more eloquently and authoritatively in the pages that follow, but I won't. Rather, I urge you to keep reading. This book contains a variety of views and debates that remind me not only of Professor Clark's contribution, but also of the rise of Canadian sociology as an intellectual enterprise. Thank you Dennis William Magill and Bill Michelson, for conceiving this magnificent tribute to the work of S.D. Clark, and thank you James Russell, for bringing it to completion. Older readers: read these pages and remember. Younger readers: read them and imagine.

So, allow me to use this space to express my own thanks and admiration for Professor Clark, who has been a teacher, colleague and friend for nearly forty years. As a teacher, Professor Clark took me on my first sociological field trip—in 1964, a one-week class trip to Kapuskasing where we learned firsthand about bi-cultural relations in a mill town, about interviewing, and about the effects of climate and topography on everyday life. (I had never before, and have never since, seen so much snow nor gotten myself so bone-chillingly cold.) Though, for the most part, not a field researcher or interviewer himself, Professor Clark knew it was important that budding sociologists at least learn what those activities looked like.

Having joined the Department of Sociology's faculty in 1970, I found Professor Clark to be a good colleague. Indeed, he did what any mentor should do for junior colleagues; namely, get them off to a good start. It was with Del's urging and intervention that I took on the Editorship of the McGraw-Hill Ryerson Series in Canadian Sociology. During the Series' 15-year life-span, we published some pretty good books. A number of our Toronto colleagues, including John Hagan, Jeffrey Reitz, Bonnie Erickson, Roger O'Toole, Warren Kalbach, and Clark himself, all contributed books, as did I. Whatever people may choose to think about that Series in retrospect, one thing is certain, my long-term association with it—almost a marriage, it seemed at times—pushed me into textbook writing and publishing far more decisively than I had ever planned or imagined. So, I ended up being a book-writer, and not a journal article writer, largely due to the influence of Professor Clark (who is also a book writer).

Finally, Del Clark's greatest influence, on me and on other students and colleagues, was by means of the example he set. Whether or not you agreed with what Clark had said or written, you knew that this was a man of integrity who took scholarship and sociology seriously. Though Clark railed (in writing and person) at a wide assortment of sociological foes—Parsons, Marx, survey researchers, symbolic interactionists, etc.—he was ready to give anyone a hearing, just so long as that person was also serious and scholarly. That's how the early Department of Sociology, which Clark established, came to resemble Noah's Ark; he made sure there were two of almost every variety. In this way, Clark showed me for the first time (though, happily, not the last) that scholarship and debate and sociology are worthy of a lifetime's effort, and that the University of Toronto is a worthy place to carry out those activities.

How fitting, therefore, that friends and family have now endowed a Chair in Sociology that will carry Professor Clark's name forever. William Michelson is the first holder of the S.D. Clark Chair in Sociology and, like Clark, he has made a truly outstanding contribution to the discipline. Michelson studies how people respond to their social and physical environments and searches for ways to improve those environments.

Many of Michelson's publications, like Clark's, have been lauded as major contributions to the field. He has represented Canada at UNESCO's Man and the Biosphere Program, developed research and policy for the government of Canada, and addressed audiences around the world. And, in one final comparison, Michelson, like his Chair's namesake, has the esteem of his peers, having been elected to the Royal Society of Canada in 1994 and to the Sociological Research Association in 1998.

With this in mind, I invite you to read on. Share with all of us who know Professor Clark personally some sense of what sociology in Canada has been, the struggles it has faced and, most importantly, what it can become. Today, sociology's future seems assured; let us never forget that Professor Samuel Delbert Clark helped get the ball rolling.

Lorne Tepperman
Professor and Chair,
Department of Sociology,
University of Toronto

Chapter One

SOCIAL SCIENCE PARADIGMS

Dennis William Magill

Introduction

The untrained mind views the social world as a maze of confused and unrelated events. The social scientific mind views the world through a framework or gestalt. It weaves fragmented events together within a systematic frame of reference. This framework is called a paradigm.

More broadly defined, a paradigm is *a set of mental images* shared by a number of individuals within an academic discipline. As Ritzer notes, a paradigm is "...a fundamental image of the subject matter within a science. It serves to define what should be studied, what questions should be asked, how they should be asked, and what rules should be followed in interpreting the answers obtained. The paradigm is the broadest unit of consensus within a science and serves to differentiate one scientific community (or sub-community) from another." [1] Thus, a paradigm facilitates communications among individuals who share the same vocabulary.

The concept of paradigm in this essay is used to convey a set of mental images that guide research. It should not be inferred that there are systematic theoretical models. For example, S.D. Clark's biographer notes that "Clark was no theorist and even rejected the idea of establishing a theory of social change." Harry H. Hiller. (1982). *Society and Change: S.D. Clark and the Development of Canadian Society*. Toronto: University of Toronto Press. p. 78.

The concept of paradigm can be used in identifying various theoretical approaches to the study of society. At a very general level, it isolates a set of mental images shared by a group of individuals. In this chapter, four paradigms that have emerged in English Canada will be considered: the Fabian, the ecological, the staple, and the frontier-social change. The first three were selected because they had an intellectual influence on Samuel Delbert Clark. At the London School of Economics, from 1932 to 1933, Clark was exposed to the Fabian socialist paradigm as well as the ideas of the Marxist Harold Laski and the Christian socialist R.H. Tawney. As a young man at the University of Toronto, he attended meetings of the Fabian inspired League for Social Reconstruction. Nock argues that the young Clark "…was a democratic socialist from a radical prairie background who clearly and explicitly rejected liberal individualism and competitive and corporate capitalism..."[2] In the early 1930s, he studied human ecology in the Department of Sociology at McGill University. Human ecology assumptions were later incorporated into his model of social change. During his later academic career, his social science images were deeply influenced by the staples paradigm of Harold Adams Innis. The frontier-social change paradigm is Clark's contribution to Canadian social sciences.

Each paradigm will be examined by focussing on: (1) the biography and academic career of the key social scientist who analyzed Canadian society using the paradigm; (2) the intellectual influences on their ideas; (3) their major publications and core ideas; and (4) their legacy. This overview will set the stage, so to speak, within which to read the papers in this volume.

The Fabian Paradigm

The Fabian approach is exemplified by the career of Leonard Marsh (1906-1982), an architect of the Canadian welfare state.

Biography. The youngest son of a British lower middle-class family, Leonard Marsh was born in 1906. He spent his childhood in a London suburb. An outstanding student, he was offered scholarships by both Oxford and the University of London, and in 1925 he enrolled in the London School of Economics. This experience molded his economic and sociological ideas. It likewise generated his interest in studying structured inequality and fostered his life-long commitment to changing society through rational social planning. Indeed, the years 1925 to 1929 shaped Leonard Marsh into a progressive social reformer who devoted the rest of his life to formulating blueprints for improving Canadian social and economic conditions.[3]

Intellectual Influences. The origin of the London School of Economics is part of the history of the British Fabians. They were a small group of socialist idealists whose goal was social reform along collectivist lines. The essence of Fabianism is represented by Sidney Webb (1859-1947) and Beatrice Webb (1859-1943).

In 1894, the Fabian Society received a bequest of ten thousand pounds to be spent "...within ten years to the propaganda and other purposes of the said society and its Socialism."[4] Sidney Webb, as chairman of the trust fund, urged that it be used to establish a School of Economics. The school opened in 1895 and five years later became part of the newly organized University of London. The school became the favorite child of the Webbs who left their imprint on its curriculum and organization.

"Lying a foundation of facts" was the Webbs' scientific approach to the study of society. In their view, a scientific sociology would emerge through the precise observation and collection of actual facts about the life history of social institutions, such as the trade union movement.

It was through social research into "facts" that scientifically valid policies would be formulated by an educated élite. Thus, the London School of Economics would not be just the first British university devoted to the study of the social sciences; it would also educate an élite who would lead the country to the promised land of collectivism. On the basis of this belief, the Webbs patronized the careers of two young men who were later to influence Marsh's intellectual development. They were William Beveridge (1879-1963) and H. Llewellyn Smith (1864-1945). Marsh learned from them the empirical social science tradition. They generated his interest in studying social inequality, and fostered his belief in welfare policy as a mechanism to reduce social inequalities.

In 1919, Beveridge, who later became the architect of the British welfare state, was appointed Director of the London School of Economics. By following two of the Webbs' intellectual aims, he built the school into an internationally known institution for the study of the social sciences. First, the social sciences were to be based on observation and analysis of facts, rather than on the analysis of concepts; and second, the school would be interdisciplinary rather than narrowly specialized. Its curriculum was to include economics, political science, statistics, geography, sociology anthropology, and law. Accordingly, ideas could be exchanged and criticized from a variety of social science perspectives.

A former civil servant, H. Llewellyn Smith, joined the London School of Economics in 1928. He assumed the directorship of the New Survey of London Life and Labour. This was a research project funded in large part by the Laura Spelman Rockefeller Foundation Memorial. The original classic London Life and Labour study (1886-1903) had been launched by Charles Booth (1840-1916), a successful British businessman.[5] The new survey was to compare the conditions with the facts in the original Booth study

Leonard Marsh enrolled in the London School of Economics in 1925. It was the school's multi-disciplinary intellectual milieu and his research apprenticeship with the New Survey study that shaped the distinctive feature of his later work. Indeed, his years at the school led to the making of a Canadian Fabian.[6]

Although Marsh read the work of theoretical social scientists, the books and articles by the Fabians made a deeper impression. His later publications reveal the impact of the Fabian fact finding approach, a tradition that stressed the systematic collection of data rather than the formulation of theoretical deductions to explain human behavior. From the Fabians, he accepted the assumption that legislation for social change should be based on scientific premises. This assumption was reinforced by studying with Beveridge who believed in "...the almost unlimited possibility of 'social engineering' or rational social planning."[7]

After graduating with first-class honors from the London School of Economics, Marsh accepted the position of assistant secretary for the New Survey. His apprenticeship with H. Llewellyn Smith had taught him the importance of systematic fact collection and how to interpret their relation to the formulation of social policy. The first volume of the study, *Forty Years of Change*, was published in 1930. Marsh collaborated on four chapters: "Cost of Living," "Wages of Labour and Earnings," "House Rents and Overcrowding," and "Unemployment and Its Treatment." The stage had been set, so to speak, for his later Canadian research.

Academic Career. In 1930, McGill University received a grant of $110,000 from the Rockefeller Foundation to study unemployment in Montreal. The project was to involve faculty from McGill's Departments of Sociology Psychology Education, Public Health, and Law. In his search for a project director McGill's principal, Sir William Currie, wrote to William Beveridge who recommended Leonard Marsh.

Marsh accepted the appointment as director of the first Canadian interdisciplinary social science research program and lecturer in the Department of Economics. He taught courses on industrial fluctuations and social legislation. Further to his research tasks, he wrote a doctoral thesis for McGill's School of Economics.

In 1941, Marsh left McGill to become research advisor to the federal government's Post-War Reconstruction Committee. After four years of wartime service in Ottawa, Marsh worked as welfare advisor and later, information officer for the United Nations Relief and Rehabilitation Administration. Returning to Canada in 1947, he was appointed the director of research at the School of Social Work, University of British Columbia. In 1965, the university appointed him a professor of educational sociology.

Marsh retired in 1973. In recognition of his intellectual contribution, he was awarded honorary degrees from York University and from McMaster University. In 1980, the Canadian Sociology and Anthropology Association elected him an honorary president.

Major Publications and Core Ideas. Strictly speaking, there is no well-defined Fabian paradigm with a set of interrelated concepts. However, there were four mental images that guided Fabian research.

(1) A belief in the social philosophy of utilitarianism, "the greatest happiness of the greater number." The utilitarianism goal was that there should be a national minimum of incomes, standards, and housing. No individual should be allowed to fall below these national minima.
(2) There should be equality in the conditions of opportunity. However, given the institutionalized nature of inequality, structural modifications in the institutions underlying the class structure were necessary to assure equality of opportunity.
(3) These modifications would emerge from a foundation of facts. The proposals for change would result from a detailed factual analysis of the nature and extent of social inequality.

(4) The modifications were to be implemented following Sidney Webb's assumption of "the inevitability of gradualness." That is, peaceful parliamentary changes through piecemeal legislation and administrative reorganization. This model of social change is rooted in an unyielding belief in rational bureaucratic planning and social engineering.

All of these images are reflected in Marsh's 1940 classic study, *Canadians In and Out of Work: A Survey of Economic Classes and Their Relation to the Labour Market.*[8] This book focussed on structured inequality in Canadian society. Social class was measured by social divisions or status groups based on the occupational structure. Using data from the census, the analysis portrayed the social class distribution on the basis of occupational status of the Canadian population in 1931. Among the dimensions considered were: (1) distribution of inequality; (2) self-perpetuating mechanisms; (3) institutional linkages; and (4) structural modification of the institutions underlying the class structure.

Marsh's detailed cross-classification revealed that Canada, a nation in 1931 with a population of about eleven million, was a society with vast social inequalities which varied along sex, regional, and ethnic lines.

Table 1 shows the extent of this inequality. The well-to-do were less than one percent of the population and the overwhelming majority of Canadians were members of the working class or farmers, farm workers, and fishermen.

Inequality was reflected in the distribution of income. Most Canadians lived below a national economic level required for a decent standard of living. To quote Marsh:

> What is often called an "American standard of living", enabling a liberal and varied diet, housing accommodation which includes a few domestic labour-saving devices, reasonable provision for health and recreation, etc., requires at the most frugal calculation $2,000.00; and some would put it considerably higher. This is characteristic only of managerial, professional, and higher-grade commercial and clerical families, the upper 15 percent of wage and salary earnings; at a generous estimate, not more than a quarter of all Canadian families.[9]

Table 1
Social Classes in Canada
Estimated Distribution of Families*

Class	Number	Percentage
Well-to-do †	*10,500*	0.6
Middle Classes	*492,000*	25.7
Business operators or owners (small and medium scale)	121,700	6.4
Professional, technical, managerial, commercial	178,200	9.3
White-collar workers, n.e.s.	110,700	5.8
Responsible and independent industrial workers	81,400	4.2
Working Classes	*815,000*	42.5
Skilled workers	257,300	13.4
Intermediate workers	213,900	11.2
Unskilled and manual workers	343,800	17.9
Farm Classes	*598,700*	37.2
Farmers, fishermen, etc	516,800	27.0
Farm workers, etc	81,900	4.2
Total	**1,916,200**	**100**

* Based on the figures for married gainfully occupied males; as at 1931.
† Including finance, industry, and professions.
SOURCE: Marsh 1940, p. 391.

To Marsh, limited access to educational opportunities was a major determinant of the self-perpetuating nature of inequality. An individual's class position in the occupational structure was, by and large, linked to his or her educational training. However, as the average cost of four years of high school was estimated to be around $500, the financial burden tended to be prohibitive for children from the working classes. Accordingly, there was a strong relationship between access to the opportunity structure and social class. Those who went to high school, and especially those who went to university, were a small, privileged, minority.

Marsh observed that: "The shape of society depends on a number of minorities who have power in the crucial spheres of life..."[10] Indirectly, his statement raises the important questions of how various classes are distributed and linked to various institutional sectors: finance, industry, the government, and the civil service. The institutional sector he selected to examine was the federal House of Commons and the Legislative assemblies of two central provinces, Ontario and Quebec. Table 2 lists the occupational class background of the elected members of these bodies.

There was a direct correlation between social class and elected membership: the higher the social class, the greater the membership. Indeed, the political decision-makers were primarily from professional (mainly legal) and business backgrounds. The most under-represented group was the industrial wage earners.

Marsh's portrait of Canada in 1931, before the height of the depression years, was a society with a bottom-heavy class structure. Given this fact, how was equality to be achieved? Marsh suggested several structural modifications necessary for a more equitable society. They included: (1) a diversity of secondary education; (2) a national scholarship program; (3) training facilities for the adolescent population; (4) a modernized federal employment service; (5) a program to dovetail employment and education experiences; (6) social insurance legislation; (7) the elimination of regressive elements of taxation; (8) the redistribution of income in the form of welfare services; and (9) public work programs.

Marsh immigrated to Canada at the beginning of the depression. During the decade from 1930 to 1940, the unemployment rate was never below ten percent of the work force. In 1933, nearly a quarter of the labor force was unemployed. Prairie farmers suffered through a lengthy drought. Unemployed Canadians were dependent on municipal relief, if it was available. Being "on the dole" was a humiliating experience. Thousands of single homeless men built roads and bridges for the federal government for a mere twenty cents a day plus food, clothing, and lodging.

As a result of the human suffering he observed in Montreal and his deeply-rooted Fabian beliefs, Marsh was drawn to a small group of individuals who had founded an organization called The League for Social Reconstruction (LSR). It was one of the first left-wing intellectual groups in Canada. Its members were "...overwhelmingly college-educated, urban, anglophone, and central Canadian."[11]

Table 2
Vocational Background of Members of the Federal House of Commons and of Certain Provincial Legislatures

	House of Commons		Candi-dates	Provincial Legislative Assemblies		
				Ontario	Quebec	
Year:	**1936**	**1940**	**1940**		**1936**	**1939**
Occupation						
Independent means	5	7	12	3	1	—
Business proprietors	23	16	42	9	6	7
Merchants	29	27	64	6	16	18
Salaried managers	6	5	23	5	1	1
Commercial agents	9	17	50	3	7	8
Lawyers	72	74	160	17	25	25
Doctors, dentists	18	18	47	12	13	8
Clergymen	4	6	11	—	—	—
Other older professions	4	3	6	—	—	1
Engineers, etc.	7	6	10	—	1	1
Teachers, principals	10	8	28	—	—	1
Lesser professions	3	1	19	2	2	4
Journalists	7	2	15	—	1	1
Public officials	3	3	10	4	2	—
Farmers	33	38	96	20	9	5
Wage-earners	9	9	57	3	6	6
Unspecified or indeterminate	3	5	22	6	—	—
Total	**245**	**245**	**672***	**90**	**90**	**86**

* Full list of candidates was not available when this list was compiled
SOURCE: Marsh 1940, p. 419. Excluded from this table is the Alberta Legislature before and after the first victory of the Social Credit Party in 1935. The 1935 election witnessed a sharp decline in farmer representation and the elimination of wage-earner members. See Marsh pp. 417-425.

Marsh was president of the LSR from 1937 to 1939. Between 1933 and 1939, he gave numerous public lectures for the league. He contributed to the 1935 multi-authored *Social Planning for Canada*,[12] and in 1938, with two other LSR members, he produced a shortened and simpler version entitled *Democracy Needs Socialism*.[13]

Social Planning for Canada was an indictment of the system of monopoly capitalism in Canada. It rejected the competitive ethic and the profit-motive. Part one contained the indictment focussed on the end of a century of progress, the nature of the Canadian economy, the structure of Canadian industry, the mechanism of the market, agriculture, and the inefficiency of the system. Part two, "What Socialist Planning Really Means," outlined structural modifications to reconstruct society through a planned and socialized economy.

Taken as a whole, *Social Planning for Canada* is a detailed analysis that should be read in its entirety. By and large, the skeleton of the argument is contained in the League's 1932 Manifesto[14]:

> The League for Social Reconstruction is an association of men and women who are working for the establishment in Canada of a social order in which the basic principle regulating production, distribution and service will be the common good rather than private profit.
>
> The present capitalist system has shown itself unjust and inhuman, economically wasteful, and a standing threat to peace and democratic government. Over the whole world it has led to a struggle for raw materials and markets and to a consequent international competition in armaments which were among the main causes of the last great war and which constantly threaten to bring on new wars. In the advanced industrial countries it has led to the concentration of wealth in the hands of a small irresponsible minority of bankers and industrialists whose economic power constantly threatens to nullify our political democracy. The result in Canada is a society in which the interests of farmers and of wage and salaried workers—the great majority of the population—are habitually sacrificed to those of this small minority. Despite our abundant natural resources, the mass of the people have not been freed from poverty and

insecurity. Unregulated competitive production condemns them to alternate periods of feverish prosperity in which the main benefits go to speculators and profiteers, and to catastrophic depression, in which the common man's normal state of insecurity and hardship is accentuated.

We are convinced that these evils are inherent in any system in which private profit is the main stimulus to economic effort. We therefore look to the establishment in Canada of a new social order which will substitute a planned and socialized economy for the existing chaotic individualism and which, by achieving an approximate economic equality among all men in place of the present glaring inequalities, will eliminate the domination of one class by another.

As essential first steps towards the realization of this new order we advocate:

1) Public ownership and operation of the public utilities connected with transportation, communications, and electric power, and of such other industries as are already approaching conditions of monopolistic control.
2) Nationalization of Banks and other financial institutions with a view to the regulation of all credit and investment operations.
3) The further development of agricultural co-operative institutions for the production and merchandising of agricultural products.
4) Social legislation to secure to the worker adequate income and leisure, freedom of association, insurance against illness, accident, old age, and unemployment, and an effective voice in the management of his industry.
5) Publicly organized health, hospital, and medical services.
6) A taxation policy emphasizing steeply graduated income and inheritance taxes.
7) The creation of a National Planning Commission.
8) The vesting in Canada of the power to amend and interpret the Canadian constitution so as to give the

federal government power to control the national economic development.

9) A foreign policy designed to secure international co-operation in regulating trade, industry and finance, and to promote disarmament and world peace.

Social Planning for Canada is a sophisticated example of research within the Fabian paradigm. Its model of democratic socialism was "...ameliorative, gradualist, and dedicated to peaceful change through the parliamentary system."[15] The book had its critics. In a forty-page pamphlet circulated throughout Canada to businessmen and newspapers, it was described as a "Marxist-inspired document."[16]

The perceived "collectivist" overtones of the research themes addressed by the Social Science Research Programme in combination with the political activities of some of its members on behalf of the LSR led some of the most powerful members of the McGill university administration to view the social science area as a centre of socialist propaganda. To rid the university of this "unfortunate reputation," the university's Chancellor and Principal decided that "the socialist-minded element among the McGill junior academics...[was] to be pressured out and replaced by less doctrinaire, 'more competent' exponents of the social sciences."[17] Accordingly, Marsh was informed that when the Rockefeller grant terminated in 1940, his position in the Department of Economics would not be renewed.

From 1941 to 1944, Marsh was a research advisor for the federal government's Advisory Committee on Reconstruction. In 1943, he published the *Report on Social Security for Canada.*[18] It was a masterpiece of social reform policies embedded in Fabian principles and centralized federal planning. The report stressed the failure of unemployment relief programs. Based on research of standard of living budgets, "...it was estimated that a minimum subsistence budget for a family of five required an annual income of $1,134 in 1940."[19] This amount placed a large number of Canadians below the poverty line.

To rectify this inequality, Marsh recommended a comprehensive system of social security and employment programs. Children's allowance, health insurance, training and guidance facilities, and a national investment of public work programs were also recommended. As a number of these recommendations later became part of the federal government's social security legislation, Marsh was one of the first architects of the Canadian welfare state.

The Legacy. Leonard Marsh's *Canadians In and Out of Work* is a significant contribution to sociology. It was the first systematic attempt to analyze the Canadian class structure.[20] Although it is difficult to assess the import of his innovative role as an advocate of social security policies, one fact is clear: a number of Marsh's social security recommendations are now part of the fabric of Canadian society.

The Ecological Paradigm

The ecological paradigm was introduced into Canadian intellectual life by Carl Addington Dawson (1887-1964). Dawson was the founder of sociology in English Canada.

Biography. Two of the important influences of Dawson's formative years were his religious family background and growing up in a rural Prince Edward Island community. Of Scottish descent, Dawson's great-grandfather immigrated from the North of Ireland to Prince Edward Island in 1812. He was the first Methodist minister to settle in the province. Dawson's father was a farmer in Augustine Cove, a small community of twenty-five families. In later years, Dawson's childhood experiences in rural Prince Edward Island communities contributed to his insightful sociological analysis of pioneer community organization in Western Canada.

In 1911, after teaching for three years in his native province, Dawson entered the Sophomore class of Acadia University. This was a Baptist-affiliated institution in Nova Scotia with an enrolment of 200 students. After graduation in 1912, he accepted a pastoral position at the Baptist Church in Lockeport, Nova Scotia. He moved to Chicago in 1916 to pursue a Bachelor of Divinity at the University of Chicago. This move had significant consequences for his career and the history of Canadian sociology.

Contrasted with life in small Prince Edward Island and Nova Scotia communities, Chicago was an enriching and stimulating experience for twenty-seven-year-old Dawson. The city was a complex metropolitan environment. It had experienced large-scale immigration of Poles, Swedes, Bohemians, Norwegians, Dutch, Danes, Croatians, Lithuanians, and Greeks.

Also, there was steady migration of Blacks from the South. The Chicago urban environment and its ethnic diversity had a tremendous impact on Dawson. During his later teaching career, "Immigration" became one of his favorite courses.

Intellectual Influences. At the University of Chicago, the Divinity School and the Department of Sociology were closely associated and Dawson was greatly influenced by Robert E. Park (1864-1944), the most dynamic individual of the "Chicago School of Sociology."

Park's most original sociological contribution was his association with the development of human ecology. This theoretical approach borrowed Darwinian ideas about the interdependence of plant and animal life within zones whose boundaries were defined by observation. This approach was defined by R.D. McKenzie[21] as:

> ...[the] study of the spatial and temporal relations of human beings as affected by the selective, distributive, and accommodative forces of the environment. Human ecology is fundamentally interested in the effect of position, in both time and space, upon institutions and human behavior.... These spatial relationships of human beings are the products of competition and selection, and are continuously in the process of change as new factors enter to disturb the competitive relations or to facilitate mobility. Human institutions and human nature itself become accommodated to certain spatial relationships of human beings. As these spatial relationships change, the physical basis of social relations is altered, thereby producing social and political problems.

Two of Park's central concepts were "natural histories" and "natural areas." Natural histories referred to an abstract procedure of analysing and categorizing social processes. They involved the construction of "ideal type" representations. Specific social realities were thus studied not to isolate a unique historical phenomenon. Instead, they were to reveal common patterns of change or typical ecological stages or "cycles" of institutional development.

Natural areas were "subcultures" which emerged as the result of social processes. These areas go through typical stages of development and have their own character and moral climate. One goal of sociology, according to Park, was to study these stages of development and through observation portray the subjective values, perceptions, and code of conduct of the inhabitants.

A former newspaper reporter, Park emphasized in his lectures the importance of exploring these natural areas as an objective observer. Chicago was viewed as a social laboratory Graduate students were encouraged "...to explore the city on foot—to walk around various neighbourhoods, occasionally talking to people they met and recording their observations afterward in detail. The purpose was to get a feel for what was out there."[22]

Examples of the natural area studies are the classic Chicago sociological studies including: *The Hobo: The Sociology of Homeless Men*[23]; *The Ghetto* [24]; and *The Gold Coast and the Slum.*[25]

From Park, Dawson learned: (1) the importance of studying the city as a sociological laboratory; (2) the relevance of investigating natural histories and natural areas, particularly those of ethnic groups; and (3) the ecological paradigm. Human ecology then became the theoretical approach Dawson taught to generations of Canadian sociology students.

Academic Career. While studying at Chicago, Dawson worked as an assistant pastor at Englewood Baptist Church. His studies were interrupted in 1918 by a telegram requesting his services in the army. For the next eighteen months he served as an honorary Captain on the Y.M.C.A. trans-Atlantic staff.

In 1919, he returned to Chicago as an instructor in the Sociology Department at the University of Chicago. From 1921 to 1922, he was head of the Department of Sociology at Y.M.C.A. College in Chicago. On September 1, 1922, he was awarded a Ph.D. sociology degree, for a thesis entitled, "The Social Basis of Knowledge."

In June 1922, Dawson accepted an offer from McGill University as assistant professor of Social Sciences and director of the School of Social Workers. In 1925, he was appointed associate professor and, under his chairmanship, a separate Department of Sociology was established with a Master of Arts program.

Recognizing the dearth of Canadian sociological publications, Dawson organized the McGill sociology curriculum around what he perceived to be important sociological issues in Canada: immigration, the city, the frontier, and the social organization of ethnic groups.

In 1927, Dawson was joined by Everett C. Hughes (1897-1983), a Chicago-trained sociologist and a student of Robert Park. Within several years, they had developed a miniature Chicago School of sociology at McGill. At the graduate level, students were expected to undertake extensive fieldwork research. Most frequently the research was based on concepts derived from the human ecology paradigm. In 1939, Hughes left Canada to assume a position at the University of Chicago. Four years later, Hughes' seminal book was published, *French Canada in Transition.*[26]

Carl Dawson retired from McGill in 1952. He died at the age of seventy-seven on January 16,1964. During his lifetime he had received continued academic recognition. He was president of the Canadian Political Science Association, a fellow of the Royal Society of Canada, chairman of the Canadian Social Science Research Council, and his alma mater (Acadia) awarded him an L.L.D.

Major Publications and Core Ideas. Dawson's publications dealt with urban life, ecological processes, and frontier settlement of the Canadian west. In a 1926 article describing the social organization of Montreal, he borrowed the ecological ideas of the Canadian born University of Chicago sociologist, E. W Burgess (1886-1966). The expansion of the urban environment was "...viewed as a selective process which distributes individuals into occupations, and sifts groups into areas of residence."[27] Cities, Dawson argued, grew from the center in a series of successive concentric zones:

Zone One: *Central Business District.* The central financial, cultural and political area characterized by high rent values and great mobility of the population.

Zone Two: *Zone of Transition.* A previous area of residence that has been invaded by light-manufacturing and business. While sites are held speculatively for sale as future business use, the residences are allowed to deteriorate. Rents are relatively low. The area becomes a slum with a shifting population. It is an area where immigrants first settle and usually houses several immigrant colonies. It is also, to use Dawson's term, the "city bad-lands" (the home of vice and crime).

Zone Three: *Working Men's Homes.* An area occupied by skilled and unskilled factory workers. Also, "...this third zone is the place of second residence for immigrant groups. They have succeeded economically; they have been disturbed by further deterioration in the area of first residence; they have been pushed out by newer immigrants and they have moved to a more stable and wholesome community. While the sudden entry of many immigrants speeds up the junking process of the second circle, it also seriously affects the social adjustment in each succeeding circle."[28] This population movement is called ecological invasion and succession.

Zone Four: *Residential.* An area of exclusive residents with single-family dwellings and high-class apartments.

Zone Five: *Commuters' Zone.* The area comprised of the suburbs and satellite cities within thirty to sixty minutes from the central business district.

Dawson noted that Montreal expanded from the center (Zone 1). However, as the city had been squeezed between the river and the mountain, it grew into a series of concentric kidney shapes.

Figure 1 illustrates the ecological process called succession. That is, as the city expanded, there was a strong tendency for each inner zone to

Figure 1
Dawson's 1926 Ecological View of Montreal

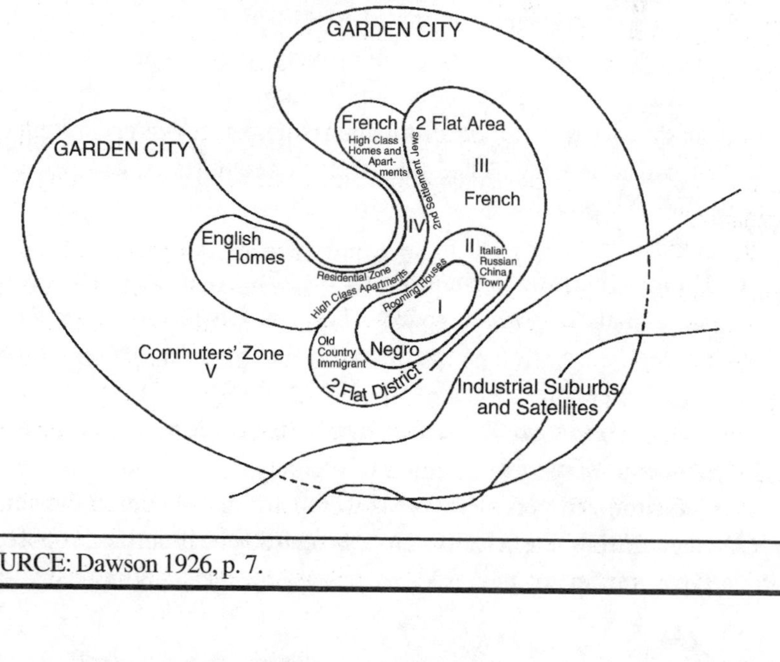

SOURCE: Dawson 1926, p. 7.

extend its boundaries by invading its immediate surrounding outer zone. In Dawson's view, the city was not a fragmented world of isolated parts; it was an organism of structural interdependence.

This pattern of concentric zones also accounts for Dawson's description of the city's social organization. Within these zones there existed a vast collection of natural areas. They were characterized by population types in respect to such factors as race, age, sex ratio, and standards of living. Each natural area had its unique social organizations, customs, group traditions, and sentiments.

Dawson's students learned these basic ecological concepts and investigated the natural histories (cycles of development) of natural areas. They also documented their internal social organization. Specifically, Montreal's ethnic mosaic was researched by graduate students working under Dawson s supervision. Immigrant studies were completed on the British,[29] the Ukrainian,[30] the Italian,[31] and the Jewish[32] communities. Other studies were completed on such topics as the French invasion of the Eastern townships[33] and the human ecology of the St. John River Valley.[34]

One of Dawson's major intellectual contributions was *An Introduction to Sociology* co-authored with Warner E. Gettys (1891-1973). The text was first published in 1929 and revised in 1935 and 1948. Rated among the ten best-selling introductory sociology texts in North America, it became the "bible" for several generations of McGill undergraduate sociology students. Drawing from a wide range of primary sources, the text explained the basic concepts of human ecology Competition was viewed as a determinant shaping the territorial distribution of human groups and institutions. The selective distribution which resulted from this competition was influenced by five ecological processes:

(1) **Concentration:** defined as the settling of a large number of individuals in a given space. The prime factors influencing this process were strategic positions in respect to transportation and great natural resources.

(2) **Centralization-Decentralization:** a form of population concentration in that there is a center of dominance as well as decentralized peripheral areas which are dependent on the center.

(3) **Segregation:** the selective process whereby well-defined population types cluster together.

(4) **Invasion:** or the entry of industry, business, residence, or population types into an area which is occupied by a different type of social organization.

(5) **Succession**: the result of invasion, is a complete change of the existing form of distribution.

Through the interconnection of these five social processes, "...the ecological order with its characteristic distribution of human tasks takes on its patterned formation."[35]

When disrupted, this ecological order was modified by the social processes of conflict, accommodation, and assimilation. To quote Dawson and Gettys[36]:

> Through competition, man discovers his place in the community and in his occupation. The institutions that guide his efforts are subject to the play of forces in the selective process. The product is an ecological order in which the different elements remain in a state of equilibrium until some force disturbs it. Selective activity in human communities is partially controlled by the social processes of conflict, accommodation, and assimilation.
>
> Conflict is the political process. Persons and groups become aware of their competitors. Issues arise which are settled by force of arms, a surplus of votes, a battle of tongues, or a barrage of looks. If the defeat is accepted, both parties to the conflict release their tensions and modify their organized activities to meet the new situation. We remember the host of readjustments that have followed in the wake of the World War. Social relationships are being reestablished in the folkways and mores of a new social order. Society is a network of such accommodations which each new generation takes over and supplements. It is through the process of accommodation that social organization takes form. Assimilation is the fundamental cultural process. Tensions fade out and the social order is established in a body of common memories. This structural

> stability is threatened constantly by forces which are never under complete social control.

The 1935 edition of the text gave more consideration to cultural areas and patterns. These were topics of specific interest to Dawson who, in 1929, had started to teach a course on culture areas in Canada. Another important addition was a study manual which provided outlines to guide student research projects in six areas: community, family, ethnic groups, strikes, organized social movements, and the individual. These outlines involved collecting data from a variety of sources such as census publications, newspapers, interviews, and life histories.

The research emphasis of this study manual provided the basis of teaching sociology at McGill. First-year students were sent into the city to observe natural areas and ecological processes. They completed a sociological analysis of their family, or wrote individual life histories. These assignments were the direct result of Dawson's belief that one learned sociology by "doing it." He was committed to the idea that it was necessary to do more than study abstract concepts. It was also essential to complete first-hand observation and analyze the data using concepts from the text.

Dawson's major research project was a comprehensive study of frontier settlement of the Canadian west. Initiated in 1929 under a grant from the Social Science Research Council, New York, the project involved some of the major Canadian scholars of the day: W A. Mackintosh (1895-1970), A. R. M. Lower (1889-1988), and Harold Innis (1894-1952).

To complete the field work, Dawson spent part of the summer of 1929 and all of the summer of 1930 with his research assistants in western Canada. He visited the communities under study and interviewed key informants. A number of his research assistants, who interviewed the pioneer families and studied the social organization of ethnic groups, were McGill sociology graduate students who wrote their theses under Dawson's direction.[37, 38, 39]

From this research, Dawson published three of the eight volumes in the Canadian Frontiers of Settlement Series.[40] His three volumes implicitly and explicitly employed an ecological paradigm. One of the volumes focussed on the Peace River Country, an area of approximately 47,000,000 acres in northwestern Alberta and northeastern British Columbia. Population distribution and the nature of social organization were interpreted in terms of how typical agricultural regions passed through successive stages of settlements: the outpost; isolated agricultural areas; the integration of agricultural areas; and the period of centralization and regional autonomy. These were successive stages. Each linked in an organic manner to the previous and prepared the way for its successor. Using the ecological processes of segregation, assimilation, invasion and succession, another volume compared the group settlement of five ethnic communities in western Canada: the Doukhobors, Mennonites, and Mormons who settled in farm villages; and the German Catholics and French Canadians who settled on scattered farmsteads in segregated areas.

The Legacy. Marlene Shore's book on McGill, the Chicago School, and the origins of social research in Canada, documents Dawson's legacy to Canadian sociology.[41] The sociology department that he founded in 1925 trained most of the next generation of Canadian-educated sociologists. Many of those individuals were his students. A number of them adopted the ecological paradigm. One of his students, Rex A. Lucas (1924-1978), who published an insightful book on one-industry Canadian communities highlighted Dawson's influence with the following dedication: "To the memory of Carl Addington Dawson, 1887-1964, pioneer Canadian sociologist and the teacher who introduced me to Canadian Communities."[42] The dedication speaks for itself. One of the greatest legacies that can be left by a scholar is his or her intellectual influence.

The Staples Paradigm

The staples paradigm is the original intellectual contribution of Harold Adams Innis (1894-1952). He was Canada's foremost political economist.

Biography. The son of a Baptist farming family, H. A. Innis was born on November 5,1894, near Otterville, Oxford County, Ontario. His early education was in southern Ontario. He attended the then Toronto-located McMaster University from 1912 to 1916, with the exception of five months in 1915 when he was a primary school teacher in Londonville, northern Alberta.

His brief teaching appointment outside Ontario had an impact on his view of Canadian society. As his biographer noted: "He had made the acquaintance of the new West. He had learned something of the West's peculiar problems. The anxieties and vexations of high interest rates and transport problems had become familiar to him through very real examples. He brought back with him some understanding of the West's conception of its own nature, and of its attitude to the nation as a whole."[43]

At the age of twenty, H. A. Innis graduated from McMaster and enlisted in the Canadian army. He was wounded while on active duty in France. After convalescing in England, he returned to Canada and earned his M.A. in Economics from McMaster. In 1918, he enrolled at the University of Chicago. The Chicago experience exposed him to ideas that he would later weave into an original contribution to Canadian social science.

Intellectual Influences. Although Innis had planned a career in the legal profession, his interest in economics intensified and the die was cast. At the University of Chicago, he wrote his Ph.D. thesis which was later published in 1923 as *A History of the Canadian Pacific Railway.*[44]

Innis was influenced by a number of Chicago economists[45]:

> ...[He] studied with Frank Knight, who taught economic theory and statistics with such scepticism that, 'one could never again become lost in admiration of statistical compilations...'; J. M. Clark, from whom he learned of 'overhead costs,' which assumed a central importance in Innis's studies in Canadian economic history; C. S. Duncan, who emphasized in his lectures on marketing the connections 'between the physical characteristics of a commodity and the marketing structure built up in relation to it'; and Chester Wright, who taught courses on trusts and American economic history and who supervised Innis's doctoral thesis on the Canadian Pacific Railway.

At Chicago, he studied the iconoclastic views of Thorstein Veblen (1857-1929).[46] Innis admired Veblen's attack on static economics, the emphasis on the dynamics of economic change, the developmental approach to the study of economic systems and institutions, and the style of academic craftsmanship which integrated economic history and theory.[47] Veblen also sensitized Innis to the impact of technology on societal organization.

In the formulation of the staples perspective, Innis' ideas were molded by other scholars. One of these was the Scottish political economist Adam

Smith (1723-1790) who stressed the importance of commodity specialization in new countries.[48] The Canadian historian William A. Mackintosh (1895-1970) who focussed on the role of staple products in Canadian history[49] was a further influence on Innis. So was the Scottish geographer Marion Newbigin (1869-1934) whose book, *Canada: The Great River, The Lands and the Men*,[50] alerted Innis to the geographical effect of the St. Lawrence River and the Pre-Cambrian Shield.

Academic Career. In 1920, Innis accepted an appointment in the Department of Political Economy at the University of Toronto. During the next twenty-two years, he became Canada's senior academic statesman. At the University of Toronto, he held key administrative roles. He was chairman of the Department of Political Economy and Dean of the School of Graduate Studies. He was a member of the 1934 Nova Scotia commission on the province's economy and the 1949 Royal Commission on Transportation. He was a driving force behind the 1940 establishment of the Canadian Social Science Research Council. Innis was elected president of four prestigious learned groups: the Canadian Political Science Association, the Economic History Association, the Royal Society of Canada, and the American Economic Association. He was awarded honorary degrees from New Brunswick, McMaster, Laval, Manitoba, and Glasgow.

Innis died prematurely on November 8,1952. Twelve years later, the University of Toronto established Innis College in his honor. A quarter of a century after his death, he was still regarded as Canada's greatest economic historian. In 1977, *The Journal of Canadian Studies* published a special issue assessing his ideas.

Major Publications and Ideas. *A History of the Canadian Pacific Railway*,[51] Innis's first book, was an exhaustive factual study of finance, debt structures, overhead costs, and speed of expansion of the Canadian Pacific Railway. The book was critical of the dominance of the West by eastern Canada.

The staples approach was outlined in three economic histories: *The Fur Trade in Canada*[52]; *Settlement and the Mining Frontier*[53]; and *The Cod Fisheries.*[54] The rationale underlying the three volumes was explained over half a century ago when Innis wrote about the teaching of economic history in Canada. He argued that a serious obstacle to research in Canadian economics and economic history was the tendency to use economic theories that applied to older industrialized nations but not to Canada. Canada, he argued, must be examined in the light of its trade patterns within an international economy[55]:

> ...it would appear that Canadian economic history must be approached from the standpoint of trade with other countries, France in the beginning, later Great Britain and the United States, and finally the Orient and the world generally. Economists will be safe in following the political scientist and the historian in their studies of the relationship of Canada to other countries. Canada's development in relation to other countries meant the development of trade from the Atlantic seaboard in commodities accessible by water transport. With primitive transportation fish and furs occupied a dominant position and the exhaustion of furs was followed by lumber. Economists cannot pretend to an understanding of Canadian economic history without an adequate history of transportation. A history of transportation must be accompanied by history of trade and especially of the trade relations between Canada and old countries. Further Canadians will find it necessary to work out the economic history of each industry especially in technique and capital organization.

This argument contains two central interrelated themes of the staple paradigm. First, is the idea of center-margin relations. Such relations involved the process whereby the colony supplied staple commodities in the form of raw materials to the mother country. The latter used these materials in the manufacture of both a finished product and goods in demand in the colony. Second, this center-margin relation resulted in a so-called staple domination in the colony. In other words, the predominant activity of colonists was the production of the staple or the facilities that promoted its production. The economic history of the Canadian colony, then, could only be understood through an examination of the influence of a series of staples. They were fish, fur, timber, wheat, and minerals.

In general, the staple commodity—its technological nature and relation to geography—molded the character of the newly forming society. The production of the staple for the manufacturing nation shaped the colony's agricultural patterns; investment patterns; transportation growth and costs; and its industrial, financial, and political institutions. Canada was a prime example of a colonial society that had never been self-sufficient. Throughout her history Canada assumed a marginal economic relation, first with Britain, and then with the United States.

The Fur Trade exemplifies the staple paradigm. It stressed the relation between geographical, technological, and economic forces. Demand for beaver fur in Europe shaped the evolution of New France and its institutions. The fur trade affected New France's transportation patterns and costs, contact with the Indians, population settlement, agricultural policies, and military conflicts.

In the post-conquest period, the centralized Northwest Company was the dominant institution in the fur trade. By the early 1820s, its organization extended from the Atlantic to the Pacific and it laid the foundation of contemporary Canada. As Innis wrote[56]:

> It is no mere accident that the present Dominion coincides roughly with the fur trading areas of northern North America. The basis of supplies for the trade in Quebec, in western Ontario, and in British Columbia represent the agricultural areas of the present Dominion. The Northwest Company was the forerunner of the present confederation.
>
> Canada emerged as a political entity with boundaries largely determined by the fur trade.... The present Dominion emerged not in spite of geography but because of it.

In describing the relation between capitalism and the staples, Innis noted how Canadian political institutions were shaped by staple production and transportation. To facilitate staple movement before Confederation, external capital investment was required for canals and railways. This investment required the development of a strong centralized government. It emerged through the Act of Union and the British North America Act.[57] Thus, the political origin of Canada was rooted in centre-margin economic relations and staple domination.

During the latter part of his life, Innis moved beyond the study of Canadian economics. His *Bias of Communication*[58] and *Empire and Communication*[59] focused on the technology of communication and the stability of empires.

The Legacy. Although the staples paradigm contains a set of mental images to guide economic history, Innis never integrated the ideas into an explicit framework. Despite this lack of formal codification, Innis' ideas stamped the Toronto School of Economic History. It started from the assumption that staple commodities molded Canadian historical development and sociological organization. This premise has served as the springboard for a formally developed staple theory of economic growth[60] and it has been criticized.[61]

Despite the criticism, Innis' political economy tradition has stood the test of time. He is Canada's most widely quoted economic historian.

The Frontier-Social Change Paradigm

The frontier-social change paradigm, developed by Samuel Delbert Clark, is the sociological by-product of the staple approach.

Biography. S. D. Clark was born on an Alberta farm on February 24, 1910. He grew up in a rural environment near Lloydminster on the Alberta-Saskatchewan border. This agricultural background was undoubtedly a factor shaping Clark's later research interests in agrarian protest movements.

In 1930, Clark was awarded a B.A. (honors) in history and political science from the University of Saskatchewan. The next year he earned an M.A. in history. His thesis was entitled, "Settlement in Saskatchewan with Special Reference to the Influence of Dry Farming." He moved to Toronto and from 1931-1932 was a Ph.D. student in history at the University of Toronto.

The depression cut short the funding for his studies and he accepted a scholarship from the Saskatchewan committee of the Imperial Order Daughters of the Empire to study in England. The depression had raised questions in his mind about capitalism and because of its radical reputation he decided to study at The London School of Economics.

In 1933, Clark returned to Canada. For the next two years he completed M.A. studies in the Department of Sociology at McGill University. He studied with Carl Dawson and Everett Hughes. He wrote a second M.A. thesis on The Canadian Manufacturers' Association as a pressure group. He returned to the University of Toronto as a Ph.D. candidate in political science. From 1937-1938, he was a lecturer in political science and sociology at the University of Manitoba. He completed his Ph.D. thesis in 1938 and returned to the University of Toronto to teach sociology until his retirement in 1976.

Intellectual Influences. Early in his academic career, Clark was exposed to radical social thought. At the University of Toronto in the early 1930s, he attended meetings of The League for Social Reconstruction. At The London School of Economics, he studied Marx and the works of the Fabians. The latter argued for rational social planning to reconstruct society. Although these ideas opened new intellectual horizons and stressed the economic underpinnings of society, they did not provide the assumptions upon which Clark constructed his later sociological explanations.

Clark's biographer, Harry H. Hiller, has pointed to the multiplicity of influences in Clark's paradigm and its origins.[62] Three influences, however, are predominant. The first is the frontier thesis of the American historian, Frederick Jackson Turner (1861-1932). American development, Turner argued, was related to the movement of population to the West. The frontier was the furthermost settlement in the West where social organization and government were loosely organized. The frontier itself was a process which transformed customs, institutions, and behavior. Without formal controls, individualism and democracy emerged and were shaped by the frontier.[63] Clark studied the frontier thesis as an undergraduate and later during graduate work at the University of Toronto. He read the work of Canadian historians such as Arthur Lower who utilized the frontier argument.

The second influence emerged from his studies at McGill of the "Chicago School of Sociology." Clark became familiar with the theory of social disorganization-reorganization as developed by W. I. Thomas (1863-1947) and Florian Znaniecki (1882-1958) in their classic study *The Polish Peasant in Europe and America* (1918-20).[64] Thomas and Znaniecki pointed to disruption of life in new environments. Here existing rules of behavior had a decreasing influence on the behavior of individuals and groups. The resultant state of social disorganization, however, was temporary. It was followed by reorganized behavior and institutions.

A study of immigrant movement to the United States, *The Polish Peasant*, examined family and community disorganization. Society was viewed as a process that moved along a three-stage process from organization to disorganization to reorganization. Clark drew upon this model but with differences. As Hiller notes[65]:

> Clark did not focus on a particular ethnic group or discuss social life in the old world as Thomas and Znaniecki had, but he did find historical evidence for the thesis that settlement on the new Canadian frontiers was a socially disorienting experience just as it was for the Polish peasant, and he assumed then that social disorganization was evidence of the effects of residence in a new environment.... The major difference between Thomas and Znaniecki and Clark was that Clark stressed the context of economic expansion and new forms of economic exploitation rather than just immigration as the cause of disorganization, and in this way he retained the Innisian perspective. He argued that new forms of production resulted in both geographical and occupational shifts in the population leading to social breakdown. Clark took from Thomas and Znaniecki the idea that a former state of stability or organization could be taken for granted and that the disorganizing process would eventually lead to another state of equilibrium. What needed investigation then was the social change from one integrative state to another in which the interstitial period was necessarily problematic. Clark also found in the Polish peasant study a sociological legitimation for the use of personal documents (e.g., letters, diaries, biographies) as evidence of basic social processes, which appealed to his research dispositions.

Third, Clark's work was heavily indebted to the ideas of his intellectual mentor H. A. Innis. Clark and Innis had first met at the London School of Economics when the Canadian political economist delivered a lecture on economic materialism. Clark later studied under Innis and for over a decade they were colleagues at the University of Toronto.

Innis had noted that "...the shift to new staple invariably produced periods of crisis in which adjustments in the old structure were painfully made and a new pattern created in relation to the new staple."[66] Clark built upon the staple paradigm starting with Innis' economic view of staple exploitation and examining the resultant social disruptions. Clark's work, then, is a fusion of the frontier thesis, the social disorganization-reorganization approach, and the staples paradigm.

Academic Career. Clark spent most of his thirty-eight-year academic career at the University of Toronto. When sociology split from political economy in 1963 he was made chairman of the Sociology Department, a position he held until 1969.

Clark became a dominant figure in the development of sociology in Canada. From 1944 to 1959, he was editor of the Social Credit in Alberta Series, sponsored by the Canadian Social Science Research Council through a special grant from the Rockefeller Foundation. The series produced ten books: W. L. Morton, *The Progressive Party in Canada*[67]; D. C. Masters, *The Winnipeg General Strike*[68]; Jean Burnet, *Next-Year country*[69]; C. B. MacPherson, *Democracy in Alberta*[70]; J. R. Mallory, *Social Credit and the Federal Party in Alberta*[71]; W. E. Mann, *Sect, Cult and Church in Alberta*[72]; V. E. Fowke, *The National Policy and the Wheat Economy*[73]; L. G. Thomas, *The Liberal Party in Canada*[74]; S. D. Clark, *Movements of Political Protest in Canada*[75]; and J. A. Irving, *The Social Credit Movement in Alberta.*[76]

In recognition of his intellectual contributions, Clark was elected a member of the Royal Society and served as president during 1975-1976. He received the Tyrrell Medal from the Royal Society of Canada in 1960. He was made an honorary president of the Canadian Sociology and Anthropology Association (1967), and Foreign Honorary Member of the American Academy of Arts and Science. He was appointed Officer, Order of Canada. He was awarded honorary degrees from the universities of Calgary, Dalhousie, St. Mary's, and the University of Toronto.

Major Publications and Core Ideas. Clark's major publications were: *The Canadian Manufacturer's Association: A Study in Collective Bargaining and Political Pressure*[77]; *The Social Development of Canada*[78]; *Church and Sect in Canada*[79]; *Movements of Political Protest* *in Canada, 1640-1840*[80]; *The Developing Canadian Community*[81]; *The Suburban Society*[82]; *The New Urban Poor*[83]; and *Canadian Society in Historical Perspective*[84].

In his early writings there was a set of mental images that guided Clark's study of social change in the Canadian frontier. In 1939, he suggested that a defining characteristic of Canadian social history "...has been the recurrent emergence of areas of social life involving new patterns of social re-adjustment and social life."[85] Much of this social re-adjustment occurred in the frontier.

The frontier was used to refer to an area which developed *a new form of economic enterprise (staple production)*. Examples include the fur trade in New France, the fisheries in the Maritime colonies, the timber trade in Upper Canada, and mining in British Columbia and the Yukon. The frontier could also be a location which used *new techniques of economic exploitation*. In these areas there are "...special kinds of demands upon social organization, and the failure to fully meet these demands resulted in disturbances in social relationships which may be described as social problems."[86] The disturbance reached its peak when economic development was at its most rapid pace.

Clark listed some of the factors which led to social disorganization: (1) distance from centres of control and supply; (2) the allocation of capital to the new economic enterprise rather than to community services; (3) the lack of school teachers, clergy and medical practitioners; and (4) the type of individuals attracted to the frontier, such as the different age and sex compositions or the emigration of "social misfits."

Given this social disorganization, a state of normlessness in which behavior was not guided by institutionalized codes of conduct could emerge. In these circumstances, a set of reformers frequently came to the forefront. They were outside the traditional institutions and could challenge existing authority.

When the reformers' ideas articulated real and long-term social needs and dissatisfactions, "...the vague and inarticulate feelings of large numbers of people were crystallized and identified with a clear-defined goal."[87] Thereafter social movements could emerge. Clark argued that, "It was the need for social expression rather than the character or motives of reformers which gave rise to reform movements."[88]

These social reform movements provided a solution to individual and social needs. With time, the reform movement became institutionalized. It appointed officials and developed an ideology that was accepted by its followers. The reform movements became part of the established order and a final phase of social reorganization was reached.

This movement from disorganization to reorganization was a process which brought about a new social equilibrium; however movement toward equilibrium was never totally attained. New disturbances led to further problems of social organization and adjustment.

Clark used the disorganization-reorganization argument in his *Church and Sect in Canada*, a study of religious movements and social change. The basic premise of the research was that "the church has grown out of the conditions of a mature society; the sect has been the product of what might be called frontier conditions of social life."[89] In the frontier—which was associated with a particular form of economic endeavor—the traditional codes of behavior and institutions were challenged. The result was social disorganization. Through an examination of evangelical movements, Clark illustrated how sects integrated unattached frontier populations. The sect was a mechanism for reform and a social means of reorganization. With stability however, sects took on church-like formal characteristics.

Clark did not limit his analysis to rural areas. In response to poverty and unemployment, sects arose in urban frontiers such as in the shipbuilding industry in the Maritimes. In any frontier, then, sects emerged as the consequence of social disorganization.[90]

The same frontier social change model was less explicitly used in *Movements of Political Protest in Canada, 1640-1840*. Clark was concerned with the breakdown of old established political organizations and the re-establishment of the social order with new forms of behavior and institutions. He extended his analysis by comparing political social movements in Canada and the United States. The frontier revolts succeeded in the United States. In Canada, he argued, there were forces which led to their defeat. One was the geography of the St. Lawrence that shaped a pattern of centralized authority. Another was the Canadian counter-revolutionary character which evolved as a reaction to American revolutionary movements.

The Legacy. As often happens with the works of an influential scholar, Clark's ideas have been assessed and criticized.[91] *Church and Sect in*

Canada and *Movements of Political Protest in Canada* illustrated the importance of historical research to the social scientist and how any explanation of social change must be rooted in its historical realities. However, Clark's most lasting contribution may well be his attempt to link forms of social organization and disorganization to Innis' ideas on staple development.

Notes

1 Ritzer, George. (1975). *Sociology: A Multi-Paradigm Science*. Boston: Allyn and Bacon. p. 7; see also Kuhn, Thomas S. (1970). *The Structure of Scientific Revolutions*, 2nd Ed. Chicago: University of Chicago Press; Kuhn, Thomas S. (1970). Reflections on My Critics. In A. Musgrave (Ed.), *Criticism and the Growth of Knowledge*. Cambridge: Cambridge University Press; Kuhn, Thomas S. (1977). Second Thoughts on Paradigms. In T.S. Kuhn (Ed.), *The Essential Tension*. Chicago: University of Chicago Press; Eckberg, Douglas L. and Hill, Lester, Jr. (1979). The Paradigm Concept and Sociology: A Critical Review. *American Sociological Review*, 44, p. 6.

2 Nock, David. (1993). *Star Wars in Canadian Sociology*. Halifax: Fernwood. p. 39.

3 For a summary of Marsh's lifelong commitment to the causes of social justice and rationality through progressive social reform, see Dennis William Magill and Richard C. Helmes-Hayes. Leonard Charles Marsh: A Canadian Social Reformer. *Journal of Canadian Studies*, 21:2 (Summer 1986), pp. 49-66.

4 Cain, Sydney. (1963). *The History of the Foundation of the London School of Economics and Political Science*. London: G. Bell and Sons Ltd.

5 Simey, T.S. and Simey, M.B. (1960). *Charles Booth: Social Scientist*. London: Oxford University Press.

6 Marsh did not view himself as a doctrinaire Fabian. He argues that, "I've always searched for facts; and for descriptive analysis not generalizations. I quite understand your use of Fabian labels…but I'm sure you understand I was never a Fabian per se." Correspondence from Leonard Marsh to Dennis William Magill, 2 January 1981.

7 Harris, José, (1977). *William Beveridge: A Biography*. London: Oxford University Press. p. 106.

8 Marsh, Leonard C. (1940). *Canadians In and Out of Work: A Survey of Economic Classes and Their Relation to the Labour Market*. Toronto: Oxford University Press.

9 Ibid. pp. 198-9.

10 Ibid. p. 417.

11 Horn, Michael. (1980). *The League for Social Reconstruction: Intellectual Origins of the Democratic Left in Canada 1930-1942*. Toronto: University of Toronto Press. p. 14.

12 *Social Planning for Canada*. (1975). New Edition with Introduction. Social History of Toronto. Toronto: University of Toronto Press.

13 Marsh, Leonard et al. (1938). *Democracy Needs Socialism*. Toronto: Nelson.

14 (1935). *Social Planning for Canada*. Toronto: Nelsons. pp. ix-xi.

15 Berger, Carl. (1976). *The Writing of Canadian History: Aspects of English Canadian Historical Writing: 1900 to 1970*. Toronto: Oxford University Press. p. 69.

16 Irving, Allan. (1986). Leonard Marsh and the McGill Social Science Research Project. *Journal of Canadian Studies*, 21:2 (Summer), pp. 6-25.

17 Frost, Stanley B. (1984). *McGill University and the Advancement of Knowledge*, Vol. 11, 1895-1971. Kingston/Montreal: McGill-Queen's University Press. pp. 378-418. See also Horn, Michael. (1999). *Academic Freedom in Canada: A History*. Toronto: University of Toronto Press. pp. 128-144.

18 (1975). *Social Security for Canada*. New Edition with Introduction by Leonard Marsh. Foreword by Michael Bliss. Social History Series. Toronto: University of Toronto Press.

19 Guest, Dennis. (1980). *The Emergence of Social Security in Canada*. Vancouver: University of British Columbia Press.

20 *Canadians In and Out of Work* has been largely ignored by mainstream and radical sociologists. See Richard C. Helmes-Hayes and Dennis William Magill. A Neglected Classic: Leonard Charles Marsh's Canadians In and Out of Work. *The Canadian Review of Sociology and Anthropology*, 30:1 (February 1993), pp. 81-109. Marsh's book will be available in 2000 from Canadian Scholars' Press.

21 McKenzie, Roderick D. (1925). The Ecological Approach to the Study of the Human Community. In R. Park et al. (Eds.), *The City*. Chicago: University of Chicago Press. pp. 63-4.

22 Carey, James T. (1975). *Sociology and Public Affairs: The Chicago School*. Beverly Hills: Sage Publications. p. 178.

23 Anderson, Nels. (1923). *The Hobo: The Sociology of the Homeless Man*. Chicago: University of Chicago Press.

24 Wirth, Louis. (1928). *The Ghetto*. Chicago: University of Chicago Press.

25 Zorbaugh, Harvey W. (1929). *The Gold Coast and the Slum*. Chicago: University of Chicago Press.

26 Hughes, Everett C. (1943). *French Canada in Transition*. Chicago: University of Chicago Press.

27 Dawson, Carl A. (1926). *The City as an Organism with Special Reference to Montreal.* Montreal: McGill University Publications, Series XIII, No. 10, p.4.
28 Ibid. pp. 5-6.
29 Reynold, Lloyd G. (1933). *The Occupational Adjustment of the British Immigrant in Montreal.* Master's thesis, McGill University, Montreal.
30 Mamchur, Stephen W. (1934). *The Economic and Social Adjustment of Slavic Immigrants in Canada with Especial Reference to the Ukrainians in Montreal.* Master's thesis, McGill University, Montreal.
31 Bayley, Charles M. (1939). *The Social Structure of the Italian and Ukrainian Immigrant Communities in Montreal.* Master's thesis, McGill University, Montreal.
32 Seidel, Judith. (1939). *The Development and Social Adjustment of the Jewish Community in Montreal.* Master's thesis, McGill University, Montreal
33 Hunter, Jean I. (1939). *The French Invasion of the Eastern Townships: A Regional Study.* Master's thesis, McGill University, Montreal.
34 Lewis, James N. (1939). *The Human Ecology of the St. John River Valley.* Master's thesis, McGill University, Montreal.
35 Dawson, Carl A. and Gettys, Warner E. (1929). *An Introduction to Sociology.* New York: The Ronald Press Company. p. 219.
36 Ibid. pp. 556-557.
37 Tuttle, Harry G. (1931). *Frontier Religious Organization with Special Reference to the Peace River Area.* Master's thesis, McGill University, Montreal.
38 Craig, Glen H. (1933). *The Means and Modes of Living on the Pioneer Fringe of Land Settlement, with Special Reference to the Peace River Area.* Master's thesis, McGill University, Montreal.
39 Younge, Eva R. (1933). *Social Organization on the Pioneer Fringe, with Special Reference to the Peace River Area.* Master's thesis, McGill University, Montreal.
40 Dawson, Carl A. and Munchie, R.W. (1934). *The Settlement of the Peace River Area.* Toronto: The Macmillan Company of Canada Limited; Dawson, Carl A. (1936). *Group Settlement: Ethnic Communities in Western Canada.* Toronto: The Macmillan Company of Canada Limited; Dawson, Carl A. and Younge, Eva R. (1940). *Pioneering in the Prairie Provinces: The Social Side of the Settlement Process.* Toronto: The Macmillan Company of Canada Limited.
41 Shore, Marlene. (1987). *The Science of Social Redemption. McGill, the Chicago School and the Origins of Social Research in Canada.* Toronto: University of Toronto Press.
42 Lucas, Rex A. (1971). *Minetown, Milltown, Railtown, Life in Canadian Communities of Single Industry.* Toronto: University of Toronto Press.
43 Creighton, Donald. (1957). *Harold Adams Innis: Portrait of a Scholar.* Toronto: University of Toronto Press.

44 Innis, Harold A. (1923). *A History of the Canadian Pacific Railway*. London: P.S. King.

45 Berger, Carl. (1976). *The Writing of Canadian History*. Toronto: Oxford University Press. pp. 87-88.

46 For a critical interpretation of Veblen's ideas, see Riesman, David. (1953). *Thorstein Veblen: A Critical Interpretation*. New York: Charles Scribner's Sons.

47 Innis, Harold A. (1929). The Work of Thorstein Veblen. In Mary Q. Innis (Ed.), *Essays in Canadian Economic History*. Toronto: University of Toronto Press.

48 Smith, Adam, (1976, originally published in 1776). *The Wealth of Nations*. Chicago: University of Chicago Press.

49 Mackintosh, William A. (1923). Economic Factors in Canadian History. *Canadian Historical Review*, IV, p. 1.

50 Newbigin, Marion. (1926). *Canada, The Great River, The Lands, and the Men*. London: Christophers.

51 Innis, Harold A. (1923). *A History of the Canadian Pacific Railway*. London: P.S. King.

52 Innis, Harold A. (1956, 1970, 1975). *The Fur Trade in Canada: An Introduction to Canadian Economic History*. Toronto: University of Toronto Press.

53 Innis, Harold A. (1936). *Settlement and the Mining Frontier*. Toronto: The Macmillan Company of Canada Limited.

54 Innis, Harold A. (1978). *The Cod Fisheries: The History of an International Economy*. Toronto: University of Toronto Press,

55 Innis, Harold A. (1929). The Teaching of Economic History in Canada. In Mary Q. Innis (Ed.), *Essays in Canadian Economic History*. Toronto: University of Toronto Press. p. 112.

56 Innis, Harold A. (1956) and (1973). *Essays in Canadian Economic History*. Toronto: University of Toronto Press. pp. 392-393.

57 Ibid. pp. 396-402.

58 Innis, Harold, A. (1951). *The Bias of Communication*. Toronto: University of Toronto Press.

59 Innis, Harold, A. (1950). *Empire and Communications*. Oxford: Clarendon Press.

60 (1967) A Staples Theory of Economic Growth. In W.T. Easterbrook and M.H. Watkins (Eds.), *Approaches to Canadian Economic History*. Toronto: McClelland & Stuart Ltd.

61 McNally, David. (1981). Staple Theory as Commodity Fetishism: Marx, Innis and Canadian Political Economy. *Studies in Political Economy: A Socialist Review*, 6 (Autumn).

62 Hiller, Harry H. (1982). *Society and Change: S.D. Clark and the Development of Canadian Sociology*. Toronto: University of Toronto Press.

63 For an interpretation of Turner, see Hofstadter, Richard. (1968). *The Progressive Historians*. New York: Knopf.

64 Thomas, William I. and Znaniecki, Florian. (1918). *The Polish Peasant in Poland and America*. New York: Knopf. For a discussion of the social disorganization see Carey, James T. (1975). *Sociology and Public Affairs: The Chicago School*. Beverly Hills: Sage Publications. pp. 95-120.

65 Hiller, Harry H. (1982). *Society and Change: S.D. Clark and the Development of Canadian Sociology*. Toronto: University of Toronto Press. p. 71.

66 Innis, Harold A. (1950). *Empire and Communications*. Oxford: Clarendon Press. p. 5.

67 Morton, W.L. (1950). *The Progressive Party in Canada*. Toronto: University of Toronto Press.

68 Masters, D.C. (1950). *The Winnipeg General Strike*. Toronto: University of Toronto Press.

69 Burnet, Jean. (1951). *Next-Year Country*. Toronto: University of Toronto Press.

70 MacPherson, C.B. (1953). *Democracy in Alberta*. Toronto: University of Toronto Press.

71 Mallory, J.R. (1954). *Social Credit and the Federal Party in Alberta*. Toronto: University of Toronto Press.

72 Mann, W.E. (1955). *Sect, Cult and Church in Alberta*. Toronto: University of Toronto Press.

73 Fowke, V.E. (1957). *The National Policy and the Wheat Economy*. Toronto: University of Toronto Press.

74 Thomas, L.G. (1959). *The Liberal Party in Alberta*. Toronto: University of Toronto Press.

75 Clark, S.D. (1959). *Movements of Political Protest in Canada*. Toronto: University of Toronto Press.

76 Irving, J.A. (1959). *The Social Credit Movement in Alberta*. Toronto: University of Toronto Press.

77 Clark, S.D. (1939). *The Canadian Manufacturers' Association: A Study in Collective Bargaining and Political Pressure*. Toronto: University of Toronto Press.

78 Clark, S.D. (1942). *The Social Development of Canada: An Introductory Study with Select Documents*. Toronto: University of Toronto Press.

79 Clark, S.D. (1948). *Church and Sect in Canada*. Toronto: University of Toronto Press.

80 Clark, S.D. (1959). *Movements of Political Protest in Canada, 1640-1840*. Toronto: University of Toronto Press.

81 Clark, S.D. (1962 and 1968). *The Developing Canadian Community*. Toronto: University of Toronto Press.

82 Clark, S.D. (1966). *The Suburban Society*. Toronto: University of Toronto Press.
83 Clark, S. D. (1978). *The New Urban Poor*. Toronto: McGraw-Hill Ryerson.
84 Clark, S.D. (1976). *Canadian Society in Historical Perspective*. Toronto: McGraw-Hill Ryerson.
85 Clark, S.D. (1939). *The Canadian Manufacturers' Association: A Study in Collective Bargaining and Political Pressure*. Toronto: University of Toronto Press. p. 351.
86 Clark, S.D. (1942). *The Social Development of Canada: An Introductory Study with Select Documents*. Toronto: University of Toronto Press. p. 2.
87 Ibid. p. 15.
88 Loc. Cit.
89 Clark, S.D. (1948). *Church and Sect in Canada*. Toronto: University of Toronto Press. p. xii.
90 For a more detailed analysis of Clark's analysis of religion, see Hiller, Harry H. (1982). *Society and Change: S.D. Clark and the Development of Canadian Sociology*. Toronto: University of Toronto Press. pp. 79-89.
91 See essays in this volume by Campbell, Harrison and Helmes-Hayes.

Chapter Two

S.D. CLARK: "THE DEAN OF CANADIAN SOCIOLOGY"[1]

Douglas F. Campbell[2]

Introduction

S. D. Clark is a "Made in Canada" sociologist. Born in Alberta, he was educated from grade school through university in Alberta, Saskatchewan, Ontario and Quebec.[3] He taught for one year at the University of Manitoba and then, except for periodic leaves of absence, for more than thirty years at the University of Toronto. This was followed by two years at Dalhousie University.[4] His books and his thirty-some published articles are almost exclusively on Canadian subjects. A Westerner by birth, he married an Easterner and they brought up their three children in Central Canada. He is typically Canadian in that he did not easily achieve his present eminent position in the Canadian academic community. For years, he was considered a historian by many sociologists and seen by historians as one who jumped on a bandwagon just as the wheels were falling off.[5]

All that has changed. Professor Clark no longer is placed in an ambiguous category; he is a *sociologist* who has developed a unique perspective on social change and applied it to the study of Canadian society. In order to

---

Campbell, Douglas F. (1983). S.D. Clark: The Dean of Canadian Sociology. From *Beginnings: Essays on the History of Canadian Sociology*. Port Credit: The Scribblers' Press. pp. 138-198. Reprinted with permission from the author. References have been removed from the text and replaced as endnotes.

facilitate our understanding of this Canadian sociologist, we will divide the paper into three main parts: 1) Clark the Person, then 2) Clark the Organizer, and finally 3) Clark the Sociologist.

Clark the Person

Samuel Delbert Clark was born the second in a family of three boys and two girls, on a farm at Lloydminster, Alberta, on February 24, 1910. The Clarks farmed in Ontario after their arrival in the New World around 1840, but Clark's father, along with many other Ontarians of his time, was attracted to the newly established province of Alberta in 1905. These were pioneering days. The West was a brand new country, a frontier, and the East, in comparison, was old, institutionalized and predictable. No doubt Clark's childhood experiences had a major impact on his research interests.

From the first, the farm did not seem to be the place for the second son. He couldn't compete with his older brother in the farm chores but he was second to none in his schoolwork. His parents, recognizing that the second son was not "cut out" for the farm, encouraged him in his schoolwork. Early in his school career, history caught his imagination, and despite the pioneering days, S.D. had very good teachers (he cites three) who nurtured his new-found interest. The last of these was a graduate of the University of Saskatchewan who encouraged Clark to do his undergraduate work at his alma mater rather than at the University of Alberta.

S.D. was the first in his community to go on to university, but that did not prevent people from giving him advice. As Clark tells the story, one of the forward-looking members of the community convinced Clark's father that Delbert could, and should for practical reasons, combine a Bachelor of Commerce with the Bachelor of Arts and the father, in turn, convinced his son, at least temporarily. But when he arrived at the University Registration desk, as Clark put it, "I decided I was going to do what I wanted to do and I stuck with that pretty much from then on." The seventeen-year-old student registered for an Arts program with honours in History.

While at the University of Saskatchewan, he was greatly influenced by two professors, the political scientist R. MacGregor Dawson[6] and particularly by the Presbyterian minister-turned-historian, Arthur S. Morton,[7] who was a historian of the western frontier. He involved Clark in his studies, and even convinced him to spend a part of his summers investigating the old fort sites around Lloydminster. Professors are often tempted to map out the future of their bright students even when such interventions are unsolicited or unwelcome. In Clark's case, Morton decided that upon graduation S.D. should go to Normal School, then become a high school teacher and eventually run for politics as a member of the Farmers' Party. For the second time in his life, Clark listened respectfully to his elder, then proceeded to do what he wanted.

During the first train trip from Lloydminster to Saskatoon, he confided to a former teacher that his goal in life was to become a university professor. His teacher-travelling companion found the idea silly but Clark was undeterred. He knew what he wanted; the problem, as the country sank into an economic depression, was how to get it. Morton's plan had been rejected. Clark had heard, more than likely from Morton, of the Canadian Frontier Project which was an interdisciplinary project of study and research which was funded by an American foundation. The directors of this project were offering fellowships. Clark applied to one of the project leaders, Professor Chester Martin of the University of Toronto, for assistance and he was flattered to receive a long distance phone call from Martin who offered him a $500 fellowship at his university. Morton, however, persuaded Clark to return to the University of Saskatchewan for a Master's degree. Since the fellowship was valid at any Canadian university, Clark agreed and did an M.A. thesis under Morton on *Farm Settlement: Dry Land Farming and Settlement in Saskatchewan* (1931).

With his M.A. in history completed, Clark capitalized on his contact with Chester Martin, and no doubt the Martin-Morton friendship,[8] to continue his graduate work in history at the University of Toronto in 1931-32. This was the year Clark described as "his wild year," during which he read Marx, Engels, and North American left-wing writers such as Beard and Myers. It was the year of his disillusionment with the constitutional-political brand of history so popular up to that time, and of which Chester Martin was a leading exponent. Clark, for example, wanted to do a thesis on the Western Farmers' Movement but he was told that that topic was not history. He had harboured a persistent love for political science as a result of his courses with R. MacGregor Dawson in Saskatchewan, and during this exciting, yet disappointing, year at Toronto, Frank Underhill and the members of the League for Social Reconstruction were making much more sense to the young man from the depressed prairies than was Chester Martin.

However, in the end, Clark was assigned a "suitable" dissertation topic in history. (The topic so impressed him that, some forty years later, he cannot remember what it was). Fortunately, he did not have to research the assigned topic.

Clark is understandably proud of having won a Saskatchewan IODE scholarship which took him to the London School of Economics in 1932. The year at Toronto had been both stimulating and disillusioning. One thing was certain: the brand of history that was taught at U of T's History Department was not his "cup of tea." One year abroad might be just what was needed to get things in perspective. His year at the London School of Economics, however, might be summed up in this manner: most Canadians at that time who studied at LSE were captivated by Harold Laski; Clark, too, was very impressed. But the scholar who commanded greater attention from him was the Christian Socialist, R. H. Tawney.[9] All too quickly the year was over. Was it back to Toronto and more institutional history?

Professor Clark's recollection of this very important crossroads makes his career appear accidental. When he disembarked in Montreal, S. D. was in financial need. However, he remembered that a Saskatchewan confrere, who had borrowed thirty-odd dollars from him some time earlier, was studying at McGill. He went to the university only to find that his student-friend was not at home. To while away the time until his return, Clark looked up Professor Carl Dawson, the sociologist, whose work was familiar to Clark. After hearing his story, Dawson suggested that if Clark was as good as he seemed, he would give him sufficient financial support to do graduate work in sociology. Clark accepted immediately. (Incidentally, he did get a cheque from his friend but it "bounced"). Thus, the following two years (1933-35) were spent at McGill studying sociology[10] under the direction of Carl Dawson and Everett Hughes. Clark wrote his second M.A. thesis, this one in sociology, on The Canadian Manufacturers' Association and the National Interest,[11] a topic apparently chosen in discussion with Dawson.

Dawson, too, had his plans for Clark. He wanted S. D. to go to the University of Chicago for his doctorate and even arranged a fellowship. However, once again, Clark had his own plans. In one of the author's interviews with Clark, he confessed that he had fallen in love with the University of Toronto from his very first day on campus. He also looked forward to working with several members of the Toronto faculty. He had seen Harold Innis and had read some of his work during his year at Toronto.

He met and talked with him a year later in London. He wanted to work with Innis and Underhill,[12] so he applied for a Ph.D. fellowship, got it and went to Toronto. (This action apparently caused considerable stiffness in Dawson's relationship with Clark for a number of years.[13]) So in 1936 Clark started (or resumed) his Ph.D. studies at Toronto, but this time in political science rather than history or sociology.

During the two years he took to complete his Ph.D., Clark had a seminar course with Innis and a reading course from Brady.[15] Then he wrote a dissertation on The Canadian Manufacturers' Association, completing it in 1937. A member of his defense committee who was deeply involved with industry took exception to Clark's labeling of the CMA as a lobby. Indeed, he held up the dissertation and the spring graduation deadline passed; as a result, the Ph.D. degree was conferred the following year in 1938.

The academic year 1937-38 was Innis's first as chairman of the Department of Political Economy. E. J. Urwick had already set up the honours program in sociology in 1933, despite the fact that there were no sociologists on the staff.[15] C. W. M. Hart,[16] an anthropologist trained in the functionalist style of Radcliffe-Brown, was hired in 1934 to teach sociology. Clark was invited to join him along with Urwick and Ketchum (a social psychologist). The latter had been in this program for several years as a full-time Instructor in sociology. The salary offered was $1,000.

As curious as it may seem today, Clark was reluctant to be hired as a sociologist. He had earned an honours B.A in history and political science, an M.A. in history, an M.A. in sociology, but a Ph.D. in political science. He wanted an appointment in political science. He also was of the opinion that he was worth more than $1,000. When he returned to Toronto from his father's farm in the fall of 1937, however, he found waiting for him an offer of the position of Lecturer in sociology and political science at $1,600 from Professor McQueen of the University of Manitoba. Two days later, with Innis's blessing, he was on the train to Winnipeg. Clark, however, was Innis's "fair haired boy"; he did the kind of sociology of which Innis approved. So, in 1938, Clark was back in Toronto as Lecturer but in sociology alone and in the Department of Anthropology. "This was the one and only appointment I could get; I was forced back into sociology." While it did not take place exactly as he had expected, nevertheless he had achieved his dream; he was a university professor. A year later sociology was placed under the umbrella of political economy where it stayed until 1963. We shall continue the story of Clark's career under the title "Clark the Organizer."

Clark the Organizer (1937-1970)[17]

Before we start discussing Clark's contribution to the development of sociology at the University of Toronto, we should say a word or two about sociology in the pre-Clark period.

Sociology was viewed with skepticism in the University of Toronto. Certain of its colleges, Victoria and St. Michael's for example, years after the subject was allowed on the university curriculum, actively discouraged students from taking courses in sociology. Professor Jean Burnet recalled being told by an officer at Victoria College (University of Toronto) that her grades put her in a position for a major award but for the fact that her subject was sociology.[18] In view of this, it is not surprising that the University of Toronto did not establish a separate department of sociology until 1963. McGill in contrast had one in 1922 and Laval in 1943.

As early as 1915, however, Toronto did have at least one professor who was identified as a sociologist and another who taught it (Macmillan at Victoria). Robert M. MacIver worked in the Department of Political Science from 1915-1927, after which he went to Columbia in New York, thereby establishing a link between Toronto and Columbia in the areas of political science and sociology. Despite the fact that MacIver wrote several of his well-known works, acclaimed by political scientists and sociologists alike, while at Toronto, he "does not seem to have had any influence in furthering the cause of sociology at the university.[19] E. J. Urwick, a "gentle" Englishman, was a member of the political science department and a social philosopher by persuasion. To him goes the credit for establishing the honours program in sociology in 1933, despite the fact that there were no sociologists on the faculty at the time. Initially, sociology seems to have been a focus around which interested faculty members from other disciplines lectured.[20] In 1934, Ketchum,[21] a Canadian social psychologist trained at Chicago, Urwick and Hart made up the "sociology" team. In 1938, Clark joined the team as the first full-time staff appointment in sociology. Within a year, sociology found a home in the Department of Political Economy under the rule of Innis.

Many people have discussed the consequences to a weak discipline, such as sociology, of being given a stall in the political economy stable.

Some of the conclusions have been that it reinforced the historical approach to the study of society; that it slowed the growth of the discipline in numbers both of faculty and graduates; that it prevented sociology from being accepted within the university as a *bone fide* distinctive discipline worthy of grants, bursaries, etc. It would be a mistake, however, to stress only negative effects. The sociologists enjoyed some of the benefits of being part of one of the most illustrious departments in the faculty. Further, when Innis became Graduate Dean, the sociologists had a strong voice in the Administration to speak on their behalf. (Incidentally, up to 1963 at least, Clark claimed that, with one exception, he had his way in every appointment made in sociology.)

Nevertheless, the growth in the sociology faculty was slow. Throughout the 1940s, while some names changed, the number remained constant at four until 1949-50 when there were five listed on the staff. Although the numbers changed little during this period, the name changes were significant. By the early 1940s, the names Urwick and Ketchum disappeared from the list and for two years (1940-42) the name E. C. Devereux appeared. Devereux was a young, Harvard-trained sociologist who was one of Talcott Parson's early missionaries. Aileen Ross spent three years (1942-45) and Eva Younge one year (1943-44) at Toronto. The year 1945-46 marked the first time that a Toronto graduate in sociology returned to take up a staff position. From that time to 1967, Jean Burnet was a core member and for many years the only woman on the sociology staff at the University of Toronto. (See her *Minorities I Have Belonged To*, (1974)). She was writing her dissertation for the University of Chicago on a dry-land area of south-eastern Alberta when Professor Seymour Martin Lipset joined the Toronto Department. He, too, was writing a dissertation on the West, the rise of the CCF in Saskatchewan. Both theses became classics in Canadian Sociology.[22] Lipset stayed for two years (1946-48). The final name to be mentioned in the 1940s was Eli Chinoy; he stayed four years before returning to the United States.

The 1950s were very much like the 1940s; the number of permanent staff stayed at five, but again, there were a number of name changes. Both John Seeley and R. Alexander Sim became part-time members of the staff while they were doing their research for *Crestwood Heights*. Theodor Geiger, a German theoretician of note, spent one year in Toronto.[23] Another Toronto graduate, Jim Giffen was listed the same year. In fact, he was listed on the permanent staff first in the academic year 1948-49. Leo Zakuta, another graduate of Chicago, joined the core staff of Clark, Burnet and Giffen in 1953, and Dennis Wrong, a Canadian who became well-known in American sociological circles, was listed for the year 1955-56. Two other significant appointments were made in the 1950's. Oswald Hall, a graduate of Chicago and by that time well-established in his field, joined the core staff in 1956 and Nathan Keyfitz, another eventual export to the U.S., came to Toronto in 1959 to stay for three years.

If the '40s and '50s were decades of stability and slow development, the '60s was a decade of change and mushrooming growth. Even before 1963-64, the year in which the department of sociology was established, the number of sociologists had grown considerably. One of the new additions made the year prior to separation was Rex Lucas, a graduate of Columbia, who remained in the department until his sudden death in 1978. By the last year of Professor Clark's chairmanship (1968-69), the number had shot up to thirty-five and continued to climb during the next decade. The new sociologists included such well-known names as Charles Tilly, Louis Feuer, E. K. Francis, Norman Bell, John Porter, Ray Breton, Bill Michelson, and Warren Kalbach. Tilly, Francis, and Porter stayed for relatively short periods of time, Feuer stayed until he resigned in 1978 to take a position at the University of Virginia.

There remain several questions which should be addressed, no matter how provisionally, before this section on the shaping of sociology at Toronto can be closed: 1. Why was the department established when it was? 2. Why were so many American sociologists appointed during the 1960s? 3. Why did Professor Clark resign the chairmanship in 1969?

1. There were remote and proximate reasons for the change. One remote reason was that practically every university in Canada had or was about to establish such a department. Secondly, the discipline was becoming more visible; there was even talk of the sociologists breaking away from the Canadian Association of Political Scientists and Economists. (This in fact happened in 1963.) Thirdly, the number of students taking sociology increased dramatically. Fourthly, the number of sociologists on the faculty had reach such a number (ten in 1962-63), that they had developed a separate enclave within the Department of Political Economy.[24] Professor Clark found while consulting each member in 1963 that there was unanimity on the desire to have a separate department. Finally, Harold Innis, the unifying force in the

social sciences, had long since passed on and his successors did not possess his vision. The proximate cause for the new department in 1963 was the rapid increase of staff in all departments and the pressure on offices in the new Sidney Smith Building. There was no room for sociologists in the new building so they were shunted off to the old Borden Building and a departmental structure of their own became part of the package. According to Professor Clark, the Dean appointed him chairman without consulting the members of the staff. The choice was never disputed but the manner of the appointment seemed to temporarily ruffle some feathers.

2. The 1960s produced a bonanza of "baby boom" students all of whom, it seemed, wanted the answers to burning social questions and sociology was seen as the discipline to provide them. Government leaders also came to the conclusion that a well-educated youth was a prerequisite to an expanding industrial economy. As a result, government funding to the university became more generous. Quite suddenly, after years of struggle to make all too infrequent appointments, sociology departments in Canadian universities were provided substantial funds to expand their departments. But where were trained sociologists to be found? In theory at least, there were four basic sources: a) recent graduates from Canadian universities; b) experienced sociologists in other Canadian universities; c) recent graduates from non-Canadian, particularly American, universities; d) experienced sociologists from non-Canadian, particularly American, universities. Unfortunately, Canadian universities were producing practically no Ph.D.s in sociology. McGill did not have a Ph.D. program at the time and Toronto might have had a half-dozen graduates with Ph.D.s in sociology. All the Canadian universities were scrambling for additional staff. It had been a long-standing tradition that "the call" would go out to lecturers who were making names for themselves in the hinterland universities to come to Toronto. (Rex Lucas was one in the 1960s who answered this call.) But, unlike the earlier years, Toronto found itself competing with many of the old and new universities in Ontario such as York and McMaster for new staff members. Canadian universities, the University of Toronto's Sociology Department included, turned to American universities for recruits; there was, for all practical purposes, no alternative.[25] When Toronto's Sociology Department was established, its staff was Canadian. Whether he could have found sociologists elsewhere or not, Clark claimed that it was his deliberate policy to hire Americans in order to pump new life into a rather

ingrown department. They did breathe new life into the department, perhaps more than anyone bargained for.

3. Clark had been responsible for sociology in the Department of Political Economy for years. After the Department of Sociology had been established, however, he served as chairman for six years (1963-64 to 1968-69). While there are many stories emanating from this period of time in the department, very little has been committed to print. Until now, Clark has not given his view of the story but, if he should decide to do so, it would make for very interesting reading. It is somewhat ironic that Clark's own "frontier" model has some explanatory value for the happenings of this period, but we shall leave this topic for another time and go on to a discussion of Clark's scholarship.

Clark The Scholar

There are six subject categories into which Clark's work can be placed[26]:

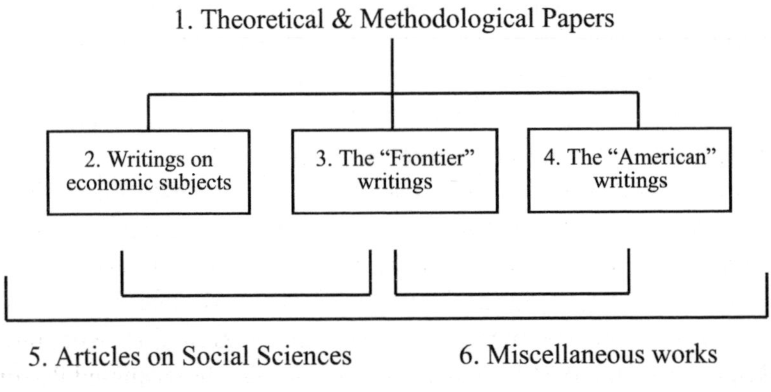

[See Appendix]

The first four categories are closely interrelated. Almost from the very beginning of his scholarly career, Clark wrote key papers in these four categories which set down the perspective, method and materials for his academic enterprise. Over the years, modifications were made but they were not substantial. Almost forty years separate the "Introduction" to *Social Development in Canada* (1942) from the "Introduction" for *Canadian Society in Historic Perspective* (1977) and what is most striking about the works is the similarity. Almost from the beginning as well, his academic peers' reactions were mixed; all his reviewers applauded his scholarship but had serious reservations about his method and/or model.[27]

Category 1: Theoretical and Methodological Papers.

What then are the ingredients of Clark's sociology? They can be found in Category 1: his four theory and method essays, his key essay "Economic Expansion and the Moral Order" (1941) as well as in the Introductions to his major works.[28] From these works, it is clear that Clark had substantial reservations about the training he received in the ecology school of sociology at McGill.[29] Human ecology and American sociology generally ignored history and because of this, Clark found it superficial and even misleading. The great works in sociology almost without exception, Clark argued, were European and historically-based. But, for Clark, it was not enough that sociologists use the findings of history in their work. Instead, sociologists should do historical research themselves. The historian does not look for the materials which are of interest to the sociologist nor does he have the perspective through which he could present his historical materials in a manner meaningful to the sociologist. The trained sociologist must take his own perspective to the historical data and arrive at a sociological understanding of the historical phenomenon.

The second major building block in Clark's sociology was that social reality is not static but dynamic. Yet most sociologists present their study as if it were static. In fact, social change has been one of the weakest areas on American sociology and the problem has been how to capture social change within the available sociological models. Clark was familiar with Talcott Parsons' work from the beginning.[30] In a 1952 essay, he discussed Parsons' solution to the social change problem. This in part is what he had to say[31]:

> "...following Parsons, it is possible to talk about 'change within the system' and to analyse such changes in terms of the concept of moving equilibrium.... All change can be viewed as change within the system, but so as well can all change be viewed as change of the system. By making so indeterminate the boundaries of the society being analyzed that there remains nothing that cannot be made part of the

> society, the problem of change of the society is effectively excluded from consideration.... It has been the failure of Parsons to see his model of society within clearly defined physical and temporal boundaries..."

Clark solved this problem within his historical approach to sociology.

Change takes place within the confines of space and time but American sociology is most frequently written without consideration for either. Historians, on the other hand, tend to study a series of events within a specified time frame and within a geographical location. Therefore, for the sociological study of social change, the location must be established and the sociological phenomenon must be studied from one specified period of time through to a later specified time. Since social change is a continuous process, the historical sociologist must begin his study at a time period of relatively little change in order to establish the state of social reality at that point. The events must then be followed through the period of most protracted change, and the study terminated only when a period of relative calm has returned and this latter state of "static" social reality has been studied.

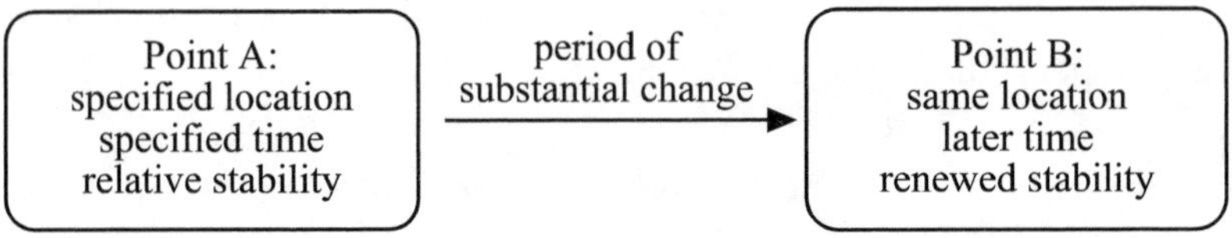

Given these two pillars to Clark's sociology, it is not surprising that he turned his historical interests to situations of rapid, even dramatic change. The largest category of his work is Category 3, The "Frontier" Category, in which he chose periods of Canadian history in which there were "great rushes of people." These would be his foci for developing his sociology of social change.

Categories Two and Four: Writings on Economic Subjects and The American Writings

Before investigating the works which form the principal category of Clark's scholarship, attention should be given to two subsidiary and interlocking areas—Canadian economic institutions and "American" literature. The initial work in his economic studies was his doctoral dissertation, *The Canadian Manufacturers' Association* (CMA) (1939). This was a case study in which Clark researched the career of this institution from its tentative beginnings in the 1850s up to the 1920s. Since he was not given access to the Association's files, he had to fetter out pertinent data from newspapers, magazines and special reports as well as from interviews. This relatively unknown work of Clark's provided insights into 1) the peculiar problems of Canadian manufacturing; 2) the difficulties of a national organization in Canada; and 3) the dangers involved in manipulating public opinion.

The relatively unsuccessful attempts at organizing industrial enterprises grew out of economic depression rather than expansion. Each subsequent attempt was provoked by the squeeze applied by the powerful Canadian banking, transportation and commercial systems on Ontario industrialists. The root problem for the Industrial system in Canada from the 19th century was stated by Clark to be[32]:

> "Manufacturing grew up within the sheltered system of national depression, developing in response to the demands of national enterprises such as railway building and, to the protection afforded by increasing customs tariffs. It remained subordinate to the major developments within the Canadian economy, and dependent upon the system of aids growing up within the Confederation structure."

From the time of Confederation on, the CMA had to fight off each threat to the tariff by attempting to convince public opinion and governments that what was good for Canadian manufacturing was good for the general public.[33]

Internally the national organization faced severe tests as well. The complex tariff system did not deal equally with manufacturers of various categories of unfinished, semi-finished and finished products. Additionally, the CMA was strongly associated with eastern manufacturers, thus appearing to discourage industrial growth in other regions of the country. Both problems produced extensive internal conflict. In fact the national office, for survival sake, removed itself from specific and troublesome issues and focused more on providing expert advice for manufacturers at the national and regional offices.

The series of events which severely damaged the CMA's public image occurred after the First World War. A very strong attack had been launched against the tariff which the CMA perceived as a grave threat. Murray's Editorial Report Service, an agency established in 1919, was thought to have been closely associated with the CMA. This Service pursued a practice whereby a newspaper was monitored over a period of time in order to relay to various industrial firms which advertised in the newspaper its views on the tariff. Although the connection between Murray's and the CMA was never proven once Murray's practice became known, public opinion turned strongly against the CMA. "In some respects the Association has never recovered the position of influence it held previously to 1919."[34]

At the same time that Clark was studying the CMA he was also interviewing representatives of the English-minority in Montreal concerning their views of the United States. He had no trouble integrating the two projects. Many of the attitudes found among the English Montrealers could be explained by vested interests, particularly the economic sphere.

> "While on the political side we see three currents of opinion, which at times diverge sharply from one another: imperial, national and North American; so on the economic side there has been a struggle between British, Canadian and American interests for the Canadian market.... In the course of this competition strong vested interests have grown up in Canada dependent on one or another of these three competitors" [35, 36]

Canadian nationalism, as Clark found among the English-speaking Montrealers, was based on the celebration of the British Empire and stereotyping the perceived negative characteristics of the United States.

> "Thus Canadian life can almost be said to take its rise in the negative will to resist absorption in the American Republic. It is largely about the United States as an object that the consciousness of Canadian national unity has grown up. And yet the cultural life of English-speaking Canada is strikingly similar to that of the United States."[37]

In his "American" papers, Clark persisted in pointing out time after time that Canadians are North Americans. Geography made Canada one with the United States but history made it different. What are these differences imposed by history? In a number of papers, perhaps in "The Canadian Community" (1950b) particularly, Clark attempted to isolate the differences between the two countries. He argued that Canada's frontier tended to be a controlled, somewhat "closed" frontier, thereby putting checks on revolutionary tendencies; Canadians were more "conservative" and maintained a "tradition of respect for institutions and law and order"; they achieved "greater stability in family organization"; they tended to favour "the aristocratic principle"; and the religion of established churches. Above all, Canada was different because of its "two chief cultural groups." In subsequent papers (1964a, 1965) Clark pursued these themes further.

> "Canadians have not so much wanted to be Canadians as to be North Americans.... Their interest found truer expression in those movements of a liberal-democratic character directed to the end of making Canada a much more integral part of the larger North American society". [38, 39]

Anti-American nationalism was not only a reflection of economic vested interests but also of the interests of Canadian bureaucrats who all but made up the middle class. In the middle 1960s, Clark agreed, the size of the middle class had grown substantially, but he did not take consolation from this fact because he saw the newly enlarged middle class as distant from the masses as ever.

> "The present is a time [1969] of political and social ferment in Canada. If good is to come out of that ferment, the beneficiaries must be the great masses of Canadian people, not a favoured few able to better their position within a strengthened bureaucratic order." [40]

He worried as well that, because of perceived threats to their vested interests, the middle class both in English and French Canada[41] would try to defy geography even more rather than compete with Americans. This Clark opposed.

> "...our strength as a nation will come not by turning our back upon the larger North American society but by our full and free participation in it."[42]

During his stay in Canada, Professor Lipset became very familiar with Clark's writings as well as with those of other Toronto academics such as Underhill, Innis, Lower, etc. In his works, Lipset often wrote extensively about Canada in comparison with the United States. In his *First New Nation* (1963), *Turner and the Sociology of the Frontier* (with Hofstader, 1961), and *Revolution and Counter-Revolution* (1968), Lipset cited Clark's work frequently.[43] Interestingly enough, Lipset's views on the Canadian value system sparked considerable debate both in the U.S. and Canada.[44]

We can now turn to the large corpus of his work, the "Frontier" writings.

Category Three: The "Frontier Writings"

From his earliest works (see 1939a), Clark used the frontier label but it seemed to cause confusion.[45] In the first footnote on the first page of *Social Development in Canada* (1942) Clark wrote[46]:

> "It should perhaps be emphasized that considerable liberty has been taken with respect to the term 'frontier.' Because of the variety of meanings which have been attached to it, its use would have been avoided if a more convenient term had suggested itself. Instead of being employed in the Turner sense to designate the furthest extended line of settlement, it is taken here to refer to the development of new forms of economic enterprise. Thus 'frontier economic expansion' means simply the expansion of new forms of economic enterprise and the 'frontier' the area in which such expansion is taking place. The emphasis is not upon the period of early settlement—what might be called the pioneering stage of development—but rather upon that period when new techniques were being fully employed in economic exploitation, what is here called the frontier stage."

Thus, Clark's use of "frontier" was much broader than Turner's because it represented the dynamics resulting from a new economic expansion, rural as well as urban, in an industrial or mining setting, in the past or in contemporary times. Clark explained the manner in which he employed the concept time and time again. He made some adjustments by distinguishing between "closed frontiers" such as early Quebec and some Scottish communities of Upper Canada and the "open frontiers" of the backwoods of Ontario, but he never fully escaped Turner's camp nor the criticisms leveled at this School. His concept of the frontier may be schematized as follows:

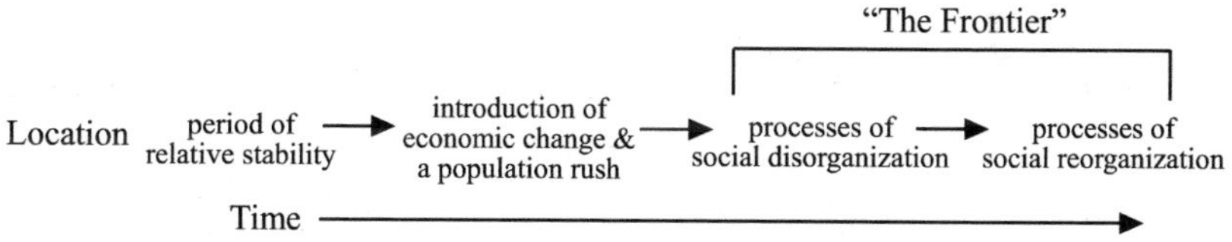

It is not at all clear that Clark wanted to escape entirely because he used the "frontier" at times in a manner not unlike Turner. Nonetheless, his fundamental concern was with social change in areas which experienced rapid economic change, thus disrupting the social organization employed in earlier situations.[47]

The Trilogy:

Clark was a student of Harold Innis. Whereas his influence is somewhat remote today, in the 1930s and 1940s the influence of Innis was far more immediate and powerful. In his early major works, Clark went over the ground broken by Innis in order to put a social face on it. This effort, carried out in great part under Innis' gaze, occupied a period of more than twenty years and resulted in the following trilogy: *The Social Development of Canada* (1942); *Church and Sect in Canada* (1948), and *Movements of Political Protest in Canada* (1959). The territories investigated were various settlements in the Maritimes, Lower and Upper Canada, British Columbia and the Yukon. The time frame was 1640-1920. The general thesis for the trilogy is contained in the following statement: "An emphasis, therefore, has been placed upon the particular problem of the relationship of frontier economic expansion in Canada, or more strictly the opening up of new areas or fields of economic exploitation, to the development of social organization."[48] We will look at this thesis as developed in each of the three works which make up the trilogy.

I. *The Social Development of Canada* is unique in Canadian sociology because, while it has an introduction and five essays, most of it is made up of historical and archival excerpts.[49] It was written ostensibly to convince sociologists that there was a rich storehouse of Canadian historical material available for their use. What it in fact did was 1) to stake out the parameters of Clark's sociological research space and 2) to demonstrate his model of social change in five case studies:

a) The Fur Trade and Rural Society in New France
b) The Fisheries and Rural Society in the Maritime Colonies
c) The Timber Trade and Rural Society in Upper Canada
d) Mining Society in British Columbia and the Yukon
e) Transcontinental Railways and Industrial-Capitalist Society

While Innis had written extensively on all these areas as an economic historian, Clark filled in the picture with his study of social relationships.

a) In his first case study of this work, the structures and relationships of the Quebec agricultural community and the habitant of the late seventeenth and early eighteenth centuries are compared with those of the fur trade and the *coureurs de bois*. The latter represented processes diametrically opposed to agriculture involving innovation, deviance, and freedom, particularly for young men. All this represented a threat to a sedentary society. A degree of disorganization resulted in the social relations of the youth within the rural and urban societies. Eventually, monopoly in the fur trade and growing distance brought some control over these disruptive influences.

b) The communities of the Maritime colonies of the pre- and post-American Revolution period were characterized by isolation, a direct result of the fishing industry. The New Englanders brought their aggressive ways to a number of Nova Scotian villages around 1760. This impaired cohesion within the province but England's policy attempted to provide a focus in Halifax. Despite all efforts, however, Halifax remained a military and naval community and was unable to integrate the various communities spread along the Nova Scotian coast. Lumbering and shipbuilding introduced further disorganization because of the tendency of the settlers to neglect their farms in favour of lumbering. The pattern of social relationships developed in the lumber camps militated against farm life with the end result that, with the collapse of the ship-building and timber industries, many experienced bankruptcy.

c) Upper Canada went from a population of 33,000 in 1812 to 952,000 in 1851. This agricultural frontier was filled with Loyalists, Americans, Scots, Irish and English. The communities of 1812 had developed structures around the frontier family, but many of the new arrivals came as individuals without the experience of frontier life. In this open frontier, considerable personal and community disorganization took place until the new homesteaders took on the proven ways of their predecessors.

d) The gold rushes of 1858-62 in British Columbia and of 1897-1905 in the Yukon are Clark's archetypical frontier. Thousands of men from all over the world descended on these areas. They fanned out over the rivers and streams during the summer living relatively isolated lives but retiring to the local town or cities to idle away their winter time. Everyone thought he was going to strike it rich but only the lucky few did and many of the latter quickly squandered their riches. Deviance of all kinds flourished, but even in these circumstances, re-organizational processes arose. For example, the Mounted Police, particularly in Dawson Creek, played an important reorganizing role. "Institutional controls derived from outside, however, were effective only as a result of the development of an underlying social consciousness favourable to the establishment of order within the community."[50]

> e) "The great number of new frontiers—manufacturing, agricultural, mining, lumbering, pulp and paper, and fishing—which emerged after the turn of the [20th] century was indicative of the wide sweep of industrial-capitalist expansion. Problems of social organization in various Canadian communities were evidence of the disturbing effects of such expansion."[51]

The disorganization resulting from these new 20th Century frontiers was manifested in the slums of the rapidly growing cities, the rural people depopulating the farms and settling uncomfortably into city life, the immigrant ghettoes, the all-male mining camps, the agrarian movements of the West, and the trade union movements of the industrial cities. Yet, in the midst of all this disarray, Clark found reorganization taking place, particularly through the growth of national organizations.

In *The Social Development of Canada*, Clark for the first time displayed in some detail his model for the study of social change through historical sociology. For the most part, the work was only suggestive; the essays touched on many ideas supportive of Clark's thesis and the many excerpts at the conclusion of each essay of course supported the approach. Clark's next work, however, *Church and Sect in Canada* (1948), more explicitly demonstrated his technique.

II. The main reason for the success of *Church and Sect* was that Clark employed an additional specifying set of concepts. He was familiar with Troelsch's church-sect dichotomy but he seemed to be more impressed by Niebuhr's *The Social Sources of Denominationalism* (1929). Niebuhr had said it all in one sentence: "Doctrine and practices change with the mutations of social structure, not vice versa; the ideological interpretation of such changes quite misses the point."[52] Clark had come across a great deal of sect-like religious activities in his research of the archival documents. He saw that Neibuhr's sect-denomination-church conceptual set could be used to specify the processes of disorganization and reorganization more clearly than did the case studies of the previous work. Clark also introduced into this work an idea found in some of the earlier frontier histories, i.e. the frontier was not bound by national boundaries. Therefore, an advancing American frontier could be seen to have flooded into the Canadian side, and the spirit, techniques, and leaders born of the American frontier "infected" people on the Canadian frontiers as well. In sum, North American frontier people on both sides of the 49th parallel had a great deal in common.

Church and Sect in Canada (1948) was a work bounded by a specific timeframe (1760-1900) and geography.

Great Awakening in Nova Scotia (1760-1783)
Great Revival in the Maritime Provinces (1783-1832)
Great Revival in Canada (1783-1832)
Break with American Sectarianism (1783-1832)

Conflict with Church and Sect (1832-1860)
New Frontiers and New Sects (1832-1860)
Rise of the Territorial Church (1860-1885)
The Revival in the City (1885- 1900)

The theme of the study was spelled out clearly in the first pages of this lengthy work[53]:

> "This study is concerned with the conflict between the church and sect forms of religious organization in relation to the changing community structure of Canada. It seeks to offer an explanation of religious change in terms of underlying changes in social conditions. The view set forth here is that the church has been dependent upon a condition of social stability and when such a condition has not been present it has given way to the sect form of religious organization.... The church has grown out of the conditions of a mature society; the sect has been a product of what might be called frontier conditions of social life."

I will give a cameo of each section of this work. (The Schema might prove of some assistance to the reader).[54]

(i) The Great Awakening in Nova Scotia (1760-83): By 1760 New Englanders had moved in large numbers to Nova Scotia in order to occupy the vacated Acadian lands. They took with them their village structures and Congregational religion. In the distant and newly established city of Halifax, the military-navy-Church of England monopoly held sway but was of little interest to the New Englanders. But moving into the Nova Scotian "frontier" had not strengthened their New England ways and the events leading up to 1776 disrupted the village structure on which the Congregational system rested. The year of the American Revolution was also the year Henry Alline, a layman, experienced a direct call from God to preach. With this event started the New Light movement of evangelism and by the time of his death (1784) there was hardly a Congregational group intact in the Maritime colonies. The New Englanders in Nova Scotia tried to remain politically neutral during the American-British war and chose to go strongly evangelical

Schema of Clark's *Church and Sects in Canada* (1948)

Time Frame	Place	Disorganizing Event(s)	Disorganizing Processes	Reorganizing Event(s)	Reorganizing Processes
1760-83	Villages of south N.S.	Arrival of New Englanders	The Frontier Loss of Village Control, Amer. Revolution Loss of Contact with New England	Conversion of Alline	Newlights, Great Awakening, Evangelism, Local Preacher
1783-1832	Villages of N.S. & N.B.	Arrival of New Englanders, Loyalists, Yorkshiremen	Uprooting Effects	Conversion W. Black	Newlights & Methodists Itinerant missionaries Sects
1783-1832	Backwoods Upper Can.	Arrival of Loyalists, Scots, Irish, English	The Open Frontier Dynamics	Arrival of Methodist (Presby. & Baptist) preachers	Evangelism, Conversion, Sense of belonging in Sects
1783-1832	Settled & Prosperous Villages & Towns of N.S., N.B., Lower & Upper Can.	Results of Amer. Rev., War of 1812 Events leading	The English vs. The Americans	Arrival of Wesleyan & Other English Ministers	First Steps toward Denomina-tionalism
1832-1860	Settled & Prosperous Villages & Towns of N.S., N.B., Lower & Upper Can.	Rise of Class	Shift from Primary to Secondary Relations	Community-wide work by churches	Development of education and moral reform by churches
1832-1860	Settled & Prosperous Villages & Towns of N.S., N.B., Lower & Upper Can.	Urban vs. Rural	Denominational Processes	Rise of Old or New Sects	Founding of Free Will Baptist Bible Christian, Disciples of Christ, MacDonaldites
1860-1885	Urban Maritimes & Canadas	Political Union & National Policy	Demands of a Rapidly Growing Nation	Intra-Denominational Unions	Presby. Union, & Methodist Union were achieved
1885-1900	Cities in Canada	Rise of Industrial Workers	Slums, "Zones of Transition"	Horner's refusal to take an appointment, Arrival of the Salvation Army	Holiness Movement Street Preaching

and other-worldly in compensation. In fact, they achieved reorganization through the New Light sect.

(ii) The Great Revival in the Maritime Provinces: After the American Revolution, Loyalists flooded the Maritime region but Methodist Yorkshiremen who settled in and around Amherst and Scots who moved to eastern parts came around that same time. However, all were dissenters and opposed to the Church of England. As much as the leaders of the established church might have wished to make inroads into these new communities, the church's parish structure, its educated and imported clergy, its intellectualized theology and ritual, its close association with the state, all militated against this possibility. At this time (1783-1832), what was to become the province of New Brunswick was a frontier for the New England states, and the type of religion which proved meaningful to many on this frontier was the evangelism of the New Lights and Methodists. William Black of Amherst, a layman like Alline, experienced a call to preach and did so with great success for the Methodist cause. He supplemented the local lay preachers with itinerant missionaries from the American Methodist Episcopal Church. As compared to the established church, these sects proved much more effective in the social reorganization of the scattered newcomers. This movement stressed emotional experience, conversion, and asceticism, all of which made the convert feel part of a privileged group involved in an important rebuilding crusade.

(iii) Backwoodsmen of Upper Canada (1783-1832): A very similar story to the previous one unfolded during the period of intense population growth in Upper Canada. The British and Americans came in great numbers to settle in the backwoods. The established church made feeble attempts at contacting the new arrivals but, as in the Maritimes, the Church of England did not have the structural flexibility, among other drawbacks, to act effectively. However, the American Presbyterians, Baptists, and particularly the Methodists did. Since Methodism had been founded for the marginal working people of the British industrial towns, it had developed techniques which proved very effective in the backwoods. This church in particular had the centralized control needed to establish preaching circuits for missionaries, it had a place for the local lay preacher and it could hold services anywhere. Their camp meetings, held over a period of several

days in large fields, were extremely effective revivalist services. Thus, the dissenting churches, particularly the Methodists, provided the instruments for reknitting the fabric of the society in rural Upper Canada during the early nineteenth century.

(iv) Americans vs. British: During the same period of time (1783-1832) both in the Maritimes and in Upper Canada people were experiencing great unease with the new Republic to the south. The Americans tried during the Revolution to "liberate" Canadians from the British and again in the War of 1812. Even after the war there continued to be rumblings from the American frontier. An undetermined number of Canadians and a significant number of newly arrived Americans apparently offered every encouragement to these enterprises but the Loyalists and British settlers offset them with their strong imperial sympathies. The disruptions of the War of 1812 forced many American missionaries to return to the United States. This provided the Wesleyans (i.e. Methodists) an opportunity to invite their British missionaries to the Maritimes and to both Canadas. The other dissenting churches did likewise. The shift away from the United States back to Britain was occurring both in the economic and ideological spheres as well. These dissenting churches in Britain, however, tended to be much less evangelical than the American ones. Their successes in competing and eventually displacing American sects gave evidence of the first steps by the backwoods communities toward denominational churches.

(v) The Rise of the Prosperous Villages. From 1832 to 1860, two trends were evident in the Maritimes and the Canadas: 1) the villages and towns were becoming larger and more prosperous, and a visible class structure was begun, 2) increasing social distance between rural and urban areas. In towns, church buildings became more elaborate and expensive, and the demand for a professional clergy was increasing. Evangelism either died out or was professionalized. At the same time, these churches became involved in community-wide efforts of moral reform and education. These very manifestations of denominationalism in urban areas were found to be unsuitable by the rural people who maintained the old forms or developed new forms of evangelism. During this time in the rural communities, the Disciples of Christ, the Free Will Baptists, the Bible Christian Church, and the MacDonaldites found favour. In the above development toward

denominationalism, as the colonies moved erratically toward confederation and the country became more urban, the demands of this rapidly expanding nation pushed the various Methodist, Presbyterian, Congregational, and Baptist churches into intra-denominational unions. This resulted in the loss of those adherents who found more comfort in the evangelical sect.

(vi) Revival in the City: Perhaps the most interesting chapter on sect development in *Church and Sect in Canada* concerns the Canadian city between 1885-1900. Up to this point, sects were associated with the rural environment. However, during this period, the industrial cities attracted hordes of workers, and slums and ghettoes became common place. The Anglican Church was no more capable of rising to this challenge than it had been in earlier times and by now the urban Methodist, Presbyterian and Baptist churches were all but middle and upper class as well. They had buried and did not have the will to resurrect the techniques required to contact this new population. Nonetheless, during this period there was a great religious revival in the Canadian cities, The religious sect which spearheaded much of it was the Salvation Army, which became the agency for effecting social solidarity among the industrial workers in this new "frontier."

III. The final book of the trilogy is *Movements of Political Protest in Canada: 1640-1840* (1959).[55] This substantial work covers much the same territory as the previous one, but whereas the previous one used the church-sect typology as an instrument for demonstrating the disintegration-reintegration process, this work employed the rise of the political reform movements only (i.e. the political sect) and associated this development with the American-Canadian frontier.

Despite the impressive amount of data amassed, the very interesting periods and events studied, and the introduction of very colourful personalities from both the political left and right, this work does not succeed to the very same extent as did *Church and Sect in Canada.* It might be that the very success of the latter made it a hard act to follow. Over and above this very real possibility, however, in *Movements of Political Protest in Canada*, some of the "frontiers," even with the term's widest interpretation seem forced. We are told repeatedly throughout Clark's work that frontiersmen were apolitical, which also presents a problem. Nor do we see that fundamental model of disorganization-reorganization operating as clearly in this work, perhaps because the dynamics were between the political sect which grew to an unsuccessful rebellion or died out, and the local Legislative Council and Whitehall, with the American frontier always in the background. In *Movements of Political Protest in Canada* the force of reorganization seem as much imposed as indigenous. Finally, this work tended to emphasize the American frontier and its impact on Canada.

> "...whereas in the United States these forms of political organization and instruments of political expression developing out of the frontier experience of the population became embodied in the constitution of the republic, in Canada they found no place in established political institutions. It was just here, in the extent to which the frontier spirit was able to make its influence felt upon the political organization of the community as a whole, that is to be found the chief difference between the political development of the United States and Canada" [56]

The work covered four successive time periods in Canadian history:

1660-1760—The First American War of Independence
1765-1785—The War of the United Colonies
1785-1815—The Struggle for the West
1815-1840—The Canadian Rebellions

In Clark's interpretation of the above periods, there existed the forces of democracy, represented by the United States and in particular by the American frontier, and the forces of monarchial government, represented by French and British rule in Canada. The American frontier had intruded sufficiently into Canada through American settlers or through its spirit to make many Canadians react in ways varying from ambivalence—to warmth towards the rhetoric and acts of "political liberation" originating or stimulated within Canada from the American frontier. For example, the attacks of the New Englanders on Acadia and Quebec in 1692 were attempts to "liberate" these colonies from French monarchial domination. The successful march of the American frontiersmen, without permission of their provisional Government, on Lower Canada and their occupancy of Montreal from 1775 to 1776 were further efforts at liberating Canadians, this time from British rule. The Jay Treaty of 1794 and the expanding American frontier precipitated the War of 1812, which was another attempt at liberation. Finally, the rebellions of Lower and Upper Canada (1837-1838) were for the most part home-grown. However, the Papineau Rebellion was influenced significantly by the French and American revolutions, and the MacKenzie uprising was supported by a notable number of transplanted Americans. The American border frontiers also provided hospitable retreats for launching several unsuccessful attempts by Canadian rebels to overthrow the imperialist regime.

Throughout the course of this story of political reform movements, in addition to the better known figures such as Papineau and MacKenzie, we meet lesser known, colourful personages such as Tonge in Nova Scotia, Glenie in New Brunswick, and Gourley in Upper Canada,[57] all of whom were minor heroes in the struggle for political democracy.

Why didn't any of these liberation movements from within or from outside the country succeed? Professor Clark's last hundred pages provide a complex answer to this question. First of all, there were strong forces for conservativism in Lower as well as Upper Canada. In Upper Canada, there were Loyalist and British immigrants, there was the Church and the Orange Order. In Lower Canada, there was the Church, the Montreal businessmen, ethnic rivalry, and the rural French. In both Canadas there was economic depression in the 1830s as well.

> "Lack of enthusiasm for the cause [of liberation] in the United States contributed to, and in part was a consequence of, the lack of enthusiasm for the cause in the Canadian colonies. What disaffection there was in Canada in the summer of 1839 was largely lacking in purpose and direction; despondency had replaced hope, and emigration to the United States offered the effective means of escaping the full acceptance of the status quo. The continuance of depressed economic conditions accentuated feelings of despondency developing out of political conditions and contributed powerfully to the movement of emigration across the border. The spirit of revolt had almost if not entirely died in the country."[58]

Two Later "Frontier" Works: Two more of Clark's works belong in the "Frontier" category. Clark concluded the final essay of *The Social Development of Canada* (1942) in the following manner:

> "The social maladjustments resulting directly or indirectly from these economic dislocations became the major note in the social development of Canada after 1920. They indicate the passing of the frontier stage of economic expansion; on the other hand, they emphasize the importance of such expansion in the building of the Canadian community structure."[59]

Despite Clark's reference in the above to the passing of the frontier stage, two of his more recent works employ variations of his basic "frontier" model. These were *The Suburban Society* (1968) and *The New Urban Poor* (1978). What seems to have happened is that Clark got away from the frontier terminology and moved closer to Parsons' equilibrium model while at the same time maintaining the disorganization-reorganization processes. Before he is out of the introductory part of *The Suburban Society*, Clark strikes a familiar theme: "What clearly has occurred was a great mass movement of population out of the city into the country."[60] A few pages later he states: "Thus the study of suburbanism is the study of social change."[61]

Clearly Clark maintained his basic model in the study of Metropolitan Toronto's suburban society but he reverted to methodologies he learned and used back in his McGill days, the interview and questionnaire. It also becomes clear that he substituted a contemporary subject for a historic one. Clark and his students studied fifteen different suburbs at various levels of income and degrees of maturity.[62] His understanding of the development of suburbs was that, with the growing population in urban areas, those not particularly wedded to the urban way of living as well as those who could not afford it moved to the surrounding rural areas. The subdivision developers soon caught up with and encouraged the exodus. Many of those migrating to the suburbs were young couples who had little experience of any kind. Nonetheless, they worked out their problems on the job, so to speak.

> "...the new suburban population did not bring a great deal to the task of social building. Much of the effort which

> went into this task had to develop out of experience of the job. It was this lack of a clearly perceived view or "image" of what was the good society which was the distinguishing mark of the suburban population. What was sought in the suburbs by the vast majority who settled there, was a home, not a new social world."[63]

Many of the distinctive characteristics of the frontier: indebtedness (p. 111); strangers one to another (p. 190); unwillingness to become involved in organized activities (p. 161); "families turned in towards themselves" (p. 194) were found in Clark's suburbs. But with time the processes of reorganization emerged from within "...what suburban development meant was the reproduction of the city in the country." (p. 221) And "After five to eight years the suburban residential area began to take on much of the character of an old established urban residential area." (p. 213) American sociologists knowledgeable in the works on suburban society hailed *The Suburban Society* (1968) as a substantial breakthrough, and so it was. But those who had read Clark's work over the years found no surprises in his approach to the subject.

Clark's most recent work, *The New Urban Poor* (1978) is placed in the "Frontier" Category because it was a study involving the geographical mobility of rural poor but, except for the movement of people which this study had in common with the other "frontier" studies, it was almost an inversion of the disorganization-reorganization model. The rural poor did not wish to move (and they were supported at a minimum level if they chose not to move) and many of those who moved went to the nearest town and reorganized themselves on the fringe with a lifestyle very similar to their previous rural one. The ones who made it to the big city repeated their prior experiences.

Clark documents this thesis with case studies: five marginal rural communities in northwestern New Brunswick, three urban areas in the same region, a number of rural and urban communities in northern Quebec and Ontario, and several communities in metropolitan Toronto.

In summary then, the core of Clark's work is his "frontier" publications and his perspective on social change which grew out of them.[64] On more than one occasion Clark has had to come to the defence of his framework. Here is an excerpt from one such effort:

> "What Professor Macpherson, however, seems unwilling to concede is that it is just such a population lacking in a class consciousness which has been one of the chief forces in history bringing about political change. Thus it is that the working classes in society may go on voting Tory while the social classes bring about revolution. What Mark [sic] looked for among the new working population created by industrial capitalism was a developing consciousness of class, but when such a consciousness developed the worker became less ready for revolution, not more." [65]

While the primary purpose of this essay has been to provide an explanation rather than to do a critique of his work, it is important to stress, nonetheless, that Clark's model has been challenged directly and indirectly a number of times. There are two pivotal emphases to the social change model, one stressing *equilibrium* and the other *disorganization.* A very useful book on the former concept is Russett's, *The Concept of Equilibrium in American Thought* (1966) and for the latter, Tilley et al., *The Rebellious Century, 1830-1930* (1975). Explanations at variance with Clark's on the rise of social movements in Canada can be found in Clark, Grayson and Grayson (Eds.), *Prophesy and Protest* (1975) and Brym and Sacouman (Eds.), *Underdevelopment and Social Movements in Atlantic Canada* (1979). Clark's view of ideologies undergirding Canada and the U.S. has had its critics as well. For a more critical assessment of Clark's work, the reader should consult Harrison (1981) and Hiller (1982).

Concluding Remarks

Professor Clark's contribution to Canadian sociology has been recognized in a number of ways. He won a Guggenheim Fellowship (1943) and the Tyrell Medal from the Royal Society (1960). He was elected a Fellow of the Royal Society (1953), served in a number of executive positions in the Society, and in 1975 he became the first sociologist to serve as its President. Clark also was president of the Canadian Political Science Association (1959) and was named honorary president of the Canadian Association of Anthropology and Sociology (1967). He accepted the position of Visiting Scholar at a number of universities in the United States and Great Britain and he has lectured at many universities in Canada.[66]

Professor Clark at the present time is very active in the discipline, so we are not discussing a completed career.[67] Up to this time (1979), Clark has remained faithful to his first love—history—which has been the mother lode of his sociological work. Growing numbers of sociologists in Canada and the United States have been coming around to appreciate this view of history and sociology.[68] There are even a few sociologists such as Charles Tilly who are doing history for sociological purposes and there are a number of historians such as Edward Shorter who are doing sociology for historical purposes. Everett Hughes seems uncertain as to whether Clark is an historical sociologist or a sociological historian. The question is no longer an open one; Clark has been an historical sociologist and both Canadian history and sociology have been enriched because of his hyphenated efforts.

Appendix
Six Categories of Clark's Writings (Up To 1979)

1. Theory and Methods Papers
   Sociology and Canadian Social History (1939a)
   Sociology, History and the Problem of Social Change (1959a)
   History and the Sociological Method (1962a) (1968a)
   Social Change and the Community (1963a) (1968b)

2. The "Frontier" Writings
   Economic Expansion and the Moral Order (1941)
   The Social Development of Canada (1942)
   Religious Organization and the Rise of the Canadian Nation (1944a)
   The Religious Sect in Canadian Politics (1945)
   The Religious Factor in Canadian Economic Development (1948a)
   Church and Sect in Canada (1948b)
   Religion and Economic Backward Areas (1950a)
   The Frontier and Democratic Theory (1954)
   Movements of Political Protest in Canada (1959b)
   The Suburban Community (1962b)
   Urbanism and the Changing Canadian Society (1962c)
   The Society of Suburbia (1963b)
   The Developing Canadian Community (1963c) (1968c)
   The Suburban Society (1968d)

Movements of Protest in Post-War Canadian Society (1970)
The Position of the French-Speaking Population in the Northern Industrial Community (1971)
The Post-Second World War Canadian Society (1975a)
The Canadian Society in Historic Perspective (1975b)
The New Urban Poor (1977)

3. Papers on Economic Institutions
The Canadian Manufacturers' Association: Its Economic and Social Implications (1939b)
The Canadian Manufacturers' Association (1938)
Economic Organization (1939c)
The Canadian Manufacturers' Association: A Study of Collective Bargaining and Political Pressure (1939d)
The Canadian Manufacturers' Association and the Tariff (1939e)
The Limitations of Capitalist Enterprise in Canadian Society (1966a)

4. Articles on Canada and Her Southern Neighbour
Canadian National Sentiment and Imperial Sentiment (1939f)
Opinions and Attitudes in English-Speaking Quebec (1939g)
The Social Development of Canada and the American Continental System (1944b)
The Canadian Community (1950b)
Canada and Her Great Neighbour (1964a)
Canada and the American Value System (1965)

5. Papers About the Discipline
The Support of Social Science Research in Canada (1958)
The American Takeover of Canadian Sociology (1974)
Sociology in Canada: A Historical Overview (1975)
The Changing Image of Sociology in English-Speaking Canada (1979)

6. Miscellaneous
Education and Social Change (1956)
The Employability of the Older Worker (1959c)
Group Interests in Canadian Politics (1964b)

Higher Education and the New Men of Power in Society (1966b)
The Attack on the Authority Structure of Canadian Society (1976a)
Canadian Society and Issues of Multiculturalism (1976b)

Notes

1 This title was conferred by William Johnson, feature writer for the *Globe and Mail* and a former student of Professor Clark's. Professor Clark gave Dennis William Magill and myself two extensive interviews, one in Halifax and another in Guelph. He also participated in our graduate seminar on Canadian Society at the University of Toronto in 1977. All three sessions were tape-recorded and the materials on these tapes were used extensively in this paper. We wish to thank Professor Clark for his cooperation. There is a completed Ph.D. dissertation and another work going to press on the Sociology of S. D. Clark. I deliberately resisted consulting these works because I wanted to arrive at my own understanding of Clark's work in its entirety, up to this time, (1979). It is unlikely that my views on his career and scholarship will coincide with Clark's own. Therefore, it should be emphasized that Professor Clark is in no way responsible for anything written in this paper; this has been an independent assessment of his position in Canadian sociology.

2 I would like to thank the following for commenting on the first draft of this paper: Robert Brym, Jean Burnet, Doreen Campbell, S. D. Clark, John De Roche, Ronald Gillis, Brian Joseph, Dennis William Magill, Ray MacLean, John Nicholson, Madeline Richard, Edward Silva and John Simpson.

3 He spent one year during his formal training at the London School of Economics. His Ph.D., however, was earned at the University of Toronto.

4 Upon his "retirement" from the University of Toronto, he spent two years as Visiting Professor at the University of Guelph, followed by two more at Lakehead University. At the time of writing this paper (1979) he was planning visits to universities in Japan and to the University of Edinburgh.

5 Berger, Carl. (1976). *The Writing of Canadian History*. Toronto: Oxford University Press. p. 168.

6 R. MacGregor Dawson is best known for his work *Democratic Government in Canada* (1949). See the first chapter for Dawson: (1963). Aitchison (Ed.) *The Political Process in Canada.*

7 Arthur S. Morton (1870-1945) should not be confused with H. L. Morton of the University of Manitoba. Arthur S. Morton published *The Journal of Duncan M'Gillivray of the North West Company* (1930), *Under Western Skies* (1936), *History of Prairie Settlement* (1938), *A History of the Canadian West to 1870-*

71 (1939), *Sir George Simpson* (1944) and *The Saskatchewan Wheat Pool* (1947). Morton used the frontier perspective in much of his work.

8 Morton and Martin published one work together.

9 R. H. Tawney is best known for *Religion and the Rise of Capitalism* (1926).

10 Clark started from scratch by taking Introductory Sociology.

11 At the same time he did what amounted to another thesis on the English-speaking minority in Quebec. See H. F. Angus (Ed.), (1938). *Canada and Her Great Neighbor*.

12 See the chapter on Harold Innis. A very good profile of Frank Underhill can be found in Berger (1976), pp. 54-84. Underhill was not a writer of books, but he wrote many articles for *Canadian Forum* and for other intellectual journals. He was one of the editors for *Social Planning for Canada* (1935). Some of his mature views can be found in *The Image of Confederation* (1964).

13 Eventually they got back to a first-name basis. In one of his interviews Clark said, "I don't think he quite ever forgave me."

14 Professor Alexander Brady first appeared in the University of Toronto Calendar in the academic year 1925-26. Some of the works he published are the following: *The Life of Thomas D'Arcy McGee (1925); William Harkisson and Liberal Reform* (1928); *Canada* (1932); *Canada After the War* (1942); *Democracy in the Dominions* (1947); *The British Commonwealth* (1953); *The British Governing Class and Democracy* (1954).

15 Professor E. J. Urwick (1867-1945) might be less well-known than Innis and Underhill. Some of his writings are the following: *Luxury and Waste of Life* (1908); *A Philosophy of Social Progress* (1912); *The Message of Plato* (1920); *The Social Good* (1927); *The Ethics of Competition* (1937); *Is There a Scientific Sociology?* (1938); *Liberalism True and False* (1938); *The Values of Life*, (Ed.), 2nd Intro. by John A. Irving (1948); *Freedom In Our Time* (n.d.).

16 Professor Hart was at the University of Toronto from 1934 to 1947. He was editor of *Essays in Sociology* (1941); the co-author of *The Tiwi of North Australia* (1960) and author of *Industrial Relations Research and Social Theory* (1949).

17 In this paper Clark's contribution to the organization of sociology has been restricted to his work at the University of Toronto. It should be noted, however, that Clark made a considerable contribution to the Canadian Political Science Association, to its Journal and to the Social Science Research Council.

18 Burnet, Jean. (1974). *Minorities I Have Belonged To*. unpublished paper, p. 5.

19 Robert Morrison MacIver (1882-1972) came to the University of Toronto from the University of Aberdeen where he had an appointment in political science and sociology. The appointment at Toronto was in the former discipline noted above. Professor Mavor was chairman at the time. While at Toronto he wrote

Community: A Sociological Study (1917); *Labor in the Changing World* (1919); *Elements of Social Science* (1921); *The Modern State* (1926). Other well-known publications of his are: *Society* (1931); *Social Causation* (1942); *The Web of Government* (1997). In addition to these titles, MacIver has to his credit approximately 25 more books and monographs many of which were published by the Institute for Religion and Social Studies, Jewish Theological Seminary of America. For a compendium of MacIver's writings up to 1969, see David Spitz (Ed.), *Politics & Society* (1969).

In his autobiography, *As a Tale That Is Told* (1968), MacIver stated his philosophy and practice of social science thus: "I have 'professed' various subjects, political science, economics, sociology, in various seats of learning, but never a subject in which I myself had any serious instruction during my lengthy university training." (p. 64)

> "I thought of myself as a social scientist—not as a sociologist or a political scientist or an economist. I had come to the conclusion that the demarcation of the social sciences into separate departmental boxes was artificial... (p.73)

Yet when talking about his decision to leave Toronto to take a position as chairman of the Department of Economics and Sociology at Bernard College, he gave as part of his reason for going: "I had not been able to introduce sociology at Toronto." (p.76)

MacIver's statement about his inability to place sociology on the curriculum is explained to some extent by an interchange which took place a decade after he had left Toronto. In early 1937, MacIver published a revised work called *Society* and subtitled it *A Textbook in Sociology*. In a 1938 issue of the *Canadian Journal of Economics and Political Science*, Professor Urwick, MacIver's contemporary and replacement as Head of the Department of Political Economy at the University of Toronto, published an article entitled *Is There A Scientific Sociology?* which in fact was a rather critical, debunking review of *Society*. In sum, he said MacIver was a fine social philosopher and he should stick to what he is good at doing. Furthermore, scientific sociology is an impossibility and MacIver knows it. MacIver replied to this review in the next issue. While it is not important to present his defence at this time, the first sentence perhaps gives the clue as to why MacIver failed to introduce sociology courses at Toronto. He began: "Professor Urwick...looks down on the pretensions of sociology with aloof and exquisite disdain." (IV, p. 549)

Yet it was Urwick who instituted the honours program in sociology at Toronto. This apparent contradiction can be resolved by eliminating the word "scientific." It was *scientific* sociology which was impossible according to Urwick.

John Irving, in a profile of Urwick, explained Urwick's thinking on sociology. "The sociologist may observe, he may generalize, he may analyse the social structure and social process with all the aids...but he is inevitably foredoomed to failure. He fails not because he attempted too much but because of the fatal limitation of scientific method which makes him so content with mere 'facts' that he 'closes his eyes to the end, the good, the ideal, the things that are not of this world, the things that are God's which (although the sociologist does not know it) are the only things that seriously matter ultimately.'" (Irving, John A. (1948). The Social Philosophy of E. J. Urwick, In *The Values of Life*, iv.

Apparently Professor Urwick contributed to the slow development of sociology in England as well. (See Abrams, Philip. (1968). *The Origins of British Sociology, 1934-1914*. Chicago: University of Chicago Press. pp. 160-61.)

Urwick's view of sociology persisted at the University of Toronto long after he had departed the scene. Clark in his *Suburban Society* (1968) wrote in part:

> "What there is about suburban society that lends itself to study by precise scientific methods is not worth study, if what is sought is understanding of how this society comes into being and develops." (p. 19)

In fact, Clark never seemed very concerned about the methodological questions of scientific sociology in any of his work.

20 The Sociology Honours Program appeared for the first time in the 1933-34 University of Toronto Calendar. The Program was outlined in the following manner:

1st year	2nd year	3rd year	4th year
English	One of English	One of Greek and	One of Greek and
Zoology	Or French	Roman His.	Roman His.
One of French	Or Oriental Lit.	Or Oriental Lit.	Or Oriental Lit.
Or Oriental	Or Rel. Knowledge	Or Rel. Knowledge	Or Rel. Knowledge
Or Re. Knowledge	History	History	History
Economics	Economics	Economics	Economics
Anthropology	Psychology	Psychology	Philosophy
Psychology	Zoology	Sociology	Psychology
			Sociology

21 John Davidson Ketchum (1893-1962) was a very interesting Canadian scholar. A student of music, he went to Germany in 1912 only to be interned, along with

some 4,000 British, in a civilian prison camp by the Germans in 1914. The camp had been a race track called Ruhleben and Ketchum and his fellow captives remained in this abnormal setting for four years. Upon his return to Toronto, he pursued his interests in social psychology and sociology, relegating his music to the "back burner." After some graduate studies at the University of Chicago he accepted an appointment at the University of Toronto. He wrote sparingly. He was editor of the *Canadian Journal of Psychology* for five years (1953-58) but he invested almost all his research interest in Ruhleben. The work was published three years after his death (1965). *Ruhleben* is a work which deserves much more attention from sociologists than it has received. In a: much as it is a study of a "society" built under extraordinary circumstances it has some kinship to Rex Lucas' *Men in Crisis* (1969). For a review of *Ruhleben*, see Herbert Blumer (1965). An Unusual Prison Society Realistically Observed. *Canadian Review of Sociology and Anthropology*, 2:3, 1965-67.

22 *Next-Year Country* has recently been reprinted by the University of Toronto Press.

23 I understand that Professor Gerd Schroeter, Lakehead University, is working on a book about Geiger.

24 In 1939, an issue of *Canadian Journal of Economics and Political Science* appeared which was devoted to five sociological essays, one each by Hart, Clark, Talcott Parsons, Carl Dawson and Robert Park. Later the essays were published as a book, edited by Hart with an introduction by Innis. (1941) Clark's contribution was his very important "Economic Expansion and the Moral Order." In 1961, another book of sociological essays appeared, but this time Clark was the editor and all the essays were written by sociologists who were (or had been, in Mann's case) at the University of Toronto. Clark's essay was "The Sociology of the Suburbs." In the "Introduction" Clark wrote: "This little volume is intended to convey some idea of what is going on in sociology at the University of Toronto" (1961, p. iv).

25 Clark published one paper on the American presence in Canadian sociology. See Clark, S.D. (1973). The American Takeover of Canadian Sociology: Myth or Reality. *Dalhousie Review*, 53, pp. 205-18. Clark spent the academic year 1960-61 at the University of California (Berkeley). It would seem that Clark drew heavily on the contacts made that year when making appointments to the department during the middle 1960s.

26 Professor Clark read the first draft of this paper and made extensive comments on it. He saw the development of his work through the following stages: (a) Early Works—the C.M.A., and those of a mixed sociological, political science and economic history character; (b) the elaboration of the "frontier" thesis: (c) the increasing emphasis on the differences in the frontier development of

Canada and the U.S., growing into *Movements of Protest in Canada*; (d) the theoretical and methodological writings—Clark claimed that his framework matured during his year at Berkeley (1960-61); (e) the return to the frontier theme: *The Suburban Society* (1968) and *The New Urban Poor* (1978); finally (f) the papers relating to the discipline of sociology and the social services as a category. Except for the last category, Clark's categories are developmental and chronological. Mine are not; I have tried to present a synthesis of the writings of Professor Clark as a totality while ignoring the time dimension.

27 Clark has been a sociologist on the margin; he acquired one M.A. in history, another in sociology, and a Ph.D. in political science. His difficult task was to build bridges between and among the social sciences with sociology at the base. His audience applauded the effort but frequently only with one hand. This reaction can best be seen by looking at the reviews. His first book, *The Canadian Manufacturing Association* (1990) was cited as:

> "...more a contribution to sociology and political science than to economics, but the study of an association of this character probably defies classification." (Curtis, in *Canadian Journal of Economics and Political Science*, 6, pp. 115-6)

Professor Cooper of McGill wrote a very positive review in *American Sociological Review* for The Social Development of Canada (1942) saying in part "...the author has got far away from the conventional political or constitutional interpretation of the Canadian scene." (7, p. 891) Everett Hughes, however, in his review of the same work which appeared in *Canadian Journal of Economics and Political Science* worried whether "...the research inspired by the book will be of a sociological character.... But I do not think that the particular hypothesis stated and the presentation of select documents will really inspire students to a fundamental sociological investigation of Canadian society." (IX, p. 97) *Church and Sect in Canada* (1949) received acclaim from all sides; Brebner called it "a pioneering work of great importance, a monumental mile-stone of Canadian historical writing." (*Canadian Historical Review*, 30, p. 76); Abrams was very laudatory (*American Sociological Review*, 14, pp. 175-6); so was Wach, but he did make a caveat that "The conceptual framework seems not quite differentiated and strong enough for so great an amount of historical detail." (*American Journal of Sociology*, LV, pp. 110) Everett Hughes again will be given the last word on this book:

> "This is a good book, one that will remain as the definite thing in the field for a long time and one of which Professor Clark may be proud.... Dr. Clark is a stiff-necked fellow. Once he had taken to himself the role

> of Canada's sociological historian (reverse the terms if you like), and once he had started on the problem of religious movements in Canada, it was inevitable that he should sooner or later write this book, and that it would be the thorough book that it is.
>
> ...he has given us a much more thorough account of the sectarian movements than of the settling down, institutionalizing process." (*Canadian Journal of Economics and Political Science*, 15, p. 421).

Morton of Manitoba, in his review of *Movements of Political Protest* (1959) stated that the work was "a major work of analysis and revision...." but went on to criticize the work. "Dr. Clark commits himself...to an application of the frontier thesis to two centuries of Canadian history. As the thesis tends to emphasize environment rather than institutions and to be deterministic rather than contingent, Dr. Clark is using a blunt instrument to perform a delicate operation." He went on to state that sociological and historical methods "...are not easily made compatible." (*Canadian Historical Review*, 4, p. 293) Morton continued to worry about the relationship between history and sociology in his review of Clark's *The Developing Canadian Community* (1962) (*Canadian Historical Review*, 14, p. 235-36) Dennis Wrong, in his review of the same work, asked whether there was any difference between historical sociology and sociological history (*American Sociological Review*, 29, p. 765). *The Suburban Society* (1968) was reviewed only in *American Sociological Review* but it was a review calculated to warm the cockles of an author's heart. "The student of the suburbs will ignore it at his peril. Finally (all hail!) the book is well-written." (*American Sociological Review*, 31, p. 558)

These reviews expose the problems, particularly the historians' problems, with Clark's work. It cannot easily be pigeon-holed. It seemed important to determine whether it was history done by a sociologist or sociology done by a historian. The frontier thesis bothered historians. Historical studies done by a sociologist annoyed some sociologists. But when Clark appeared to abandon historical subjects and the frontier model, as in *The Suburban Society*, both historians and sociologists were content. Historians could ignore it and sociologists felt secure. Dawson is supposed to have said on hearing about *The Suburban Society*, "At last, ...he is doing sociology."

28 For Clark's theoretical and methodological essays, see Clark, 1968c, pp. 269-313.

29 For confirmation of this point, see Clark's review of *Pioneering in the Prairie Provinces: The Social Side of the Settlement Process*, in *The Canadian Historical Review*, (1940), 21, pp. 336-38.

30 Clark cites Parsons' *The Structure of Social Action* (1937) in a 1939a essay. Clark maintained a fruitful dialogue with Parsons over the years until Parsons' death (1979). In a number of ways, they were trying to do the same thing in their respective countries, particularly in providing legitimacy for the discipline in the academic community.

31 Clark, S.D. (1952). pp. 299-300.

32 Clark, S.D. (1939). The Canadian Manufacturers' Association and the Tariff. *Canadian Journal of Economics and Political Science*. p. 11.

33 Apparently, around the turn of the 20th century, some leaders of CMA thought themselves capable of doing much more as this excerpt from a speech quoted by Clark indicates:

> "We are not manufacturers," said the President of the Association in 1903, "merely of articles of wood and stone, and iron and cotton and wool, and so on, we manufacture enthusiasm; we manufacture Canadian sentiment; we manufacture feeling of pride in our country, and we manufacture a spirit of independence and a spirit of national pride. We have been doing that for some time." (1938, p. 226)

34 Op. Cit. p. 88.

35 Angus, H. F. (Ed.). (1970, original 1938). *Canada and Her Great Neighbor*. New York: Russell & Russell. p. 199-200.

36 The interested reader will find this study in *Canada and Her Great Neighbor*, edited by H. F. Angus. The work is subtitled *Sociological Surveys of Opinions and Attitudes in Canada concerning the United States* (1938). This study truly was a national study with at least twelve social scientists from all the regions of Canada participating. It documented American influences on Canada in areas of education, motion pictures, radio, periodicals as well as the opinions and attitudes of Canadians on the U.S. as found in the press, Hansard, books, in schools and areas such as English-speaking Quebec, rural Manitoba and British Columbia.

37 Op. Cit. p. 243

38 Clark, S.D. (1968). *The Developing Canadian Community*. Toronto: University of Toronto Press. p. 226.

39 This paper was read at the American Sociological meetings held in Montreal.

40 Op. Cit. p. 232.

41 This paper was read at Laval University.

42 Op. Cit. p. 231.

43 In his 1950 paper Clark wrote: "Whereas the American nation was a product of the revolutionary spirit, the Canadian nation mainly out of forces of a counter-revolutionary character." (1968c, pp. 190-91) Lipset clearly relied on Clark's

writings for Canadian data. It is curious that in his 1965 paper Clark cites Lipset as the source of Canadian-American values debate, almost as if he himself had nothing to do with it.

44 Some might argue that this is an example of the Canadian problem. The ideas developed by Clark became valuable in Canada only after they had been exported and employed by American scholars. Then they were worthy of discussion and debate.

45 The American historian, Frederick Jackson Turner, read a paper, *The Significance of the Frontier in American History* at the American Historical Meetings in 1893 which became the inspiration for the Frontier School of History. For Turner, American greatness could best be explained from the perspective of the frontier which he presented as a *location*, specifically "the outer edge of a wave—the meeting point between savagery and civilization" or generally the West, and as a *process* of overcoming difficulties, conquering a vast and free land, and above all making progress. This was an environmental and continental perspective, a landlocked perspective.

> "American social development has been continually beginning over again on the frontier. This perennial rebirth, the fluidity of American life, this expansion westward with its new opportunities, its continuous touch with the simplicity of primitive society, furnish forces dominating American character." (Turner in Cross (Ed.), (1970), p. 12)

In the U.S., this thesis had a great following but also a great many critics who ultimately had their way. In Canada, the Turner thesis had a direct and, perhaps more importantly, an indirect impact on Canadian intellectual thought. We will look at the direct impact first. Walter Sage in 1928 and John Bartlett Brebner in 1931 stressed the continental aspect of the frontier thesis. Canada shared North America with the U.S. therefore, the two nations have many geographical similarities. The frontier is not respectful of national boundaries so that study should proceed most profitably from a North American perspective. In 1930, *The Winning of the Frontier* was published, the main thesis of which was "The dominant motive in the religious life of Canada has been the winning of the Frontier." (Oliver, 1930) In the work, the frontier concept was employed both in a geographic and non-geographic manner. Lower (1936) used the frontier perspective in his study of the lumber industry and Burt used it also to show the rise of individualism in the Ancient Regime. But it has its critics too. Stanley (1940) chose the most frontier-like of all the communities he could find in Canadian history the Red River Settlement, and demonstrated that it remained a very stable and conservative society. Hofstadter (in Cross (Ed.), 1970) and Creighton (in Cross (Ed.), 1970) faulted the thesis as "an analytic device," the frontier was only a frontier to something else: There wasn't a frontier without a civilization and the frontier could only exist in dynamic relationship with civilization. These criticisms made the frontier thesis look simplistic and it was dropped or modified by Canadian historians in the 1930s and 1940s.

The frontier thesis, however, has had an indirect influence on Canadian historiography which has survived. J. M. S. Careless (1954) claimed there have been several schools of Canadian history;

1. the Britannic or "Blood is thicker than water" School
2. the School of Political Nationhood
3. the Environment School or the North American School
   a. environmental determinism
   b. modified environmental determinism
   c. the East-West modification
4. the Laurentian School—geography and commerce underlay Canadian development
5. Metropolitan-Hinterlands thesis—the frontier is dependent on the metropolis.

As Cross (1970) pointed out, the metropolitanism of Creighton is a grandson or great-grandson of the frontier thesis. "Macintosh derived the environmentalism of his staple approach from Turner; then Creighton's Laurentianism grew from the staple theory; and metropolitanism carried it a stage further into a general theory of urban growth." (Cross, (1970), p. 11)

In case this review has given the impression that Turner was a mere romantic, the writer would like to stress that this is not his opinion. Turner's history was one (some would say the only) expression of a North American, not a borrowed historiography. (See, for example, Davis, David Brian. (May 3, 1979), Marlboro County. In *The New York Review of Books*, XXVI:7, pp. 30-32.

46 Clark, S.D. (1942). *Social Development In Canada*. Toronto: University of Toronto Press. p. 1.

47 The disorganization-reorganization model has its origin in Thomas and Znaniecki's, *The Polish Peasant in Europe and American* (1918 & 20). In this classic study the authors studied the two related processes of disorganization and reorganization which was taking place in the Polish villages and the disorganization and reorganization that the Polish immigrants experienced in Chicago at the turn of the 20th century.

48 Op. Cit.

49 Innis had compiled a similar book for Canadian economic history.

50 Op. Cit. p. 326.

51 Ibid. p. 380-81.

52 Niebuhr, Richard H. (1929). *The Social Sources of Denominationalism*. New York: Meridan Books. p. 21.

53 Clark, S.D. (1948). *Church and Sect in Canada*. Toronto: University of Toronto Press. p. xii.

54 Professor Clark, like Professor Innis before him, wrote bulky books. The reader is not distracted by figures, pictures, tables as he goes through page after page, each one banked high with footnotes. Clark, it should be said, is a much better writer than was Innis, but because of the wealth of materials offered, it seems to me that the occasional schema such as this one could have been very helpful. Clark seems, however, to look askance at quantification of any kind. Only in his *The Employability of the Older Worker* (1959) and in *The Suburban Society* (1968) did he use the very occasional percentage and table. This lack does not result from his ignorance of quantification techniques. For example, in the Angus volume (1938) there is an article on Canadian and American journals and in this article there is a graph depicting the circulation of selected Canadian and American journals by province. The article was not written by Clark but the graph was credited to him. (See Angus, (1938), p. 163). Incidentally, Clark reacted in the following manner to this schema: "I do not like the schema on this page as in my view it only confused what I was trying to do in *Church and Sect*."

55 This work was part of the Social Credit in Alberta series directed and edited by Professor Clark and sponsored by the Canadian Social Science Research Council. It is not clear why this work was included except, as the author himself claimed, the social forces of the frontier which encouraged the political reform movements from 1640-1840 also undergirded the Social Credit movement. The Social Credit series produced a number of excellent, if not classic works, in the Canadian social science. The ten books comprising the series are cited as they appeared:

W. L. Morton	*The Progressive Party in Canada*
D. C. Masters	*The Winnipeg Strike*
Jean Burnet	*Next-Year Country*
C. B. MacPherson	*Democracy in Alberta*
J. R. Mallory	*Social Credit and the Federal Power in Canada*
W. E. Mann	*Sect, Cult and Church in Alberta*
V. E. Fowke	*The National Policy and the Wheat Economy*
L. G. Thomas	*The Liberal Party in Alberta*
S. D. Clark	*Movements of Political Protest in Canada*
John A. Irving	*The Social Credit Movement in Alberta*

56 Clark, S.D. (1959). *Movements of Political Protest in Canada, 1640-1840.* Toronto: University of Toronto Press. p. 6.

57 Gourlay perhaps should be cited as Canada's first social surveyor. See Gourlay, Robert, (1822). *Statistical Account of Upper Canada.*

58 Op. Cit. p. 439.

59 Clark, S.D. (1942). *Social Development in Canada.* Toronto: University of Toronto Press. p. 394.

60 Clark, S.D. (1968). *The Suburban Society.* Toronto: University of Toronto Press. p. 11.

61 Ibid. p. 14.

62 The fifteen suburbs were developed into six types:

1) Single Family Residence Development of the "Pure" Suburban Type
2) Semi-detached Residence Type
3) Single Family Residence in a Built-Up Area
4) The "Packaged" Residential Area
5) The Cottage-Type Residential Development
6) The residential Development of the "Pure" Suburban but now 5-10 Years Old.

63 Op. Cit. p. 100.

64 For the sake of brevity, I have ignored for the most part Clark's work categorized as "Papers about the Discipline" and "Miscellaneous."

65 (1963) Aitcheson, J. H. (Ed.), *The Political Press Process In Canada.* Toronto: University of Toronto Press. p. 77.

66 Additional honours: Made a Foreign honorary Member of the American Academy of Humanities and Social Sciences (1976); appointed an Officer of the Order of Canada (1978); received an honorary L.L.D. from the University of Calgary (1978), an honorary L.L.D. from Dalhousie University (1979), and an honorary D.L.H. from St. Mary's University (1979).

67 Professor Clark, during the writing of this paper, published an article on the beginnings of sociology in Canada. (Nov. 1979) We can expect a number of works on the sociology of Canadian sociology in the next few years. It will be interesting to compare the views of those who made history with those of sociologists who are studying it.

68 Clark, in his assessment of Canadian Sociology (1973), claimed that, his own works aside, there was only a handful of sociological works that were distinctively Canadian. He might be the only Canadian sociologist who could get away with making this statement. Clark, however, has never claimed to be the kind of Canadian nationalist so popular with some academics in the 1970s. In fact, while his works are deeply Canadian, they are also strongly continental.

Bibliography

Abrams, Philip.

(1968). *The Origins of British Sociology 1834-1914*. Chicago: University of Chicago Press.

Aitcheson, J. H. (Ed.)

(1963). *The Political Press Process In Canada*. Toronto: University of Toronto Press.

Angus, H. F. (Ed.)

(1970, original 1938). *Canada and Her Great Neighbor*. New York: Russell & Russell.

Berger, Carl.

(1976). *The Writing of Canadian History*. Toronto: Oxford University Press.

Blumer, Herbert.

(1965). An Unusual Prison Society Realistically Observed. *Canadian Review of Sociology and Anthropology* 2:3, pp. 165-67.

Brebner, J. Bartler.

(1931). Canadian and North American History. *Canadian Historical Association Annual Report* XII, pp. 37-48.

Burnet, Jean.

(1951). *Next-Year Country*. Toronto: University of Toronto Press.

Burnet, Jean.

(1974). *Minorities I Have Belonged To*. unpublished paper.

Burt, A. L.

(1940). The Frontier In The History of New France. *Canadian Historical Association Annual Report*, XXI, pp. 93-99.

Careless J. M. S.

(1959). Frontierism, Metropolitanism and Canadian History. *Canadian Historical Association Annual Report*, XXXV, pp. 1-21.

Clark, S. D.

(1938). Economic Organization. In *Canada and Her Great Neighbor*, H. F. Angus (Ed.). New York: Russell & Russell.

(1938). Canadian National Sentiment And Imperial Sentiment. In *Canada and Her Great Neighbor*, H. F. Angus (Ed.). New York: Russell & Russell.

(1938). Opinions and Attitudes in English-Speaking Quebec. In *Canada and Her Great Neighbor*, H. F. Angus (Ed.). New York: Russell & Russell.

(1938). The Canadian Manufacturers' Association. *Canadian Journal of Economics and Political Science*, 4:4, pp. 505-23.

(1939). The Canadian Manufacturers' Association: Its Economic and Social Implications. In *Essays in Political Economy*, H. A. Innis (Ed.). Toronto: University of Toronto Press. pp. 75-84.

(1939). *The Canadian Manufacturers' Association: A Study In Collective Bargaining And Political Pressure*. Toronto: University of Toronto Press.

(1939). Sociology And Canadian Social History. *Canadian Journal of Economics and Political Science*, 5:3, pp. 348-57.

(1939). The Canadian Manufacturers' Association and The Tariff. *Canadian Journal of Economics and Political Science,* 5:1, pp. 19-39.

(1941). Economic Expansion And The Moral Order. In *Essays in Sociology*, C. W. M. Hart (Ed.). Toronto: University of Toronto Press.

(1942). *Social Development of Canada*. Toronto: University of Toronto Press.

(1944). Religious Organization and the Rise of The Canadian Nation. *Report of The Canadian Historical Association*, pp.4486-96.

(1944). The Social Development of Canada And The American Continental System. *Culture*, 5:2, pp. 132-43.

(1945). The Religious Sect in Canadian Politics. *American Journal of Sociology,* 51:3, pp. 207-16.

(1948). The Religious Sect in Canadian Economic Development. *Canadian Journal of Economics and Political Science*, 12:4, pp. 439-53.

(1948). The Religious Factor in Canadian Economic Development. *Tasks of Economic History* (Supplement to the *Journal of Economic History*), pp. 89-103.

(1948). *Church And Sect In Canada*. Toronto: University of Toronto Press.

(1950). The Canadian Community. In *Canada*, G. W. Brown (Ed.). New York: Books for Libraries Press. pp. 375-89.

(1950). Religion And Economic Backward Areas. *Papers and Proceedings of the American Economic Association*, 41:2, pp. 258-65.

(1954). The Frontier And Democratic Theory. *Transactions of the Royal Society of Canada* XXVIII, Series III, pp. 65-75.

(1956). Education and Social Change in Canada. In *Transactions of the Third World Congress of Sociology, V*, pp. 69-70.

(1958). The Support of Social Science Research in Canada. *The Canadian Journal of Economics and Political Science*, 24:2, pp. 141-51.

(1959). Sociology, History and the Problem of Social Change. *Canadian Journal of Economics and Political Science*, 25:4, pp. 389-400.

(1959). *Movements of Political Protest In Canada, 1640-1840*. Toronto: University of Toronto Press.

(1959). *The Employability of the Older Worker*. Ottawa: Department of Labour.

(1962). The Suburban Community. In *Urbanism And The Changing Canadian Society*, S. D. Clark, (Ed.) Toronto: University of Toronto Press. pp. 20-38.

(1962). (Ed.) *Urbanism and the Changing Canadian Society*. Toronto: University of Toronto Press.

(1963). The Society of Suburbia. In William Petersen and David Matza (Eds.), *Social Controversy*. Belmont: Wadsworth. pp. 304-15.

(1963,1968). *The Developing Canadian Community*. Toronto: University of Toronto Press.

(1964). Group Interests in Canadian Politics. In J. H. Aitchison (Ed.), *The Political Process In Canada*. Toronto: University of Toronto Press. pp. 64-78.

(1964). Canada and Her Great Neighbour. *Canadian Review of Sociology and Anthropology*, I:4, pp. 193-201.

(1965). Canada and the American Value System. *La Dualité Canadienne A C'Heure Des États-Unis*. Quebec: Les Presses de L'Université Laval, pp. 93-102.

(1966). *The Limitations of Capitalist Enterprise in Canadian Society*. Sixth World Congress of Sociology, Evian, France.

(1966). *The Suburban Society*. Toronto: University of Toronto Press.

(1969). *Higher Education and The New Men Of Power in Society*. I;2, pp. 77-87.

(1970). Movements of Protest in Post-War Canadian Society. *Transactions of The Royal Society of Canada*. VIII, Series IV, pp. 223-37.

(1971). The Position of the French-Speaking Population in the Northern Industrial Community. In Richard J. Ossenberg (Ed.), *Canadian Society*, Scarborough: Prentice-Hall.

(1973) The American Take-over of Canadian Sociology: Myth or Reality. *Dalhousie Review*, 53, pp. 205-18.

(1976). *Canadian Society in Historical Perspective*. Toronto: McGraw-Hill Ryerson.

(1976). The Attack on the Authority Structure of the Canadian Society. *Transactions of The Royal Society Of Canada*, XIV, Series IV, pp. 1-15.

(1978). *The New Urban Poor*. Toronto: McGraw-Hill Ryerson.

(1979). The Changing Image of Sociology in English Speaking Canada. *Canadian Journal of Sociology*, 4:4, pp. 393-403.

(1979). Cross, Michael (Ed.) *The Frontier Thesis and the Canadas*. Toronto: Copp Clark.

Dawson, R., MacGregor.

(1949). *Democratic Government In Canada*. Toronto: University of Toronto Press.

Harrison, Deborah.

(1981). *The Limits Of Liberalism: The Making Of Canadian Sociology*. Montreal: Black Rose Books.

Hart, C. W. M. (Ed.)

(1940). *Essays In Sociology*. Toronto: University of Toronto Press.

Hiller, Harry H.

(1976-1977). The Contribution of S. D. Clark to the Sociology of Canadian Religion. *Studies In Religion*, 6:9, pp. 415-27.

(1982) *Society And Change: S. D. Clark and the Development Of Canadian Sociology*. Toronto: University of Toronto Press.

Irving, John A.

(1948). The Social Philosophy of E. J. Urwick. In *The Values Of Life*. Toronto: University of Toronto Press.

Ketchum, J. Davidson.

(1965). *Ruhleben: Prison Camp Society*. Toronto: University of Toronto Press.

Lipset, Seymour Martin.

(1950). *Agrarian Socialism*. Berkeley: University of California Press.

(1963). *First New Nation*. New York: Basic Books.

(1968). *Revolution And Counter Revolution*. New York: Basic Books.

(1968). and Richard Hofstader (Eds.), *Turner and the Sociology of the Frontier*. New York: Basic Books.

Lower, A. R. M.

(1936). *Settlement and Forest Frontier in Eastern Canada*. Toronto: Macmillan.

Lucas, Rex.

(1969). *Men In Crisis*. Toronto: University of Toronto Press.

MacIver, Robert.

(1917). *Community*. London: Macmillan.

(1921). *Elements of Social Science*. London: Methuen.

(1931). *Society*. New York: R. Lang & R. R. Smith.

(1947). *The Web of Government*. New York: Macmillan.

(1968). *As A Tale That Is Told*. Chicago: University of Chicago Press.

Morton, Arthur S.

(1909). *The Journal of Duncan McGillavray of the North West Company*. Toronto: Macmillan.

(1936). *Under Western Skies*. Toronto: Nelson.

(1938). *History of Prairie Settlement*. Toronto: Macmillan.

(1939). *History of the Canadian West to 1870-71*. London: Nelson.

(1944). *Sir George Simpson*. Toronto: Benfords-Mort.

Niebuhr, H. Richard.

(1957, original 1920). *The Social Sources of Denominationalism*. New York: Meridan Books.

Oliver, E. H.

(1930). *The Winning of the Frontier*. Toronto: The United Church Publishing House.

Parsons, Talcott.
(1937). *The Structure of Social Action*. Glencoe: Free Press.
Seeley, John R. et al.
(1956). *Crestwood Heights*. Toronto: University of Toronto Press.
Spetz, David (Ed.)
(1969). *Politics And Society*. New York: Atherton Press.
Stanley, George F. G.
(1940). Western Canada and the Frontier Thesis. *Canadian Historical Association Annual Report* XXI, pp. 105-17.
Tawney, R. H.
(1926). *Religion and the Rise of Capitalism*. New York: Harcourt, Brace and Company.
Thomas, W. I. and F. Znaniecki.
(1918 & 1920). *The Polish Peasant in Europe and America*. Chicago: University of Chicago Press.
Underhill, Frank et al.
(1975, original 1935). *Social Planning For Canada*. Toronto: University of Toronto Press.
Urwick, E. J.
(1938). Is There A Scientific Sociology? *Canadian Journal of Economics and Political Science*. IV:2, pp. 231-40.
Zaslow, Morris.
(1948). The Frontier Thesis In Recent Historiography. *Canadian Historical Association Annual Report*, XXIX, pp. 153-67.

Chapter Three

'CRUSHING THE POWER OF FINANCE': THE SOCIALIST PRAIRIE ROOTS OF S.D. CLARK

David Nock

The Changing Image of S.D. Clark

S.D. Clark played a pivotal role in the development of Canadian sociology. As one of the few academic sociologists in Canada before the expansion of the subject in the 1960s, he founded and was the first chair of the Department of Sociology at the University of Toronto. Prior to that he had been the main sociologist in the celebrated interdisciplinary Department of Political Economy at the same university. From 1939 onwards, while in this position, Clark wrote a series of works which commented on the nature of Canadian social development in the context of the Canadian staples and frontier economy, engaging in what can be regarded as a type of macrosociology.

Clark's contributions have been acknowledged by both academic and government bodies. He became the president of the élite Royal Society of Canada in 1975, having previously been the president of its Humanities and Social Sciences section. He was awarded membership in the Order of Canada, was invited to be the editor of the Rockefeller series on the

---

Nock, David A. (1993). 'Crushing the Power of Finance': The Socialist Prairie Roots of S.D. Clark. From *Star Wars in Canadian Sociology*. Halifax: Fernwood. Pp. 37-54. Reprinted with permission from the publisher. References have been removed from the text and replaced as endnotes.

development of the Social Credit in Canada, and was made an Honorary Life Member of the Canadian Sociology and Anthropology Association. The only comparable figures in English Canadian sociology are Carl Dawson and John Porter.[1]

Yet Clark's impact had not been without controversy or dispute. His method of research is thoroughly historical in nature, and he became increasingly conservative at a time when Canadian sociology was becoming more and more materialist and even Marxist. Clark's work is often not read at all, is read superficially, or is misinterpreted because readers assume that what Clark came to represent in the 1960s and 1970s was the same or similar to what he had stood for in the 1930s, 1940s and 1950s when his scholarly reputation was first established. Clark did not alleviate this sort of misinterpretation when he published a number of works which seemed intended to discourage aspirants to the new materialist, neo-Marxist sociology now predominant in Canadian sociology.[2]

The assessment of Clark as a conservative is revealed in Dusky Lee Smith's comment that, "Some readers will have difficulty accepting the view that Clark was a young radical as well as in accepting the radical or critical nature of his [earlier] sociological form."[3] R. James Sacouman states that "S.D. Clark's works are a major example of the idealist perspective,"[4] that Clark "consistently develops a non-Marxist classless theory,"[5] and that "his principles and focus of analysis are the antithesis to those of Marx."[6]

No doubt the most ambitious presentation of this interpretation of Clark is provided by Deborah Harrison who devotes an entire book, *The Limits of Liberalism: The Making of Canadian Sociology*, plus a major article (1983) to the proposition that, "while ostensibly operating from a wholistic and historical conception of his society, Clark has nevertheless become trapped within the American functionalist assumption that sociology is fundamentally about individual behaviour and decision making. How, while being passionately preoccupied with his society, Clark has at the same time attempted to be a liberal individualist, in a country where one cannot do both."[7]

This dichotomy leads Harrison to outline two traditions of scholarship: the collective and the individualist. The former tradition includes such a mixed bag of Canadian scholars as Donald Creighton, Stanley Ryerson, Harold Innis, Mel Watkins, R.T. Naylor and Carl Cuneo, and is considered positive and progressive by Harrison; she feels the work of these scholars dwells on the survival of "the collective lives of groups and societies in terms of their abilities to survive over time"[8] rather than on "individuals on the make." For Harrison it is extremely important that Canadian scholarship identify with the collective tradition because of the precariousness of the Canadian state as it stands face to face with the American imperialist juggernaut. The individualist tradition which Harrison decries includes such scholars as F.J. Turner, Harry Johnson, Frank Underhill, Marcus Hansen, and the structural functionalist school of sociology in general, in addition to Clark himself. The impact of such an assessment is to dismiss Clark's work as essentially un-Canadian in its content, as pro-American in its individualistic orientations, and essentially as pro-imperialist and therefore unprogressive and un-Marxist. Such an interpretation by Harrison, Sacouman and Smith dismisses Clark as a figure in the progressive, materialist, neo-Marxist Canadian sociology movement and could remove him from his pedestal as a founder of Canadian sociology.

In the later part of his career, these characterizations of Clark begin to take on more validity. In 1953, in his mid-forties, Clark joined the establishment party in federal politics, the Liberal party of Canada, leaving behind him his former identification with the social democratic and quasi-socialist party, the Co-operative Commonwealth Federation (CCF). This transition came about at the same time as his promotion to full professor at the University of Toronto. Shortly after, his writings changed abruptly from the historical study of social development in frontier Canada to a modern study of urbanization and its consequences for urban poverty. He also became an essayist writing on Canadian social issues and problems such as multiculturalism, social protest and poverty.

His later analyses do not focus on the unequal development of capitalism, but tend to stress the inadequacy of hinterland values in adapting to an industrial and urban society. He tends to dismiss Marxist ideas as "un-Canadian" and, somewhat oddly, as American imports. He states that the best stance for the Canadian social scientist is in the middle of the political spectrum. He could hardly understand the student movement and denounces it, claiming it was produced by the sons and daughters of the affluent. According to John Conway[9]:

> Sadly his later career came close to undoing his reputation among many of the present generation of sociologists. His

> late turn to American sociological methods; his continentalism and his unthinking opposition to all nationalism, even the new progressive nationalism which had as its aim a return to many of Clark's own original commitments; his fear and disdain of mass movements; his incredibly blind and hostile response to the student movements; his late convergence with established opinion: all served to undermine what could have been the greatest period in his career.

Many members of the student movement went on to become social scientists themselves after a spell in graduate schools and have become influential in the Canadian sociology movement. While many are aware of the foundation laying and cornerstone work undertaken by Clark to develop sociology in Canada, there is often an uneasiness about Clark as an establishment figure who produced establishment thought.

Clark's early political and social thought is radical, progressive, socialist and collectivist and his major scholarly writings up until the late 1950s have to be seen as reflecting the centrality of such values. There was a shift towards a personal conservatism and scholarly accommodation of establishment sociology, but this was a development of the 1950s that did not reach complete fruition in his published work until after 1959 (with some minor indications first emerging in 1953). It was not until then that Clark became a liberal individualist, and a supporter of corporate capitalism and the academic establishment.

In the 1930s and 1940s, Clark was a democratic socialist from a radical prairie background who clearly and explicitly rejected liberal individualism and competitive and corporate capitalism. This prairie radical socialism of S.D. Clark has been largely hidden from critics who have come to judge him on his impact in more recent years. It can be argued that this early radical prairie socialism provided the underlying paradigmatic grounding for all his scholarly writings up to and including *Movements of Political Protest* published in 1959. It thus becomes clear that there are two Clarks: one whose sociology is infused with his early democratic socialist ideology, and a later one whose work is ideologically tinged with a conservative-Liberal outlook and an acceptance of mainstream American professionalized sociology. Since Clark's longer and pathbreaking scholarly works date from the earlier period, there is every reason for progressive Canadian sociology and the Canadian sociology movement to continue to incorporate this work into its interpretative framework.

The Young Clark in His Context

S.D. Clark was the son of a farming family living near Lloydminster, a prairie town that straddles the border of Saskatchewan and Alberta. He was born in 1910 and thus as a boy had seen the United Farmers of Alberta come to power in 1921. The farmers' revolt against the prevailing economic and political system had been going on for some time when Clark reached his twenties. Farmers formed the governments in Ontario and Manitoba, as well as in his own province, and they had become the second largest party at the federal level in 1921. (Because many of their reforms could only be effected in Ottawa, and due to their inexperience in political life, the farmers in politics were only successful to a limited degree.) The depression simply reinforced the young farm boy's conviction that the prevailing system was rigged against the real producers in society.

The beliefs of the young S.D. Clark are laid out in a series of letters to the editor of the *Lloydminster Times* in 1932 and 1933, as well as in an article in the *Canadian Forum* in 1932. He had by this time been at university for five years and had studied under such well-known academics as Hilda Neatby, A.S. Morton and R. MacGregor Dawson at the University of Saskatchewan (1927-31), and with Frank Underhill, George Brown and Chester Martin at the University of Toronto.

Clark was a wordy correspondent with the *Lloydminster Times*. He found it difficult to restrain himself as he was strongly committed to a message that he felt others needed to share. What S. Delbert Clark (as he signed himself) wrote about was a clear exposition of a socialist outlook. He did not identify himself as a Marxian communist, but did suggest that he was "a sympathizer of Communism," that "Socialism and Communism" were not "irreconcilable" (27 April 1933) and that if socialism failed, then "perhaps we shall join the ranks of Tim Buck. It won't be our fault" (14 January 1932, Tim Buck was a leader of Canadian communism). Perhaps enough has been said to point out how different S.D. Clark was at this time from the politically Liberal and less radical figure he became in the 1960s and 1970s. The system of thought that Clark espoused in the 1930s followed a coherent pattern. He suggested that the prevailing economic system only benefited "the self-interest of greedy capitalists" (18 February 1932) and the "profits of the exploiting class" (29 March 1932). In general he denounced "the inadequacy and incompetency of capitalism" (11 February 1932) and the nature of our "pernicious economic system" (18 February 1932). He pointed specifically to the predominance in modern capitalism of the financial sector. Thus he revealed how "our financial leaders … now enjoy despotic and regal power" (ibid.), the western countries are falling under "a financial dictatorship," and North America is falling under "the dictatorship of a financial Plutocracy" (18 August 1932). Clark believed that only by "crushing the power of finance" could "the individual assume a rightful share of the control of his destiny" (ibid.).

The political sector, for Clark, gave no relief from the dominance of economic power since, for him, the finance capitalists controlled the parliamentary and state systems. His view of the relationship between economic and political interests would be characterised today as "instrumentalist" by modern political sociologists, with the financiers directly controlling the political system. The House of Commons itself was "merely a debating forum" (28 July 1932) and the Prime Minister had "been reduced to the position of a figurehead of the financial interests" (ibid.). Clark looked back one hundred years to when there had been no such great financiers, a time when the "economic life of the country was dominated by small individualist capitalists" and the parliament was "elected by the people" (18 August 1932). In the 1930s he felt that, "Today, both functions are performed by a small group of self-appointed financiers" (ibid.). The youthful S.D. Clark vigorously denied the "pluralistic" view of political and economic life which became so influential in the political sociology of the 1950s.

Since Clark has been typified by Deborah Harrison as a liberal individualist stressing individual mobility and competition, and writing about "individuals on the make" as she puts it, it may be important to look at young Clark's comments on such matters to see whether his outlook is better described as liberal individualist or socialist collectivist. In fact, Clark denounced "economic individualism" as taught by J.S. Mill and Jeremy Bentham, claiming it had led "the world into anarchy and resulted in the chaos of an international war" (28 July 1932). He felt that social progress would be made only when "competition would be eliminated" (29 March 1932) and he denounced "the waste of competition." He felt that economic individualism and competition led to a waste of energy, such as the proverbial "four gasoline stations … situated on the four corners of intersecting streets" and the "dozen commercial travellers" who competed to sell the same supplies, "the only difference in the brands being the names on the outside labels" (ibid.). He commented, "There is scarcely any end to such instances of waste in competition" (ibid.), and looked forward to the day when "private property is subordinate to the interests of the state" (ibid.). In Clark's vision, "With the realization of a Socialist Commonwealth, everyone would be producing something, not for his own pecuniary gain nor that of his nations but for the gain of civilized mankind" (11 February 1932). Such opinions fit better with the radical collectivism advocated by Harrison herself than with liberal individualism.

Clark was fearful for the future because he felt war was inevitable. He felt this not because of the actions of Germany or the threat of Nazism as such, but because the capitalists needed a war to solve the problems that were being caused by the Depression. He felt that war would help "our great industrial capitalists" (18 February 1932) in several ways. They would be able to "amass large fortunes" by producing war materials. War would also encourage a greater degree of social control as "dissatisfaction … will now be allayed since the malcontents and agitators will be conscripted for cannon fodder." Furthermore, "the remnants of our armies would return home disappointed, broken and lacking in spirit" no longer able to give "effective resistance to the capitalist order." Clark felt that "the financial leaders … realise that they must plunge the world into another great war." They had the precedent of the First World War when war "saved the situation except Russia." But Clark saw revolution was "looming in the background" since "that another war could be staged without revolution is highly unlikely"(ibid.). Clark felt that the only solution to this grim problem was to advocate that socialism "be given another trial" as it "appears to hold out the more certain salvation for future society" (14 January 1932). By 1933 the CCF had appeared and, according to Clark, "has accepted a Socialist programme. Let us send them to Ottawa with an absolute majority" (27 April 1933).

But the success of socialism was somewhat doubtful according to Clark as "the privileged classes would wage war rather than surrender their inheritance." In addition, the popular response to a Depression was "conservative rather than radical because of the fear engendered"; fear which Clark felt was people's "most pronounced trait" (14 January 1932). Nevertheless, the effort to achieve socialism would be worthwhile since the alternative would be war and either violent revolution or continued domination of the financial plutocracy.

It must be clear from Clark's early ideology that this was no establishment figure speaking. He described himself as a firm democratic socialist and not simply a social democrat. In the context of the Canadian political culture, Clark was solidly on the left as he sympathized with the agrarian movements and was on the left wing of the CCF itself.

That the young Clark expressed such views is not so astonishing. Even before the Depression exacerbated the situation, the farmers' revolt against the established economic and political system had been going on for some decades, although it gained strength and impact after the First World War. While the social thought of S.D. Clark had been affected by his experience with urban democratic socialist and social democratic movements (for example his connection to the League for Social Reconstruction in Toronto in 1931-32), he had been imbued with the ideals and viewpoints of the farmers' revolt. The radical agrarian petite-bourgeoisie had little do with Marxist ideas directly, but many of their written documents dealing with monopoly capitalism and large scale capitalists still sound as radical as any produced by social movements in Canada[10]. As Harry Hiller has written, "Clark grew up in the midst of this agrarian political activity replete with its ideology of protest, and the leaders of the UFA [United Farmers of Alberta] such as William Wise Wood were his heroes. As a young boy, he had even kept a scrapbook about them and their ideas. Somewhat later, he also became familiar with the writings of William Irvine."[11]

William Irvine played a key if chequered role in the period of agrarian revolt which has been surveyed by Anthony Mardiros in his biography. Originally a UFA member, he came to wider notice through his book *The Farmer in Politics* published in 1920, the year before the UFA swept in to power and shut the established parties in Alberta out of power for half a century. An analysis of Irvine's thought shows how deeply the young Clark relied on this older prairie mentor.

One of Irvine's themes was the true nature of political democracy. For Irvine, "The history of Canada is the record of the rise, development, and supremacy of class rule" with the ruling class reaching a peak under the Borden government of the First World War which was "in reality nothing more than the cooperation of the plutocratic classes for the domination and exploitation of the dominion."[12] He suggested that at an earlier time some "degree of competition among the plutocratic classes" had existed, but since the emergence of the Union Government of Sir Robert Borden with its domination by "the plutocratic classes ... every semblance of democracy vanished from Canadian life."[13]

The "plutocrats" were identified as "twenty-three money kings who control the whole arterial system of Canadian commercial life." The political system, for Irvine, directly represented the wishes of the money kings. In his words, "These kings of commerce and industry are the commanders of the political parties. They dictate the policies, and they make the laws, and they do both in the sole interest of property rights and business."[14] Irvine went on to detail how much legislation was "enacted by and for our twenty-three money kings"[15] including the disposition of natural resources, and the role of the tariff (which he characterised as "of enormous benefit to manufacturers but *equally disadvantageous* to everybody else") in setting up the rights to private property above the needs for health and education of the people.[16] The tariff was always of concern to farmers since it acted as an extra tax on foreign goods, thus keeping their prices artificially high. The resulting prices on foreign products helped Canadian manufacturers but hurt farmers.

For Irvine, farmers and industrial workers must organise to counter the control of parliament by "the selfishness of manufacturers" and the "plutocrats." Unless they did so, the government and its economic policy and laws would always go against the vast majority of the population who did not belong to the dominant classes. He held no modern Althusserian-Poulantzasian doctrine of the relative autonomy of the state, but instead a direct (and perhaps vulgar) instrumentalist theory of the state.

After the farmers and allied classes had taken over the government, they could set about to change the economic system, a system based on "individualism in industry,"[17] competition and profit-making. For Irvine, the profit motive denied service to the community: "our competitive system is one grand race for profit-making. There are no competitors for service. Service is incidental in the industrial scheme."[18] The alternative Irvine was advocating was a system based on a radical collectivism.

As noted above, Clark felt that socialism was the only answer. Yet he feared the social contradictions of the farmers' position, especially the farmers' individualism. In words that correspond with but predated those of C.B. Macpherson in later years, he pointed out in an article that appeared in the *Canadian Forum* that it "is impossible to say whether the Western Farmers are the most radical or the most conservative people in Canada."[19] On the one hand, the farmer "remained from beginning to end an individualist—an embryo capitalist" who always sought "independence"; he or she was an entrepreneur who remained "a small capitalist in a highly capitalized world."[20] As such, the farmer often constructed an individualist philosophy, was "almost arrogantly individualist in his outlook ... and looked with suspicion upon cooperative effort."[21] More recently (since the traditional low-tariff Liberal Party had maintained high tariffs between 1896 and 1911), many farmers had realized that their independence "remains but a fiction" and that they were dependent on the banks, railways and farm implements companies. Because of this realization, many farmers "have now become proletarians" who have adopted a collectivist philosophy.

Clark believed that this division of opinion was unresolved, creating "a muddled and contradictory philosophy." He worried that the individualism of the majority of farmers would prevent the CCF from becoming truly socialist, pointing out that the farmers had ensured that private ownership of agricultural land would remain a CCF plank. "It is no sin for the Government to own the systems of transportation, manufacturing and banking; but the farmer must be absolute boss over his own broad fields."[22] For Clark this conservatism of farmers meant that a true socialist party could not be achieved: "In short the new Federation may be a valuable contribution to social reform; but for some time at least, it cannot be a cohesive Socialist party."[23]

Clark's writings of 1932 and 1933 were essentially politically motivated. His first truly academic articles and books appeared in 1938. By this time he was a lecturer at the University of Toronto. His parents were running the family farm and would continue to do so until 1942 when his brother took over.[24] Clark retained his identification with the CCF until 1953, at which time he changed his allegiance to the Liberal Party of Canada. By 1953 he had published three of the books which contributed substantially to his reputation. The book which is arguably his best,[25] *Church and Sect in Canada*, was published in 1948, five years before his political break. His later book, *The Developing Canadian Community* (1963), was a collection of his more important essays, many of which had been published prior to

1953. Thus a major portion of his writing, including much of that for which he was celebrated in the world of Canadian scholarship, was published while he still considered himself to be an adherent to the democratic left. *Movements of Political Protest* appeared in 1959, but still utilized the framework he had worked out in the 1940s (although, as will be pointed out later, his shift in political stance was reflected in some subtle but important ways). It is the thesis of this chapter that the early social views of Clark, as reflected in the *Lloydminster Times*, continued to have an important influence on the subject, tone and paradigmatic approach of his more consciously academic writing until his conversion to the Liberal Party and for some time after, that is to say, until the publication of *Movements of Political Protest*.

The Young Scholar

The scholarly writings of the young Clark are academic in style and tone, and are seemingly written in the detached "neutral" voice usually adopted in academic prose. Distinctly lacking are the polemical tone and phrases that appear in his journalistic writings as a socialist advocate. Clark had learned his lessons of academic socialization well. Yet no matter how detached the tone, the sociology of knowledge holds that a world-view and ideology stands behind all writing, including that of the social sciences (see Nock and Nelsen 1982, for a further discussion of this point). Such world-views do not (necessarily) lead a social scientist to lie or to alter facts. But he or she chooses what questions to ask, what subjects to study, and what interpretations to make of the observed facts on the basis of the world-view and ideology.

Clark's earliest publication looked into the Canadian Manufacturers Association (CMA). This interest was in evidence as early as 1933 when, following a year at the London School of Economics, he began working at the McGill Department of Sociology on his M.A. thesis on this subject. Harry Hiller comments, "The selection of this topic for the focus of his M.A. research in sociology was also consonant with his historical and economic interests even if it was not very sociological in the Chicago tradition. In spite of his exposure to Dawsonian sociology (McGill's senior sociology professor), the thesis turned out to be very unecological and was clearly an exception to the emphasis in McGill's program."[26] He continued to work on the CMA for his Ph.D. dissertation in the Department of Political Economy at Toronto from 1935 to 1938.

Given his radical agrarian and democratic socialist background, this was a logical and perhaps even an inspired choice. It was the tariff issue more than any other single issue which had consistently annoyed farmers. They were convinced that a high protection tariff kept them in poverty, resulted in ruinously high prices, caused rapid depopulation of rural areas because of the ruin of farmers unable to pay artificially high prices, produced social problems in the city because of the swelling of the urban population, and resulted in the emergence of an employee society, sometimes referred to by the farmers as the "new feudalism." To the modern reader, the tariff might seem an important but dry and technical issue. However, it was an issue that rallied most farmers to a common cause, from moderate farm leaders such as T.C. Crerar and E.C. Drury to more radical leaders such as William Irvine.

The issue led many farmers to the conclusion that both old-line parties were unresponsive to the popular demands placed upon them and that the older parties had "sold out" to the plutocratic classes (although the more moderate leaders always seemed to hold out the hope that the Liberal Party, which had started life at least in part as a farmer-supported low tariff party, might return to the fold and see the light). In turn, this led to the demand for group representation by which farmers and workers would represent their own interests directly instead of being minor players in parties which were dominated by the money kings or even by liberal professionals. Thus, combined with his agrarian background, a study of the CMA would tell Clark much about how and why farmers had been excluded from influence in the political system. Obviously such a topic would also appeal to an urban socialist as the manufacturers were seen by the socialist movement as of central importance in modern capitalism—with such exemplars as the Fords. Clark's chosen topic allowed him to observe just how much influence manufacturing capitalists had in the political system.

Clark was very interested in the issues surrounding the tariff, the lobbying of the CMA, and the resulting union of purpose between the government and manufacturers. As Clark suggests "Dependence tended to be placed upon the lobbyist rather than upon the industrial engineer or sales promoter; the struggle for higher tariffs or bounties provided a rallying point which brought manufacturers together. These privileges established the close connection of the manufacturing industries with the government."[27]

Clark analysed the ideology behind the CMA and its tactics. It practiced neutrality and nonpartisanship in relations with the two old parties but actively favoured parties supporting a high tariff. The Association tended to identify its own need for a high tariff with the national interest, while denouncing farmer-labour movements. For example, a president of the CMA said, "We do not want warring groups in Canada but rather a union of all groups to advance the interests of our common country."[28]

A second article by Clark looks directly at "the CMA and the tariff" and states bluntly, "Protection as an economic creed has been largely an expression of industrial capitalism in Canada."[29] "The tariff systems developed with the growth of [the] manufacturing industry and it was pressed upon the Government as a necessary policy by organizations formed to advance the interests of manufacturers."[30] Clark went on to defend this thesis with a myriad of details. Such an argument obviously was in harmony with Clark's radical agrarian background.

In *The Social Development of Canada* (1942) Clark presented an analysis which he was later to elaborate more fully in religious and political contexts. What had to be explained, as Clark saw it, was the tendency for frontier populations to reject traditional institutions and methods of social organization. Frontier populations tended to see monopolistic institutions supported by the state as "coercive controls" and as "privileged."[31] Whether the subject at hand was an established church, trading companies granted royal charters, or the leadership of "family compacts" of politically connected and nepotistic kin, the frontier settlers saw such developments as encroachments on their own liberty. Social innovation was natural on the frontier as these populations were "less dependent upon traditional institutions even after they were established."[32] Farmers who supported and recruited circuit-riding preachers, for example, might be less than enthusiastic to see one-seventh of all land given over to the Church of England for its maintenance. Small French-Canadian fur traders resented the monopoly given to royal-chartered companies and resisted what they saw as an unjust imposition from a state which seemed alien to their interests. Thus on the frontier, "nonconformist attitudes," "habits of independence" and "new patterns of behaviour" emerged which combated "traditional systems of institutional control."[33] Such forces on the frontier produced "the weaknesses of economic monopolies, colonial class systems, established churches, or authoritarian systems of government."[34] All such traditional institutions were introduced but were resisted by frontier residents. Clark concludes, "the newly developing Canadian communities ... were outcasts of some sort from older societies."[35]

Given the resentment felt by the frontier population regarding the alien state, it was natural that reformers and even "social revolutionists" emerged on the frontier to challenge what Clark called the "vested interests." While Clark realized that a variety of factors, from the "boredom of routine tasks" to the "love of power," might influence such leaders, he emphasized that they could only succeed with community support. Clark stressed that "the reformer differed from the 'crank' in that he gave expression to genuine and persistent social needs and dissatisfactions" and that it was "this need for social expression" experienced by the community "rather than the character or motives of reformers which gave rise to reform movements."[36] By 1954, Clark much more readily viewed such frontier leaders as lacking in "political intelligence"[37] and as representing "not a rich and progressive but a poor and retarded society."[38] In this earlier work, however, the frontier reformers and radicals are presented as logical responses to the more or less just objections of frontier populations to alien bureaucratic and monopolistic states which burdened rather than aided the frontier population.

The appeal of such an analysis to the young Clark should be clear. He had grown up in a period of constant agrarian and frontier unrest. It must have seemed almost natural for such a population to be at odds with conventional society. As a boy and young man, for example, he had seen the UFA and Social Credit supplant the Liberal and Conservative parties. His student, W.E. Mann, later wrote a book outlining the strengths of sects in Alberta as opposed to the relative weakness of more conventional denominations and churches (1955). In exploring the frontier protest against the monopolistic state and traditionalistic institutions from the time of the French regime to the settlement of the prairies at the turn of the century, Clark was also studying the nature of the social forces which had led to the ubiquitousness of reformist and revolutionary movements on all of the Canadian frontiers, right down to his own Alberta.

In his early writings Clark denounces the plutocratic classes. He comes back to this theme rather pointedly in his major work *Church and Sect Canada* (1948). This is a study which ranges in time from 1760 almost to his own day, and from Nova Scotia westward to William Aberhart's Alberta. Each chapter centres on the social significance of religious affiliation in hinterland areas. In each new area of settlement on the frontier, there was an effort in Canada by the dominant classes emanating from Britain to support religious bodies which reflected their own establishment views. Such a religion , as espoused by the dominant classes was relatively unemotional, hierarchical and patriarchal in its organization, and laid considerable stress on the expertise and education expected of men of God. In provinces such as Ontario and Nova Scotia, there was also a direct process of affiliating the church and state as had been the case in Britain itself.

Most settlement frontiers were inhabited by uneducated men and women who not infrequently had left (even fled) the older settled areas of Europe and the Americas for a more democratic milieu where people could expect to own land individually rather than be tenants or worse for aristocratic landowners; thus, it was not surprising that church-forms of religion seemed culturally inappropriate, and politically and socially symbolic of the dominant classes trying to spread their control. The sects, with their greater emotional appeal, with their emphasis on a personal call from God that could override formal training and studies and the costs of advanced education, with their democratic rather than hierarchical and episcopal organization, naturally had greater appeal. As Michael S. Cross puts it[39]:

> S.D. Clark ... gives a broad spectrum approach, relating the conflict of the established churches and the evangelical sects to the nature of the frontier society, and linking it to other challenges to traditional institutions—particularly the rejection of the British class system and the frontier reaction against undemocratic forms of government. In discussing what he considers the failure of the traditional churches to provide the social leadership needed by a frontier society, to develop 'a more inclusive philosophy,' Clark seems to come down squarely as a supporter of the evangelicals and their democratic approaches. As with the orthodox frontierists, then, there is a strong moral content to his history.

In his introduction to *Church and Sect in Canada*, Clark points out that some large religious denominations[40]:

> ...have struggled to secure a dominant position. Some of them have enjoyed the protection and assistance of the state. All of them have had the support of powerful economic and social interests.... Throughout the development of Canada, from the early settlement of New France to the present day, undercurrents of unrest in religious organizations have found expression in the break from established religious authority and in the emergence of new religious forms.

A good example of this process was the fuss caused by the ministry of Henry Alline, the son of a New England farmer who had settled in Nova Scotia in the 1770s. As an uneducated frontier farmer, Alline would not have been of good enough background to obtain the education needed for ordination from the established churches, but his direct call from God meant he could bypass the worldly and ecclesiastical authorities. According to Alline, "Although many (to support the ministry of Antichrist) will pretend there is no such thing as a man's knowing in these days he is called to preach any other way than by his going to the seats of learning to be prepared for the ministry, and then authorized by men: yet blessed by God, there is a knowledge of these things, which an educated man knows nothing of."

As Clark comments, "In responding to this call, he challenged the prerogative of the Church to perform ordination." Alline's perspective is clear, "I saw I needed nothing to qualify me but Christ."[41]

As a settlement matured, as the outside metropolis asserted its control, as a greater degree of socioeconomic differentiation created greater degrees of wealth and poverty, the population was more likely to be incorporated into the wider system of authority. The frontier moved west (or, at least, away in a different direction) and the same process began anew.

The subject matter of *Church and Sect in Canada* surely appealed to the agrarian radical that Clark had been and still was. In such works he explored the radical and deviant roots of agrarian and frontier communities from the past and sought to grapple with why such periods of unrest always seemed to pass on and why former areas of unrest, such as the Maritime Provinces, were relatively quiescent by his own time. *Church and Sect in Canada* could be seen as the logical outcome of the combining of Clark's early political and social views and his academic influences. As an academic personally interested in movements which question the status quo, it is not surprising that he should study other times and places which have undergone similar struggles or movements.

The Epistemological Break in S.D. Clark

It may be of interest to take a close look at a paper Clark presented to the annual meeting of the Royal Society of Canada in 1954, a year after he decided to support the Liberal Party of Canada. It cannot be accidental that, for the first time in Clark's published work, there is a note of doubt and even of condemnation of the radical agrarian movements. In talking about his home province of Alberta, where twenty-two years earlier he had been fanning the flames of protest in a rather supportive milieu, he now committed to print before his intellectual peers this judgement[42]:

> We have been too much inclined perhaps to exaggerate the political intelligence of frontier populations. It comes hard to one brought up in Alberta to suggest that the people of that province who thought of themselves as in the vanguard of reform actually had only a limited appreciation of the complexities of modern government and no great understanding of the conditions necessary for the preservation of individual rights and a sense of community responsibility. In a cultural sense, the frontier was not a rich and progressive but a poor and retarded society.

Clark points out that political reform was "only one of many forms of frontier protest which also included medical quackery, vigilantism, mob rioting." He goes on to suggest that what characterised the UFA was "an underlying attitude of irresponsibility with respect to the larger affairs of the community," and even indicates that the UFA sought to make the individual "in a sense a poor citizen" and that "poor citizenship" became with the Social Credit "almost a condition of membership of the party."[43]

Later in this essay, Clark portrays McCarthyism in the USA as a logical outcome of American radical agrarian radicalism. Thus he writes, "The attack of Joseph McCarthy upon communist influences in the government of the United States was a clear and genuine expression of the American frontier, isolationist spirit. It was no accident that McCarthy came from the Middle West and represented an ethnic-religious minority population in the United States."[44] These words, delivered in 1954, surely tell us more about the mind of S.D. Clark than about the McCarthy phenomenon. After all, Wisconsin in the 1950s was hardly on the edge of any frontier, and McCarthy, a Roman Catholic, did not come from the hard sectarian Protestantism that Clark himself had characterised as a natural development of the frontier.

This new rejection of a more radical or socialist viewpoint is also in evidence in Clark's foreword in C.B. Macpherson's *Democracy in Alberta: Social Credit and the Party System* (1953). In his 1932 *Canadian Forum* article, Clark voices a number of ideas which were similar to those of Macpherson. Macpherson and Clark were colleagues in the Department of Political Economy at the University of Toronto. Macpherson, while strictly academic in his writings, has usually been connected with the left, even the Marxist viewpoint and as such provides a class-based and materialistic explanation of the appeal of the Social Credit to a party of farmers who retained land ownership and a sense of entrepreneurship in their ideology. The older Clark reveals his doubts regarding Macpherson's perspective. He suggests contentiously that, "Not all Professor Macpherson's readers will accept his conclusions, but this is not the place to question the arguments put forward."[45] Earlier he also casts doubt by stating, "However far one may be prepared to go in accepting Professor Macpherson's explanations ...." Evidently Clark is no longer prepared to go the whole distance with Macpherson's class-based analysis.

Although the general Clarkian framework remains in his last major work which owes something to his own agrarian origin (*Movements of Political Protest in Canada, 1640-1840*), the shift in orientation is also clear in this text when Clark suggests that the frontier encouraged "a system of political irresponsibility."[46] In discussing frontier insurgents such as Papineau, Mackenzie and Aberhart, Clark describes them as "irresponsible"[47] although he does acknowledge that such leaders might "be seeking a better world to live in."[48]

Despite the major shift in Clark's views towards a questioning of frontier radicalism, his own interpretation remains largely that which he had constructed earlier. In *Movements of Political Protest in Canada, 1640-1840*, the emphasis is on looking at the "revolutionary forces" that had affected Canadian political development. According to Clark, "On the North

American continent political authority was established only in face of almost continuous resistance on the part of the population in outlying areas."[49] New areas of settlement "organized their own systems of control, and when central authority sought to establish itself, movements of revolt quickly developed."[50] Against the state, dominated by the longer-settled areas usually back east, the frontier exhibited an "intense localism" of almost "sectarian exclusiveness."[51] The state was costly to pioneers who could largely do without it, with their dependence either on local individualism or community co-operation. Like the state church, the state itself was seen as a costly and alien intrusion. Thus Clark states, "Reform on the frontier was directed against such social evils of the outside world as political patronage, the payment of excessive salaries to government officials, economic monopoly, a stringent money supply, exorbitant interest charges, and burdensome taxation."[52]

In the context of Canada, such frontier revolts against the state involved disloyalty to European powers which, up until 1840, still attempted to control the new areas of frontier development with forms of social organisation imported from a more rigidified class and state system. Clark's analysis of the rebellions of 1837-1838 in Lower and Upper Canada takes up about half the book. Other authors have described these rebellions as contests for responsible government, but Clark sees them as having, "the object of liberating the Canadian population from British rule … of freeing the population of British North America from the rule of an overseas power."[53] For Clark, these movements were by no means ones supported for individual gain, but "were very real and genuinely appealing" to frontier settlers "who, suspicious of the Federal power in the United States, were even more suspicious of the powers of an overseas empire."[54]

An interesting example of Clark's analysis is that of the Patriote rebellion in Lower Canada. Some authorities hold that this was interpreted as a war between the ethnic groups or "races" (as the older usage had it). More recently Fernand Ouellet has suggested it was due to the narrow socioeconomic self-interest of a liberal professional class whose mobility was blocked and who used a nationalistic appeal to further their own narrow views. Donald Creighton, another prominent authority on this subject, suggests the liberal professionals stood in the way of the progressive business community in Montreal because their aims were threatened by this business class. Both authors tend to deny the truly popular nature and significance of the rebellions in their focus on a small élite's class self-interest.

Clark's analysis remains based on the notion that frontier populations were struggling to overcome the coercive power of an oppressive state system that owed its existence to a foreign European imperialism. For Clark, then, the Patriote movement was a genuine response by the rural population, and not simply the élite's manipulation by French Canadian liberal professionals.

By the mid-to-late 1950s, Clark had moved a long way from his origins. He lived in Central Canada and taught at the University of Toronto. He joined a party that has always chosen its leaders from Québec and Ontario, the Liberal Party of Canada. He was a member of the Royal Society of Canada, which had been founded by a Governor General of Canada who had been a member of the British aristocracy (ironically just the sort of authority Clark critiques in his academic writings on resistance to the British class system). Of course, the times were so much better and the state had, with the Keynesian revolution, become an active state with many social benefit programs. As Hiller puts it, "The optimism that was part of the post-war era was particularly maintained by persons like Clark who had experienced the hardships of the depression years."[55] The fortunes of Canada's protest parties suffered. In some cases, as with the Social Credit, the movement ceased to be a movement of protest at all, and simply became another big business party.

Clark's early socialist radicalism had been predicated on the view that capitalism could not recover and that a war would produce a revolution or a situation worse than the 1930s. Neither of these things had happened and prosperity was general, unemployment low. In addition, Clark was far from Alberta and by now was a long-time resident of Toronto. As Hiller says, "It is important to note that his commitment to socialism was born in agrarian populism rather than industrial radicalism, and … the more Clark became removed from that agrarian environment in time and space, the more his enthusiastic zeal for it waned."[56] It is likely that Clark's turning away from topics which had been of such burning interest to a prairie radical also occurred because of his altered political, social and physical environment.

Throughout the 1960s and 1970s (and starting in the 1950s with his shift to the Liberal Party), Clark's social outlook increasingly supported the authority structures of his society. It was at this time that large numbers of activists from the Canadian sociology movement entered sociology departments as doctoral students and professors. These students were confused about the nature of Clark's heritage. The conservatism of his present outlook (and his Liberalism in politics), the general difficulty for sociology readers of his main works, and some of his actions during the fiercer days of the late 1960s and early 1970s, tended to produce doubt about whether Clark's writings could or should be incorporated as part of a progressive Canadian sociology, and whether they were compatible or hostile to a materialistic and neo-Marxist outlook. The subject matter of the new Marxist sociology often also tended to be different from Clark's concerns. Much of the new Marxist sociology was directed to understanding Canada's place and fate *vis-à-vis* the juggernaut of American imperialist capitalism. In this view, the Canadian state was accepted as a given, and movements which might threaten the Canadian state and which thereby might weaken resistance to the American threat could be interpreted in a hostile light. Thus it is evident that S.D. Clark's early writing up to 1959 (with exceptions as noted after 1953) needs to be prefaced with a proper understanding of his own agrarian radicalism and socialism to be understood.

It is my argument that Clark's early work must be incorporated into the new Canadian progressive sociology and social science. Clark's subject matter remains of importance to a progressive Canadian sociology—the rejection of the British and French class system and system of authority and social control (such as the established church, aristocratic landowners), the vitality of movements of political and social protest on the frontier, the importance of the farmer's movement, and the nature and functioning of Canadian manufacturers and capitalists are highly significant aspects of our history. The fact that Clark became socially more conservative and politically more Liberal in his outlook from 1953 onward should not be allowed to obscure the importance of the writings of the early Clark witten from the paradigmatic outlook and ideology of an agrarian radical democratic socialist.

Notes

1 Magill, Dennis William. (1983). Paradigms and Social Science in English Canada. In J. Paul Grayson, (Ed.), *Introduction to Sociology: An Alternate Approach.* Toronto: Gage.

2 Clark, S. D. (1979). The Changing Image of Sociology in English-speaking Canada. *The Canadian Journal of Sociology*, no. iv, pp. 393-403.

3 Smith, Dusky Lee. (1983). Review of D. Harrison, The Limits of Liberalism. *The Canadian Review of Sociology and Anthropology*, no. xx, pp. 359-60.

4 Sacouman, R. James. (1983). Regional Uneven Development, Regionalism and Struggle. In J. Paul Grayson, (Ed.), *Introduction to Sociology: An Alternate Approach*. Toronto: Gage. p. 159.

5 Ibid. p. 157.

6 Ibid. p. 158.

7 Harrison, Deborah. (1981). *The Limits of Liberalism: The Making of Canadian Sociology*. Montreal: Black Rose Books. p.16.

8 Ibid. p. 14.

9 Conway, Jim F. (1983). Review of Harry H. Hiller, Society and Change: S.D. Clark and the Development of Canadian Sociology. *Canadian Journal of Political Science*, no. xvi, pp. 366-7.

10 David Laycock has provided the best overall analysis of radical prairie movements in his *Populism and Democratic Thought in the Canadian Prairies, 1910 to 1945*. He identifies "crypto-Liberalism," Radical Democratic, Social Democratic and Social Credit forms of populism and points out that despite differences in the points of view of these traditions "each variant cohere(d) around principles concerning redistribution of power among social classes and groups" (Laycock 1990, 4).

11 Hiller, Harry H. (1982). *Society and Change: S.D. Clark and the Development of Canadian Sociology*. Toronto: University of Toronto Press. p.153.

12 Irvine, William. (1920). *The Farmer in Politics*. Toronto: McClelland and Stuart, p. 198.

13 Loc. Cit.

14 Ibid. p. 202.

15 Ibid. p. 203.

16 Ibid. p. 204.

17 Ibid. p. 33.

18 Ibid. p. 29.

19 Clark, S.D. (1932). *Canadian Forum*, pp. 8

20 Clark, S.D. (1932). The United Farmers of Alberta. *Canadian Forum*, XIII, p. 7.

21 Loc. Cit.

22 Loc. Cit.

23 Loc. Cit.

24 Hiller, Harry H. (1982). *Society and Change: S.D. Clark and the Development of Canadian Sociology*. Toronto: University of Toronto Press, p.152

25 Nock, David A. (1983). S.D. Clark in the Context of Canadian Sociology. *Canadian Journal of Sociology*, no. viii, p. 93; Douglas F. Campbell. (1983).

Beginnings: Essays on the History of Canadian Sociology. Port Credit: The Scribblers' Press, p. 170.

26 Op. Cit. p. 46
27 S.D. Clark. (1938). The Canadian Manufacturers' Association: A Political Pressure Group. *Canadian Journal of Economics and Political Science*, no. iv, p. 506
28 Ibid. 514
29 S.D. Clark. (1939). The Canadian Manufacturers' Association and the Tariff. *Canadian Journal of Economics and Political Science*, no. v, p. 19.
30 Loc. Cit.
31 S.D. Clark. (1942). *The Social Development of Canada*. Toronto: University of Toronto Press, p. 5.
32 Ibid. p. 6.
33 Loc. Cit.
34 Ibid. p. 7.
35 Loc. Cit.
36 Ibid. p. 15
37 S.D. Clark. (1962). *The Developing Canadian Community*. Toronto: University of Toronto Press. p. 218.
38 Loc. Cit.
39 Michael S. Cross. (1970). *The Frontier Thesis and the Canadas*. Toronto: Copp Clark. pp. 80-81.
40 S.D. Clark. (1948). *Church and Sect in Canada*. Toronto: University of Toronto Press. pp. 21
41 Loc. Cit.
42 S.D. Clark. (1962). *The Developing Canadian Community*. Toronto: University of Toronto Press, p. 219.
43 Loc. Cit.
44 Ibid. p. 216.
45 S.D. Clark. (1953). Foreword in C.B. Macpherson, *Democracy in Alberta: Social Credit and the Party System*. Toronto: University of Toronto Press, p. vii.
46 S.D. Clark. (1959). *Movements of Political Protest in Canada 1640-1840*. Toronto: University of Toronto Press. p. 8.
47 Ibid. p. 505.
48 Loc. Cit.
49 Ibid. p. 4.
50 Loc. Cit.
51 Ibid. p. 5.
52 Loc. Cit.
53 Ibid. p. 255.

54 Ibid. p. 256.
55 Harry Hiller. (1982). *Society and Change: S.D. Clark and the Development of Canadian Sociology*. Toronto: University of Toronto Press, p. 156.
56 Ibid. p. 155.

Bibliography

Campbell, Douglas F.
(1983). *Beginnings: Essays on the History of Canadian Sociology*. Port Credit: The Scribblers' Press.

Clark, S.D.
(1932a). Letters to the Editor, *Lloydminster Times*. 14 January; 9, 11, 16, 18, February; 24, 29 March; 28 July; 18 August; 3, 17 November; 15, 22 December.
(1932b). The United Farmers of Alberta. *Canadian Forum*, XIII, pp. 7-8.
(1938). The Canadian Manufacturers' Association: A Political Pressure Group. *Canadian Journal of Economics and Political Science*, no. iv, pp. 505-23.
(1939). The Canadian Manufacturers' Association and the Tariff. *Canadian Journal of Economics and Political Science*, no. v, pp. 19-39.
(1942). *The Social Development of Canada*. Toronto: University of Toronto Press.
(1948). *Church and Sect in Canada*. Toronto: University of Toronto Press.
(1953). Foreword in C.B. Macpherson, *Democracy in Alberta: Social Credit and the Party System*. Toronto: University of Toronto Press.
(1959). *Movements of Political Protest in Canada 1640-1840*. Toronto: University of Toronto Press.
(1962). *The Developing Canadian Community*. Toronto: University of Toronto Press.
(1979). The Changing Image of Sociology in English-speaking Canada. *The Canadian Journal of Sociology*, no. iv, pp. 393-403.

Conway, Jim F.
(1983). Review of Harry H. Hiller, Society and Change: S.D. Clark and the Development of Canadian Sociology. *Canadian Journal of Political Science*, no. xvi, pp. 366-7.

Cross, Michael S.
(1970). *The Frontier Thesis and the Canadas*. Toronto: Copp Clark.

Harrison, Deborah.
(1981). *The Limits of Liberalism: The Making of Canadian Sociology*. Montreal: Black Rose Books.

(1983) The Limits of Liberalism in Canadian Sociology: Some Notes on S.D. Clark. *Canadian Review of Sociology and Anthropology*, XX, pp. 150-166.

Hiller, Harry H.

(1982). *Society and Change: S.D. Clark and the Development of Canadian Sociology*. Toronto: University of Toronto Press.

Irvine, William.

(1920). *The Farmer in Politics*. Toronto: McClelland and Stuart.

Laycock, David.

(1990). *Populism and Democratic Thought on the Canadian Prairies 1910 to 1945*. Toronto: University of Toronto Press.

Magill, Dennis William.

(1983). Paradigms and Social Science in English Canada. In J. Paul Grayson, (Ed.), *Introduction to Sociology: An Alternate Approach*. Toronto: Gage.

Mann, W.E.

(1955). *Sect, Cult and Church in Alberta*. Toronto: University of Toronto Press.

Mardiros, Anthony.

(1979). *William Irvine: The Life of a Prairie Radical*. Toronto: James Lorimer.

Nock, David A.

(1983). S.D. Clark in the Context of Canadian Sociology. *Canadian Journal of Sociology*, no. viii, pp. 93.

Nock, D.A. and Nelson, R.W.

(1982). Science, Ideology and 'Reading, Writing and Riches.' *Journal of Educational Thought*, XVI, pp. 73-88.

Sacouman, R. James.

(1983). Regional Uneven Development, Regionalism and Struggle. In J. Paul Grayson, (Ed.), *Introduction to Sociology: An Alternate Approach*. Toronto: Gage.

Smith, Dusky Lee.

(1983). Review of D. Harrison, The Limits of Liberalism. *The Canadian Review of Sociology and Anthropology*, no. xx, pp. 359-60.

Chapter Four

RESEARCH BIOGRAPHY AND DISCIPLINARY DEVELOPMENT: S.D. CLARK AND CANADIAN SOCIOLOGY

Harry H. Hiller

No account of the development of sociology can ignore the fact that the autonomy of the discipline has not always been taken for granted. The rooting of sociology in humanistic inquiry usually placed the sociological perspective within more established disciplines in the academic community before its emergence as a differentiated discipline. While some initially lamented the trend towards disciplinary autonomy,[1] others have worked towards this goal as a means of furthering professional and scientific development,[2] while still others have more recently called for a revitalization of interdisciplinary alliances.[3] Perhaps once established as a legitimate field of inquiry, sociology has accepted extra-disciplinary endeavours as less threatening.

The erosion of the nineteenth century alliance of sociology with other fields was a halting yet volatile process dependent on a complexity of local factors. Wherever sociology emerged it did so in a manner and at a time that was congruent with national traditions and structures.[4] As a consequence, global differences are usually related to factors peculiar to specific national contexts. For example, DiRenzo[5] has shown how sociology in Italy was

---

Hiller, Harry H. Research Biography and Disciplinary Development: S.D. Clark and Canadian Sociology. From *The Journal of the History of Sociology*, 3(1). Reprinted with permission from the author. References have been removed from the text and replaced as endnotes.

thwarted in its development by both academic institutional structures and religio-political ideologies.

In Australia, sociology was affected by its ties to social anthropology and university structures modelled in the Oxbridge tradition.[6] If in America sociology received its impetus from teaching demands,[7] sociological practice in Greece on the other hand found no academic supports but has been maintained in research centers.[8] Or, in the case of Holland, the discipline was strengthened by the employment of sociologists as government advisors on social policy.[9]

It is generally acknowledged that it was in the United States where sociology attained its earliest and most widespread acceptance as a differentiated discipline.[10] Sociological organizations and journals in other countries preceded those in the United States but it was in the United States that the discipline attained its strongest impetus particularly in the inter-war period and immediately after World War II.[11] Most important was the fact that sociology was able to attain disciplinary autonomy and legitimation as an independent field of inquiry much earlier than elsewhere. Furthermore, the confluence of other factors including the availability of support for sociology through research funding contributed to a particular sociological style in the United States of university-based empirical research.

The battle for autonomy and indeed the question of a separate disciplinary existence was not as readily forthcoming in most other countries as in the United States. As a contribution to the literature on the various national experiences of disciplinary differentiation, it is the purpose of this paper to show how the sociological perspective emerged and the discipline developed in Canada by looking at the work of one of its long-standing sociologists. Not only is it of merit to trace his personal biography for its own sake, but it is my thesis that an examination of the work of S. D. Clark is useful because the changes his work demonstrates over time reflect changes in the discipline as it emerged from a dependent undifferentiated position to that of an autonomous highly differentiated discipline.

Most explanations of differences in disciplinary evolution stress the role of university structures or the socio-political milieu in either supporting or resisting disciplinary innovations.[12] This study attempts a somewhat different approach by demonstrating how the published work of a sociologist significant to a specific national context can be an important indicator of how the discipline has developed in that country and the issues that have shaped that development. The thrust of this paper is to show how research biography can be a useful tool in the history of sociology as a reflector of disciplinary development and differentiation.

The most typical use of biography in sociology is to describe chronological landmarks in the theoretical or methodological progression of the discipline. Hence, the intellectual development and theoretical perspective of an "important" sociologist is traced and the contribution or significance of this person and his thought is assessed in relation to the discipline as a whole.[13] Biography has also been used as an analytical focus in the sociology of knowledge by situating the ideas of a particular sociologist in a socio-political context.[14] Another role of the biography is to demonstrate how friendship networks and relationships (i.e., theory groups or cohorts) contribute to the institutionalization of ideas.[15] Terry Clark,[16] for example, has attempted to explain why Durkheim and his followers were able to become established in the French universities whereas other groups of social researchers were not successful in doing so. In contrast to these approaches, my goal is to illustrate how research biography (in addition to intellectual or personal biography) evidences important issues, perspectives, and dispositions in the evolution of sociology as a discipline in a socio-national context. By examining the published work and research of sociologists of note in a particular country, illustrative material can be gathered regarding the history of sociology in that country.

The work of Canadian sociologist S. D. Clark is particularly relevant to this thesis because his career has spanned most of the critical phases in the development of sociology of Canada. Beginning in a strong interdisciplinary context which molded his thinking, and then moving into a strictly disciplinary context with the changes that implied, Clark's career illuminates critical aspects of the historical development of sociology in anglophone Canada.

A Developmental Perspective

Elsewhere[17] I have developed a schematic framework for the evolution of sociology as a discipline in Canada. A four-fold periodization consisting of two cycles of disciplinary dependency was developed in which British conceptions of sociological research were followed by American conceptions of sociological practice in anglophone social science. In brief, the first period was that of *European transference* when anglophone social scientists emulated British models of theory and academic organization. While the legacy of this tradition remained strong in the years following the First World War, the second period of *environmental adaption* (1920s-1940s) saw numerous attempts to explore the vicissitudes and dynamics of Canadian life through the modifications of transplanted theories and approaches. Three interdisciplinary study series characterized this phase of Canadian social science which included Frontiers of Canadian Settlement, Canadian-American Relations, and Backgrounds to Social Credit in Alberta. In each instance, sociology was thought of as part of a team of social sciences (represented jointly by the interdisciplinary Canadian Political Science Association) illuminating important aspects of Canadian society rather than distinguished by its own disciplinary theory or research methodology.

Proximity to the United States meant a perpetual awareness of sociological developments there but the resistance to sociology as an "American" discipline by Canadian universities remained until the 1950s. By the latter part of that decade, the British orientations were rather convincingly replaced by American orientations which led to the reorganization of the previous academic structures to accommodate the widespread establishment of autonomous departments of sociology across Canada for the first time. Parallel to this development was the establishment of a separate journal (*The Canadian Review of Sociology and Anthropology*) in 1964, and the creation of an association (The Canadian Sociology And Anthropology Association) in 1965, all of which was part of the third phase of *disciplinary differentiation and specialization*. The sudden structural emulation of the American model of a differentiated discipline combined with increased instructional demands for the newly accepted discipline due to expanding universities produced a personnel problem (particularly in anglophone sociology) for which there were few native-trained sociologists to fill faculty positions. Recruitment from abroad but particularly the United States, the procurement of American textbooks in the absence of Canadian ones, the growth of micro (as opposed to macro) sociological interests, and the expansion in the numbers of university-based sociology faculty holding diverse substantive specializations further contributed to dramatic changes in the discipline. The effect of these rather rapid and large-scale developments led to a period of *consolidation* in the 1970s in which a second indigenizing trend took place to ensure the relevance of sociology to the Canadian context.[18] Emphasis was given to the training of sociologists in Canada (i.e., the development of graduate programs), to the development of a more adequate Canadian sociological literature including texts, and to the utilization of theoretical models and approaches more conducive to explaining the dimensions of Canadian society and the nature of social life found therein.

The work of no other Canadian sociologist so graphically displays the tensions and paradoxes contained within the history of sociology in Canada as that of S. D. Clark. Trained and matured into a position as senior scholar in the interdisciplinary period of environmental adaptation, Clark came to embody a more British conception of sociology in social science. But as the disciplinary context began to change, Clark's research also began to change from historical research to survey research, and from rejection of American sociology to greater acceptance of it. Nevertheless, his debate with Park and Parsons provided him with sufficient distance that he became an important spokesman in the period of consolidation for a sociology more attuned to the society in which it is practiced. An examination of Clark's personal and research biography reveals something of the process through which the discipline of sociology has evolved over time in Canada. But first it is important to locate Clark within Canadian sociology.

Clark Within Canadian Sociology

Clark was not the first sociologist in Canada but he was the first sociologist born, raised, and trained in Canada. Carl A. Dawson of McGill University is generally regarded as the father of Canadian sociology. Dawson was trained at the University of Chicago and soon after coming to McGill established the first Department of Sociology in Canada in 1924.[19] The uniqueness of Dawson's sociological leadership in Canadian academia is reflected in the fact that the department at McGill remained the only autonomous department of sociology in Canada for considerably more than three decades. Clark, on the other hand, represented a more interdisciplinary conception of the discipline at the University of Toronto which had much greater influence and was a better indicator of Canadian attitudes towards the discipline.[20] If Dawson had sought to replicate Chicago sociology in Canada, Clark debated with that form of sociology in deference to a more historical and macro-sociological conception of sociology-in-political economy. The publications of both Dawson and Clark contributed to developing a greater knowledge of the contours and shape of Canadian society[21] but Dawson's thirty year career (1922-1952) ended just when his own conception of sociology as an autonomous discipline in Canada began to gain greater legitimacy within university structures. On the other hand, Clark's career at the University of Toronto stretched from 1938 to 1976, thereby extending into the later phases of the development of sociology of Canada.

Among anglophone sociologists Clark has been called the "dean" of Canadian sociology. Not only has his career been a lengthy one but the strategic position of influence that he had within the Canadian social science community during its early years helped perpetuate a conception of sociology that was at odds with Dawson's. Clark was active in the interdisciplinary Canadian Political Science Association when it embraced political science, economics, and sociology in a common tradition of historical analysis. He served on the executive of the Association in various capacities for several years culminating in the Presidency in 1958. He was one of the editors of the *Canadian Journal of Economics and Political Science* from 1945-52 and served as managing editor in 1953. Clark was elected to the prestigious Royal Society of Canada in 1953, served as President of its Humanities And Social Science section in 1969-70, and was elected President of the entire Royal Society in 1975. He was made the first chairman of the newly established Department of Sociology at the University of Toronto in 1963 after having served as coordinator of the sociology section in the Department of Political Economy for many years. In 1967, Clark was elected Honorary President of the Canadian Sociology and Anthropology Association, made a Foreign Honorary Member of the American Academy of Arts and Science in 1976, and was honored by being made an Officer in the Order of Canada in 1978.

Clark's publications are also noteworthy in that they all deal with important macro questions confronting Canadian society from politics to religion to economic institutions to urbanization. He is the author of nine books including six major monographs and has written well over 30 articles or chapters in books. These published comments and analyses provide good evidence of changing conceptions of sociology in the anglophone Canadian academic community.

Foundations for Clark's Research Biography: His Academic Socialization[22]

Samuel Delbert Clark was born in 1910 in rural Alberta as the son of a struggling farm family. From 1927-30, Clark studied at the University of Saskatchewan completing an undergraduate honors degree in history and particularly learning to do historical field research from the eminent Canadian social historian A. S. Morton. As the result of funding that was made available to Morton from the Frontiers Of Settlement or Pioneer Problems project, Clark was offered a fellowship at Saskatchewan to complete his M.A. under Morton. It was here that Clark learned to use historical materials as a data source for studying social phenomenon which was to become a major career perspective for him. Data was gathered from diaries, letters, books, personal papers, newspapers, census reports, and government and land company reports. Clark's work with Morton also sensitized him to the significance of the frontier as a locus of social process and his M.A. Thesis ("Settlement In Saskatchewan With Special Reference To The Influence Of Dry Farming") attempted to relate the settlement process to environmental factors and the adaptation of farming techniques. Both history as a data source and the frontier as the cutting edge of social process were to become critical foci for him as a researcher throughout the period of environmental adaptation.

After completion of his M.A. in History, Clark went to the University of Toronto for one year where his initial intention was to embark on a Ph.D. in History. The financial hardships of the depression years and his discontent with the sterility of constitutional history enticed him to accept an IODE Fellowship for study in England. His personal knowledge and experience with agrarian discontent which had attacked the economic system, and his own growing intellectual awareness of the significance of economic factors in history[23] led him to select the London School of Economics for his year abroad. Through his exposure to Harold Laski and R. H. Tawney at the LSE during the 1932-33 school year, Clark was exposed not only to leftist critiques of society but also to an hostility to American-style sociology. From these criticisms of a methodology he attributed to the Chicago School, Clark emerged with a caricature of American sociology as "doorbell ringing" and rather trivial.

Ironically, but out of desperation as a result of the depression, Clark visited C. A. Dawson in Montreal on his way home from England and was offered a job as research assistant. Here Clark was to benefit from the second great interdisciplinary Canadian research project, that of the Canadian-American Relations study,[24] which provided the funding to hire Clark. He also enrolled as a graduate student and remained at McGill from 1933-35 where he completed his M.A. in Sociology with a thesis on the Canadian Manufacturers' Association as an organization affecting Canadian-American relations. Clark worked with both Dawson and Everett Hughes, though it was Dawson who primarily tried to teach him the social-ecological approach and the pre-eminence of sociology. Dawson put pressure on Clark to go to Chicago for his Ph.D. in Sociology but the die had already been cast and Clark resisted. His thesis at McGill had been very "un" ecological and not at all in the Chicago tradition of data collection. But more than that, Clark's Canadian reference group and personal experiences had drawn him closer to political economy and history and had established a bias against American-style sociology through the views of his earlier mentors and the prevailing academic sentiments in Canada.[25] Later when Clark applied for a position to teach sociology at the University of Toronto in 1938, this rather strong Canadian preference for a particular sociological style was reflected in Clark's appointment over that of a sociologist trained at Chicago.

At the University of Toronto, Clark was attracted by the work of Harold Innis who by this time was acquiring both a national and international reputation for his work in economic history.[26] No longer content with theories generated in other societies, Innis sought to correct the previous Britannic orientation to anglophone social science by showing how the staples (fur, fish, metals) industry linked empire metropoles with the new world and shaped Canadian society. While Alex Brady became Clark's official supervisor, the relationship which Clark established with Innis was to cement him firmly into the academically strong Canadian political economy tradition. Thus, at Toronto, Clark's interests in both economics and history came together neatly in political economy. This perspective allowed him to expand on his earlier work on the Canadian Manufacturers' Association for his Ph.D. thesis.

Clark's removal from the agrarian environment led to a gradual cooling of his leftist zeal. He had served a term as President of the Labor Club while at McGill and was still interested in the CCF (a left-wing political movement with roots in Saskatchewan) when he went to Toronto in 1935 to complete a Ph.D. in political science cum economic history. But his political interests no longer consumed him—probably largely influenced by his relationship with Innis who taught academics to beware of monopolies of truth.[27] From then on, Clark's radical spirit seemed to slowly disappear.

An undergraduate honors program in sociology had been established at Toronto in 1933 and Clark[28] has referred to it as "a splendid program of training" which defined sociology as "a body of learning bringing together history, economics, philosophy, psychology, anthropology, and biology." E. J. Urwick, a British social philosopher who had little appreciation for American sociology[29] helped set it up and an anthropologist, C. W. M. Hart, who had studied under Radcliffe-Brown, taught the sociology courses. In view of his M.A. degree in sociology, Clark was also used in the program while he was still a graduate student and he taught a course in the History of Sociological Theory emphasizing the work of European sociologists rather than American sociologists. This was the beginning of Clark's increasing professional identification with sociology for he found that sociology-in-political economy not only suited his interests but was more likely to provide a university appointment upon graduation. After a year of teaching sociology and political science at the University of Manitoba, Clark accepted an appointment to teach Sociology at Toronto where, except for brief interludes elsewhere, he remained until his retirement in 1976.

Hart was responsible for directing the sociology program at Toronto until he resigned in 1946 when Clark took over. Nevertheless, sociology was just a small program within the department of political economy and it was expected that sociology would be developed in a manner consonant with the thrust of political economy. Such a program was clearly at odds with Dawson's program at McGill but it fitted the interdisciplinary milieu within Canadian academia in which sociology was expected to exist.[30]

Research Biography Phase I: Sociology in Political Economy

The interdisciplinary conception of sociology-in-political economy is evident in Clark's four major monographs published by the University of Toronto Press during this period. Here Clark's own synthesis of the McGill-

Chicago sociological tradition and the Innisian political economy framework becomes evident. His first book, *The Canadian Manufacturers' Association: A Study in Collective Bargaining And Political Pressure* (1939), displayed parallels as a study of a major economic institution with both Innis' work on the Canadian Pacific Railway (1923) and Everett Hughes' work on the Chicago Real Estate Board (1931). Yet its rather straightforward documentation was less of a synthesis than his three following works. His second book, *The Social Development Of Canada* (1942), focussed on the locations of new economic development where Innis had obtained his staples theory. Taking a clue from F. J. Turner who identified these social locations as frontiers,[31] Clark defined a frontier as any "new area of economic exploitation" rather than just a time period or outpost of settlement. Thus he could speak of remote mining, fishing, or logging communities, backwoods agricultural settlements, or even of industrializing cities (and later suburbanization) as frontiers because new economic forces were being put to work. In engaging in socio-historical analysis of these communities of yesterday, Clark examined their social life through the analysis of original historical documents. Using the social disorganization thesis of Thomas and Znaniecki (1918), Clark found ample evidence of family breakdown, unbalanced sex ratios, social class cleavages, and psychological and social instabilities. In sum, Clark applied a sociological model to the study of historical communities in order to determine the social effects of underlying economic forces.

In addition to the existence of these disorganizing forces, Clark also noted the existence of movements of reorganization in frontier communities. Two of the most effective means of reorganization, he discovered, were through religion and politics. In his third book, *Church And Sect In Canada* (1948), Clark argued that the sect was the product of frontier instability and that the sect became more church-like over the course of time as the result of the increasing economic prosperity of its members (i.e., the church-sect thesis of Niebuhr, 1929). If sectarian religious leaders were major agents in reintegration, so also were political leaders. This theme was woven through Clark's fourth book, *Movements Of Political Protest In Canada, 1640-1840* (1959) as well. But for the powers of the central government which reduced the rampant disorganization more characteristic of the American frontier, the result of the Canadian frontier would have been similar argued Clark. This volume was a contribution to the third interdisciplinary research project of this period. As general editor of the series entitled Backgrounds

To Social Credit In Alberta sponsored by the Rockefeller Foundation,[32] Clark achieved increasing visibility in the Canadian social science community. He had been recommended for the task by Innis and this role gave him direct involvement in all three of the major social science projects of the era.

All of these books (and the journal articles that accompanied them) demonstrated untiring use of different types of historical and archival data though the sociological generalizations with which he emerged were frequently not as firmly supported as he concluded they were. While the focus of all of his research was Canadian society and his research method was most closely akin to the Canadian tradition of political economy and British historical empiricism, Clark was clearly borrowing heavily from American interpretive models. In that sense, Clark's primary aim was to contribute to a knowledge of Canadian society rather than build theories and generalizations relevant to sociology and disciplinary literature *per se*. He applied interpretive frameworks or theoretical notions from elsewhere when he thought they were useful to understanding Canadian data.

Clark's research and publications through the first twenty years of his career reveals most of the characteristics of the sociology-in-political economy era. As its most eminent spokesman, Clarkian sociology was interdisciplinary, historical in thrust and method, and effectively utilized interpretive models to explain Canadian phenomenon. Initially, Clark saw his approach as diametrically opposed to Chicago sociology and he criticized Dawson for lacking an historical perspective.[33] Some years later, he was far more charitable to the Chicago School and, in retrospect, came to view his approach as putting Park to work in the analysis of societies of the past by engaging in the same, detailed inquiry required of studies of current social life.[34] With the decline of the Chicago School and the rise of Parsons to prominence in sociology, Clark[35] also took issue with him on the grounds that Parsons only took account of change within the system and not change of the system. Clark felt that such an omission led Parsons to emphasize order rather than change. If historical sociology had low prestige in American sociology,[36] then it became increasingly clear to Clark that the notion of social change might be a new way to conceptualize his work and research interests.

Clark's primary reference group was in Canada and in political economy. Yet his personal identity as a sociologist forced him to interact with American sociological theories and theorists. Clark was thus caught between being a spokesman to disparate reference groups.[37] But such was the nature of his academic structures began to change to allow greater acceptance for sociology in Canada would Clark seek to explicitly relate the more strictly disciplinary sociological and historical traditions whose inter-relationship had previously been taken for granted in Canadian social science.[38] Symbolically, in 1960 Clark was awarded the Tyrell Medal of the Royal Society for his faithfulness to historical research.[39]

Research Biography Phase II: Sociology as an Autonomous Discipline

With the death of Innis and the decline of political economy, and the growth in university student bodies and faculty, the old interdisciplinary alliances became cumbersome and outmoded. By the late 1950s, a cluster of Canadian sociologists were meeting regularly and the outlines of a professional organization began to develop.[40] Increasing openness to American sociology was indicative of a growing disciplinary conception of sociology and the need for the enlarging group of sociologists to establish linkages with other sociologists.

Clark's work in the late 1950s-early 1960s demonstrates critical shifts that reflect this changing milieu. First, Clark turned away from the alliance of sociology and history which lacked legitimation in American sociology and instead focussed on the phenomenon of social change.[41] And second, Clark turned to the study of urbanization (particularly suburbanization) to research the contemporary aspects of social change. The acceptance of a research grant of $30,000 in 1958 from the Central Mortgage and Housing Corporation to study the new frontier of suburbanization symbolized this shift away from detailed historical analysis to a new research method more congruent with American sociology. He was never again to return to his former research method and focus.

As a means of drawing attention to the new focus at Toronto, Clark edited *Urbanism And The Changing Canadian Society* (1961) which included contributions from persons related to the sociology program there. Clark also spent the 1960-61 academic year at Berkeley as Visiting Professor where he became more thoroughly acquainted with American sociology.

As a Guggenheim Fellow, Clark had visited both Columbia and Chicago in 1943-44 but political economy was too strong in Canada at that time to encourage a more independent approach. With the decline of political economy, the consequence was what Tiryakian[42] has called "paradigm anomie" or a condition of deregulation from an orientation previously recognized as authoritative. The resultant void made it easier for sociologists to turn to American sociology for paradigmatic models.

The study of suburbanization involved a radical shift in methodology for Clark. Data was collected through questionnaires (204 items) and interviews (1,200) and, in an era when suburbanites were being stereotyped as middle class conformists, the contribution of Clark's work published as *The Suburban Society* (1966) was to show the diversified character of the many types of suburbs. A more recent work utilizing this research methodology appeared in 1978 as *The New Urban Poor*. Here Clark attempted to investigate those impoverished persons living on the margins of urban areas who lacked the resources to succeed in the city. However, in both studies Clark resisted the use of the computer in data analysis and statistical presentation arguing that "to lay claim to scientific precision...would be to falsify the competence of sociology."[43] Thus while Clark had been drawn into a strictly disciplinary American conception of sociology, he remained cautious about the merits of attempts at scientific explanation.

After a period of almost uncritical reliance on American sociology in the 1960s, the 1970s brought a new questioning of a relevance posture and style for sociology in Canada. Because of his continuous role in sociology in Canada for so many years, Clark almost took on a patriarchal position as "the grand old man"[44] of Canadian sociology. For a discipline that now had full legitimation in the university structures, had overcome the pains of rapid growth, and now sought consolidation, Clark became the primary contact with the discipline's history in Canada. Several articles on his assessment of the development of sociology in Canada were brought together in *Canadian Society in Historical Perspective* (1976) and Clark attempted to sketch his own analytical perspective for the new generation of sociologists. In speaking to the question of an American takeover of Canadian sociology, Clark argued that what the Canadian sociologist needed was a feel for his society, a knowledge of its history, and a sense of identification with it[45] in order to display a greater sensitivity to the unique traits of Canadian society.

Clark objected to the assumption that sociology was a universal science because in his assessment such an assertion played down national societal differences which in turn might thwart a developing knowledge of Canadian society. Thus the question for Clark was no longer what institutionalized shape sociology ought to take as a differentiated discipline, but what it meant for sociology to be relevant to the society in which it is practiced.

If the 1960s mean that sociology in Canada had become differentiated from other disciplines and developed characteristics similar to American sociology, Canadian sociology in the 1970s took on a more independent character with considerable internal reflection and interaction. In some quarters, new interest was expressed in a return to political economy.[46] In spite of his forays, interaction, and debate with the dominant paradigms and personages of American sociology, Clark still viewed himself as "faithful to the Toronto tradition of political economy"[47] because his expectations of sociology were more humanistic, less scientific, and more historically interdisciplinary. Even though there were numerous changes in his own research fact and methodology, it had not meant that he had divorced himself from his intellectual roots.

Conclusion

The thesis of this paper has been that research biography can be a useful tool in the analysis of disciplinary history in particular national settings. A study of the work of S. D. Clark provides important clues about the character and shape of the sociological perspective as well as the issues and debates that encompassed sociology at various stages in the history of the discipline in Canada. Clearly the life and work of no single sociologist is an adequate basis for a history of sociology in a given country, but changes and shifts in research as well as assessments by that sociologist of what has transpired can serve as convenient signposts of sociological evolution on that country. Furthermore, not all sociologists are significantly affected in their work by changed disciplinary contexts. However, it can be hypothesized that where contextual and structural alterations in an academic milieu are notable, a study in shifts in research biography are more likely to be illuminating. It may be that an examination of the research biography of sociologists in other countries where the discipline has experienced different patterns of emergence and evolution can also contribute to our knowledge of the history of sociology in that national context.

Notes

The research for this paper was done while the author was a Fellow of The Calgary Institute of the Humanities and the final draft was written while the author was a Leave Fellow of the Social Sciences and Humanities Research Council of Canada; my gratitude is expressed to both organizations for their financial support as well as to Barclay Johnson and J. Graham Morgan for their helpful comments.

1 Madge, John. (1962). *The Origins of Scientific Sociology*. Free Press: Glencoe. p. 2.

2 Odum, Howard. (1951). *American Sociology: The Story of Sociology in the United States Through 1950*. New York: Longmans Green.

3 Tiryakian, Edward A. (1979). Post-Parsonian Sociology. *Humboldt Journal of Social Relations*. 7, pp. 17-32, p. 30.

4 Eisenstadt, S. N. and Curelaru, M. (1976). *The Form of Sociology: Paradigms and Crises*. New York: John Wiley. pp. 30-43, 120-141.

5 DiRenzo, Gordon. (1975). Contemporary Sociology in Italy. pp. 329-354 in R. P. Mohan and D. Martindale (Eds.), *Handbook of Contemporary Developments in World Sociology*. Westport: Greenwood Press, p. 329.

6 Bladock, Cora and Lally, Jim. (1974). *Sociology in Australia and New Zealand*. Westport: Greenwood Press, pp. 4-14.

7 Dynes, Russell. (1974). Sociology as a Religious Movement: Thoughts on its Institutionalization in the United States. *The American Sociologist*, 9, pp. 169-175, p. 174.

8 Kourvetaris, George A. and Moskos, Charles C. (1968). A Report on Sociology in Greece. *The American Sociologist*, 3, pp. 243-245, p. 244.

9 deValk, J. M. M. (1975). Contemporary Sociological Theory in the Netherlands. pp. 47-57 in R. P. Mohan and D. Martindale (Eds.), *Handbook Of Contemporary Developments in World Sociology*. Westport: Greenwood Press, p. 48.

10 Oberschall, Anthony. (1972). The Institutionalization of American Sociology. in his *The Establishment of Empirical Sociology*. New York: Harper and Row. pp. 187-251, p. 187.

11 Mitchell, Duncan G. (1968). *A Hundred Years of Sociology*. Chicago: Aldine. pp. 217-225.

12 E.g. Shils, Edward. (1970). Tradition, Ecology, and Institution in the History of Sociology. *Deadalus*, 99, pp. 779-780.

13 E.g. Rocher, Guy. (1974). *Talcott Parsons and American Sociology*. London: Thomas Nelson; Matthews, Fred H. (1977). *Quest for an American Sociology: Robert E. Park and the Chicago School*. Montreal: McGill-Queen's University Press.

14 E.g. Alvin Gouldner's discussion of Parsons (1970). *The Coming Crisis of Western Sociology*. New York: Basic Books, p.147; Romalis' discussion of Lipset. (1972). A Man of His Time and Place: A Selective Appraisal of Lipset's Comparative Sociology. pp. 211-232 in Andrew Effrat (Ed.), *Perspectives in Political Sociology*. Indianapolis: Bobbs-Merrill.

15 Tiryakian, Edward A. (1979). The Significance of Schools in the Development of Sociology. pp. 211-233 in W. E. Snizek, E. R. Fuhrman, and H. K. Miller, *Contemporary Issues in Theory and Research*. Westport: Greenwood Press.

16 Clark, Terry. (1972). Emile Durkheim and the French University: The Institutionalization of Sociology. pp. 152-186 in Anthony Oberschall (Ed.), *The Establishment of Empirical Sociology*. New York: Harper and Row.

17 Hiller, Harry H. (1980). Paradigmatic Shifts, Indigenization, and the Development of Sociology in Canada. *Journal of the History of the Behavioral Sciences* (July).

18 Hiller, Harry H. (1979). The Canadian Sociology Movement: Analysis and Assessment. *Canadian Journal of Sociology*, 4(2), pp. 125-150.

19 McGill University Archives, Accession 1563/1

20 cf. Card, B. Y. (1975). *The Expanding Relation: Sociology in the Prairie Provinces*. Regina: Canadian Plains Research Center, p. 9; Clark, S.D. (1979). The Changing Image of Sociology in English-Speaking Canada. *Canadian Journal of Sociology*, 4, pp. 393-403.

21 It is significant to note that of the eight volumes in the Frontiers of Settlement series (or Canadian Pioneer Problems as it was sometimes called) sponsored by the Carnegie Foundation, three were written by Dawson (1934, 1936, 1940).

22 Much of the following undocumented information is based on personal interviews with Professor Clark in 1978.

23 His convictions about the imminent demise of capitalism at this point are evident in issues of his hometown newspaper, *The Lloydminster Times*, of which Clark served as an occasional correspondent from January 1932 to May 1933.

24 There were numerous volumes to this project sponsored by the Carnegie Endowment For International Peace but the sociological project was entitled *Canada and Her Great Neighbor* (Angus, 1938). The original designer of the project was R. M. MacIver while he was at Toronto but MacIver later moved to Columbia and H. A. Angus (an economist at the University of British Columbia) took over. In the published volume, Clark was the only identifiable contributing sociologist.

25 Berger, Carl. (1976). *The Writing of Canadian History*. Toronto: Oxford University Press. pp. 161-169.

26 Innis is generally regarded as the leading Canadian social scientist of the '30s and '40s. Not only was he active in organizing the Canadian social science

community through the Canadian Political Science Association and the Canadian Social Science Research Council, but he also had an international reputation as evidenced by his lectures in England (where Clark first met him) and his election to the Presidency of the American Economic Association in 1951. For three of his importance publications at this stage of his career, cf. Innis, 1930; 1933; 1940.

27 In a letter to Frank Underhill, an active socialist campaigner in 1935 as well as an academic, Innis declared that "there is much to be said for the Marxian approach to Canadian history, but not sufficient to support absolute certainty. Intellectual honesty and curiosity demand fresh interpretations and not the same interpretations" (Creighton, 1957, p. 93).

28 Clark, S.D. (1976). *Canadian Society in Historical Perspective.* Toronto: McGraw-Hill Ryerson. p. 135.

29 Urwick, E. J. (1935). The Role of Intelligence in The Social Process. *Canadian Journal of Economics and Political Science*, 1, pp. 64-76.

30 Compare the academic context of anglophone Canada with that described by John Rex (1973, p. 44, p. 56) in England where the characteristic British social science of the nineteenth century was political economy. The consequence of this dominance was that sociology existed as a pariah subject on the margins of the academic curriculum for years. Abrams (1968, p. 148) has made a similar observation regarding the relationship of sociology to political economy in England.

31 It is interesting that Odum (1951, p. 41) points out the role of the frontier thesis in contributing to a break from European thinking among American sociologists.

32 The Backgrounds to Social Credit in Alberta series (published by the University of Toronto Press) consisted of nine volumes. In addition to Clark's own contribution, two others were done by Clark's students, W. E. Mann (1955) and Jean Burnet (1951). The other studies were written by those with other disciplinary identifications.

33 Clark, S.D. (1940). Review of Pioneering in the Prairie Provinces: The Social Side of the Settlement Process by C. A. Dawson. *Canadian Historical Review* 21, pp. 336-338.

34 Clark, S.D. (1968). *The Developing Canadian Community.* Toronto: University of Toronto Press, Revised Edition. p. 306.

35 Clark, S.D. (1962). *The Developing Canadian Community.* Toronto: University of Toronto Press. p. 299.

36 Harry Elmer Barnes (1948, p. 14) had pointed out that historical sociology had declined dramatically in American sociology since 1900.

37 Wrong, Dennis. (1964). Review of *The Developing Canadian Community* by S. D. Clark, *American Sociological Review*, 29, pp. 764-765, p. 764.

38 This point is made clear in the Second Edition to *The Developing Canadian Community*, Chapters 18-21. These papers were all originally written in the late 1950s and early 1960s as the disciplinary context underwent dramatic change in Canada.
39 *Proceedings and Transactions of The Royal Society*. (1960). p. 57.
40 A sociology chapter within the Canadian Political Science Association was formed in 1956.
41 Cf. footnote 38. In 1956 a group of sociologists with Howard Becker as chairman petitioned the American Sociological Association to hold annual sessions on sociology and history. Clark was part of that group and chaired the session in Los Angeles in 1963 (Cahnman and Boskoff, 1964, pp. vii-viii).
42 Tiryakian, Edward A. (1979). Post-Parsonian Sociology. *Humboldt Journal of Social Relations*, 7, pp. 17-32, p. 24.
43 Clark, S.D. (1966). *The Suburban Society*. Toronto: University of Toronto Press. p. 19.
44 Elliott, Jean. (1977). Review of Canadian Society In Historical Perspective by S. D. Clark. *Contemporary Sociology*, 6, p. 174.
45 Clark, S.D. (1976). *Canadian Society in Historical Perspective*. Toronto: McGraw-Hill Ryerson, p. 132.
46 Clement, Wallace. (1977). Macrosociological Approaches Toward a Canadian Sociology. *Alternate Routes*, 1, pp. 1-37.
47 Op. Cit. p. 136.

Bibliography

Ahrams, Philip
(1968). *The Origins of British Sociology*. Chicago: University of Chicago Press.

Angus, H. A.
(1938). *Canada and Her Great Neighbor*. Toronto: Ryerson Press.

Bladock, Cora and Jim Lally
(1974). *Sociology in Australia and New Zealand*. Westport: Greenwood Press.

Barnes, Harry Elmer
(1948). *Historical Sociology: Its Origins and Development*. New York: Philosophical Library.

Berger, Carl
(1976). *The Writing of Canadian History*. Toronto: Oxford University Press.

Burnet, Jean
(1951). *Next-Year Country: A Study of Rural Social Organization in Alberta*. Toronto: University of Toronto Press.

Cahnman, Werner and Alvin Boskoff
(1964). *Sociology and History: Theory and Research*. New York: Free Press.

Card, B. Y.

(1975). *The Expanding Relation: Sociology in the Prairie Provinces*. Regina: Canadian Plains Research Center.

Clark, Terry

(1972). Emile Durkheim and the French University: The Institutionalization of Sociology. In Anthony Oberschall (Ed.), *The Establishment of Empirical Sociology*. New York: Harper and Row. pp. 152-186.

Clark, S. D.

(1939). *The Canadian Manufacturers' Association: A Study in Collective Bargaining and Political Pressure*. Toronto: University of Toronto Press.

(1940). Review of Pioneering In The Prairie Provinces: The Social Side Of The Settlement Process by C. A. Dawson, *Canadian Historical Review*, 21, pp. 336-338.

(1942). *The Social Development of Canada*. Toronto: University of Toronto Press.

(1948). *Church and Sect in Canada*. Toronto: University of Toronto Press.

(1959). *Movements of Political Protest in Canada, 1640-1840*. Toronto: University of Toronto Press.

(1961). *Urbanism and the Changing Canadian Society*. Toronto: University of Toronto Press.

(1962 and 1968). *The Developing Canadian Community*. Toronto: University of Toronto Press. The revised edition in 1968 contained six additional chapters.

(1966). *The Suburban Society*. Toronto: University of Toronto Press.

(1976). *Canadian Society in Historical Perspective*. Toronto: McGraw-Hill Ryerson.

(1978). *The New Urban Poor*. Toronto: McGraw-Hill Ryerson.

(1979). The Changing Image of Sociology in English-Speaking Canada. *Canadian Journal of Sociology*, 4, pp. 393-403.

Clement, Wallace

(1977). Macrosociological Approaches Toward a Canadian Sociology. *Alternate Routes*, 1, pp. 1-37.

Creighton, Donald

(1957). *Harold Adam Innis: Portrait of a Scholar*. Toronto: University of Toronto Press.

Dawson, Carl A.

(1934). *The Settlement of the Peace River Country: A Study of a Pioneer Area*. Toronto: Macmillan.

(1936). *Group Settlement: Ethnic Communities in Western Canada*. Toronto: Macmillan.

(1940). *Pioneering in the Prairie Provinces: The Social Side of the Settlement Process*. Toronto: Macmillan.

deValk, J. M. M.

(1975). Contemporary Sociological Theory in The Netherlands. In R. P. Mohan and D. Martindale (Eds.), *Handbook of Contemporary Developments in World Sociology*. Westport: Greenwood Press. pp. 47-57.

DiRenzo, Gordon

(1975). Contemporary Sociology in Italy. In R. P. Mohan and D. Martindale (Eds.), *Handbook of Contemporary Developments in World Sociology*. Westport: Greenwood Press. pp. 329-354.

Dynes, Russell

(1974). Sociology as a Religious Movement: Thoughts on its Institutionalization in the United States. *The American Sociologist*, 9, pp. 169-175.

Eisenstadt, S. N. and N. Curelaru

(1976). *The Form of Sociology: Paradigms and Crises*. New York: John Wiley.

Elliott, Jean

(1977). Review of Canadian Society in Historical Perspective by S. D. Clark, *Contemporary Sociology*, 6, pp. 174-175.

Gouldner, Alvin

(1970). *The Coming Crisis of Western Sociology*. New York: Basic Books.

Hiller, Harry H.

(1979). The Canadian Sociology Movement: Analysis and Assessment. *Canadian Journal of Sociology* 4(2), pp. 125-150.

(1980). Paradigmatic Shifts, Indigenization, and the Development of Sociology in Canada. *Journal of the History of the Behavioral Sciences*. July.

Hughes, Everett C.

(1931). *The Growth of an Institution: The Chicago Real Estate Board*. Chicago: University of Chicago Press.

Innis, Harold A.

(1923). *A History of the Canadian Pacific Railway*. Toronto: McClelland Stewart.

(1930). *The Fur Trade in Canada*. New Haven: Yale University Press.

(1933). *Problems of Staple Production*. Toronto: University of Toronto Press.

(1940). *The Cod Fisheries*. New Haven: Yale University Press.

Kourvetaris, Goerge A. and Charles C. Moskos

(1968). A Report on Sociology in Greece. *The American Sociologist*, 3, pp. 243-245.

Madge, John
(1962). *The Origins of Scientific Sociology*. Glencoe: Free Press.
Mann, W. E.
(1955). *Sect, Cult and Church in Alberta*. Toronto: University of Toronto Press.
Matthews, Fred H.
(1977). *Quest for an American Sociology: Robert E. Park and the Chicago School*. Montreal: McGill-Queen's University Press.
Mitchell, G. Duncan
(1968). *A Hundred Years of Sociology*. Chicago: Aldine.
Neibuhr, H. R.
(1929). *The Social Sources of Denominationalism*. New York: Meridian.
Oberschall, Anthony
(1972). The Institutionalization of American Sociology. In his *The Establishment of Empirical Sociology*. New York: Harper and Row. pp. 187-251.
Odum, Howard
(1951). *American Sociology: The Story of Sociology in the United States Through 1950*. New York: Longmans Green.
Rex, John
(1973). *Discovering Sociology*. London: Routledge and Kegan Paul.
Rocher, Guy
(1974). *Talcott Parsons and American Sociology*. London: Thomas Nelson.
Romalis, Coleman
(1972). A Man of His Time and Place: A Selective Appraisal of Lipset's Comparative Sociology. In Andrew Effrat (Ed.), *Perspectives in Political Sociology*. Indianapolis: Bobbs-Merrill. pp. 211-232.
Shils, Edward
(1970). Tradition, Ecology, and Institution in the History of Sociology. *Daedalus*, 99, pp. 760-825.
Thomas, W. T. and F. Znaniecki
(1918). *The Polish Peasant in Europe and America*. Boston: Goreham Press.
Tiryakian, Edward A.
(1979a). Post-Parsonian Sociology. *Humboldt Journal of Social Relations*, 7, pp. 17-32.
(1979b). The Significance of Schools in the Development of Sociology. In W. E. Snizek, E. R. Fuhrman, and H. K. Miller, *Contemporary Issues in Theory and Research*. Westport: Greenwood Press. pp. 211-233.
Urwick, E. J.
(1935). The Role of Intelligence in the Social Process. *Canadian Journal of Economics and Political Science*, 1, pp. 64-76.

Wrong, Dennis
(1964). Review of The Developing Canadian Community by S. D. Clark. *American Sociological Review*, 29, pp. 764-765.

Chapter Five

REORIENTATION: S.D. CLARK

Carl Berger

One of the most significant continuities of interest from the thirties to the later forties was the emergence of the historical sociology of Samuel Delbert Clark. Sociology, which Innis once called the Cinderella of the social sciences in Canada,[1] was a relative latecomer to the academic scene. An understanding of the particular twist that Clark imparted to it requires a preliminary digression into the background of the subject.

The study of social relations and institutions was first promoted in English Canada by clergymen and lay reformers inspired by a sense of obligation and service of the social gospel. Early advocates of social Christianity were horrified by the separation of ethics from everyday economic conduct and by problems associated with rapid urban growth, rural depopulation, intemperance, and immigration. They described and diagnosed the origins of these and other social maladies in the hope that conditions could be controlled and rectified. In 1897, the progressive businessman Herbert Ames published *The City Below the Hill*, a description of housing and living standards in a working-class quarter of Montreal. The technique of the social survey was later applied by J. S. Woodsworth in his tracts on

Berger, Carl. (1976). Originally printed as Reorientation. From *The Writing of Canadian History: Aspects of English-Canadian Historical Writing: 1900-1970*. Toronto: Oxford University Press. pp. 161-169. Reprinted with permission from University of Toronto Press.

immigration and urban reform, and in his 1917 report on Ukrainian Rural Communities for the Bureau of Social Research of the Governments of Manitoba, Saskatchewan, and Alberta. The first courses in the subject matter of sociology were taught before the First World War by clergymen in church institutions like Acadia University or Wesley College to candidates for the ministry. In other universities political economists like O. D. Skelton at Queen's regularly lectured on immigration and race relations, social-betterment schemes, charitable work, and city planning. The basis of sociological enquiry in French Canada was laid by Léon Gérin. In the mid-1880s he studied at L'École de la Science Sociale in Paris and came into contact with the followers of Frédéric Le Play, who had inaugurated research on family budgets. In the next fifty years, Gerin produced a number of monographs on the structures and functions of the traditional habitant family and the parish as the fundamental institutions of French Canada.[2]

The chief pioneer of academic sociology in English Canada was Carl A. Dawson, who founded the Department of Sociology and Social Work at McGill in 1922. Born in Prince Edward Island in 1887, and a graduate of Acadia, Dawson was a Baptist clergyman who had worked with the Canadian YMCA during the war. Afterwards he studied both sociology and theology at the University of Chicago and was converted to the social ecology of Robert Park, who envisaged the city as a laboratory in which human conduct and social processes could be examined. Park and his colleagues applied the same techniques of enquiry to urban groups as anthropologists had used in their surveys of primitive peoples. Their work on immigrant communities, hobos, gangs, the ghettos and the slums, stressed locality, neighbourhood, and community structure. They focussed on immediate problems, employed the field survey and interviews, and made use of statistics compiled for administrative purposes. They concerned themselves with metropolitan communities and the patterns of relations between the city and the region it dominated. Park, who was once a newspaperman, was the first to suggest that areas of metropolitan control could be measured by the circulation of urban newspapers. Underlying the Chicago social-ecology approach to sociology was a faith in reform and an impatience with deviation from the norms of American life.[3]

Dawson's work for the Canadian Pioneer Problems Committee, which superintended the eight studies in the Canadian Frontiers of Settlement Series that were published between 1934 and 1940, was one incident in the application of this methodology to Canada. In the thirties, the Prairies became for some Canadian social scientists what the city had been for Park—a kind of social clinic. The father of the series, Isaiah Bowman, the Canadian-born Director of the American Geographical Society, believed that the long period of undirected and wasteful expansion of agricultural settlement had ended. At the same time he rejected the notion of a closed frontier and maintained that there was still available for occupation enormous areas of land in Canada, Siberia, Manchuria, Australia, South Africa, and South America. These pioneer belts were of strategic importance as sources of future food supply and raw materials and also for relieving the congestion of population in older societies. Bowman conceived a grand design for comparative studies of the 'pioneer fringe' in various countries in the hope that certain principles of 'a science of settlement' would be established and that these in turn would inform state-directed agricultural settlement policies. The Canadian Frontiers of Settlement project originated in the same intellectual milieu as the Carnegie series on Canadian-American relations, and the organizers of both shared a faith in collaborative, inter-disciplinary research directed at practical ends.[4]

The group of books that appeared in the Canadian Frontiers of Settlement series comprised examinations of the geographical setting of prairie settlement and of contemporary economic problems by W. A. Mackintosh; a joint history of land policies by Chester Martin and of settlement patterns by Arthur S. Morton; a survey of standards of living and agricultural practices by the sociologist of rural life, R. W. Murchie; and studies of settlement on the mining and forest frontiers by Innis and Lower.[5] Dawson and his collaborators contributed three volumes. *The Settlement of the Peace River Country* (1934) presented a model of the life cycle of a pioneer fringe—from outpost, to isolated farming, to integration and organization as a region. *Group Settlement: Ethnic Communities in Western Canada* (1936) analysed the gradual integration into the western community of immigrants like the Mennonites and Doukhobors, who had originally settled in isolated blocs. Dawson had no reservations about the desirability of assimilation, which he attributed to the penetrative power of material, mainly economic, factors. *Pioneering in the Prairie Provinces* (1940) appraised the social aspects of the pioneering process, the creation of religious and educational institutions, and the emergence of local 'metropolitan' centres.

While Dawson's studies did much to sustain sociology's claim as a separate discipline, these books were the products of a particular methodology that Clark sought to qualify and amend. Social ecology, he argued, was excessively concerned with surface description; it was presentist in orientation, and conveyed a static picture of society. The bias of Dawson's writings on the Prairies was reinforced by the same techniques employed in examinations of the institutions of French Canada in a period of industrialization in Horace Miner's *St. Denis: A French Canadian Parish* (1939) and in Everett C. Hughes' *French Canada in Transition* (1943). Like Innis in economics, Clark sought to offset the fixation with current issues and to establish certain principles of social change by using the broader perspective of history. The historical detail of past Canadian social change, moreover, would make the academic teaching of sociological concepts and theories less abstract.[6]

Clark's prescription for a more historical sociology was made in reaction to a certain type of enquiry, and it also expressed his experiences and preference for history. He was born in 1910 and grew up on a farm near Lloydminster on the Alberta-Saskatchewan border. His parents, who had come from Ontario, were supporters of the United Farmers of Alberta, and he recalled that two of his early heroes were the progressive leaders Thomas Crerar and Henry Wise Wood. At the University of Saskatchewan he studied with A. S. Morton and completed a master's thesis on Saskatchewan settlement with special reference to dry-farming techniques, an undertaking that was supported by the Canadian Pioneer Problems Committee. He went to Toronto in 1931 with the intention of doing research on the history of farmers' movements, but was disappointed with the kind of history taught there. 'I must confess', he told Morton, 'that I am finding it very difficult to keep my interests alive in the work which I am doing. What with trouble looming in the orient and with our present Economic crisis, it seems almost ludicrous to spend hour after hour studying the contribution of Sydenham or Bagot to responsible government.'[7] After a year he proceeded to the London School of Economics where he took courses on politics from Harold Laski and on economic history from Eileen Power and R. H. Tawney. On his return to Canada he worked at McGill as a research assistant, wrote a thesis for Toronto on the Canadian Manufacturers' Association as a pressure group, and, after teaching two years at Manitoba, returned to Toronto in 1939. In that year, sociology became a semi-autonomous body within the Political Economy Department.

Clark carried into sociology the economics of Innis, the sociologists' preoccupation with deviance and social pathology, and an enduring interest in the frontier. Innis and others had analysed the patterns of Canadian economic development based on a succession of staple commodities and new technologies. Clark built upon their conclusions and determined to explore the social consequences of new forms of economic enterprise over time. In one of the classic works of American sociology, *The Polish Peasant in Europe and America* (1918-20) by William Thomas and Florian Znanieki, he found a suggestive clue that provided a link between staple economics and social disturbance. The life histories of these immigrants portrayed a people who had lost a sense of participating in society because their attitudes, shaped by one milieu, no longer corresponded to the economic structures of their new situation. A succession of frontiersmen in Canadian history experienced roughly similar disorientations as the immigrant Polish peasants.

The characteristic feature of Canada's social history, Clark argued, 'has been the recurrent emergence of areas of social life involving new problems of social re-organization and adjustment.'[8] These storm centres of social breakdown were identified with the 'frontier'. Clark's definition and use of this concept was somewhat ambiguous. At times he seemed to attribute to the frontier traits that Turner had identified with it. Frontier conditions, he argued, promoted democracy and stripped away inherited habits of thought and action that were inappropriate in the new environment. Writing of the United Farmers of Alberta in 1932, Clark had described the agrarian movement as 'an expression of the frontier; an expression of that rugged and enterprising individualism which is the mark of the pioneer of forest or plains.'[9] On the other hand he denied the usefulness of a conception of a Turnerian frontier defined as the furthest edge of settlement or free land. The frontier was rather an area in which new forms of economic enterprise were developed.[10] As such it could be urban as well as rural. Slightly later he would equate that zone of new economies and social disruption with 'the frontier of capitalism'.

From within this perspective the history of Canadian social development became the record of a succession of disturbances in social relations, habits, controls, and institutions caused by the intrusion of new forms of economic production. In the fur trade of the St Lawrence Valley, the fisheries of Nova Scotia, lumbering and farming in New Brunswick, farming in Upper Canada, mining in the Yukon and northern Ontario, wheat-growing on the Prairies, and manufacturing in the industrial cities, the specific modes of production determined the nature of social problems. On each of these frontiers traditional institutions were transplanted with difficulty; people tended to be independent and nonconformist and freer of social restraints. Furthermore, the imbalance between age and sex groups weakened the family, and religious controls were undermined by the inability of established churches to meet the needs of new occupational groups. Social apathy, deviant behaviour, prostitution, crime, and intemperance were thus the first short-run effects of frontier life. Clark was concerned not only with disorganization but also with the way in which institutions were reorganized by moral reform agencies and evangelical religion.

In *Church and Sect in Canada* (1948), Clark surveyed evangelical and revivalist Protestant movements that emerged on the margins of society between 1760 and 1900. The churches had repeatedly failed to respond successfully to the requirements of classes immediately affected by new economic developments. Frontier conditions destroyed old status relations and emphasized individual worth and equality. Those directly affected by the new environment were isolated and dispossessed of a past culture. In sectarian evangelicalism they expressed their protest against authority and found a sense of fellowship and a social place. This, Clark insisted, was the common experience that linked the followers of Henry Alline in Nova Scotia in the eighteenth century, the Upper Canadian backwoods farmers who supported early Methodism, the industrial working masses who responded to the Salvation Army in the late-Victorian period, and the prairie farmers who turned to the fundamentalist prophetic preaching of William Aberhart. For people in the hinterland, religious separatism was analogous to political revolts against outside control. The sects were conservative, however, rather than truly radical, for they served to focus and thereby legitimize the status of fringe groups. In due course sects tended to lose their initial separatist thrust and became instruments by which their members were assimilated into the social order. Evangelicalism also led to political indifference because it stressed the other-worldly.[11] Social and ultimately economic factors were held to be the determining influences in religious history throughout all of Clark's analysis. He was alert, however, to the reciprocal effects of religion on economic life, pointing out that religion had inhibited the free play of economic forces in Canada and that sectarianism functioned as a discipline to the labour force.

It was but a short step from these conclusions regarding the social history of sectarianism to an analysis of social credit, the main contemporary manifestation of aberrant evangelicalism and political protest. When Clark witnessed the Aberhart campaign of 1935, he could only compare its emotionalism, the absence of a rational program, and its intense appeal to insecure people, with contemporary European fascism. A series of ten volumes on the background and development of social credit in Alberta was begun in 1943-4 when the Rockefeller Foundation made a special grant to the Canadian Social Science Research Council. Innis conceived the general idea of using these funds to support a comprehensive study of agrarian protest in the west, and through his influence Clark was made editor of the series.

Like its predecessors in co-operative research, the Social Credit series,[12] which was published between 1950 and 1959, represented an alliance of social scientists and humanists who approached the same general problem from different angles. The historical contributions included W. L. Morton's history of the Progressive party, D. C. Masters' assessment of western labour radicalism and the Winnipeg General Strike, and Lewis G. Thomas's description of the dominance and breakup of the Liberal party, which ultimately led to the one-party tradition in Alberta. The historian of Canadian agricultural policy, Vernon Fowke, examined the national policy and the wheat economy, emphasizing that agriculture in Canada had always functioned as the basis for commercial and territorial empire, and that the Prairie economy was truly a colonial one. Employing a subtle Marxist analysis, the political scientist C. B. Macpherson revealed the relationship between the ideologies of the United Farmers of Alberta and Social Credit and the political economy of independent commodity producers. Another political scientist, J. R. Mallory, investigated the issues involved in the collision between the provincial legislation of Social Credit and the authority of the central government. John Irving, a teacher of philosophy, sought to explain the psychological appeal of Social Credit in the election of 1935 and contended that it fulfilled a need of people suffering from economic difficulties as well as deep-seated feelings of guilt at being unemployed and on relief. Two of Clark's own students, the sociologists Jean Burnet and William Mann, examined respectively the community life and tensions in the district of Hanna in central Alberta and the function of sects and religious cults in the province. With the exceptions of the study by Irving, and to a lesser extent the books by Mallory and Macpherson, the series concentrated on the background of the Social Credit movement rather than on the period in which it came to power.

This tendency was equally manifest in Clark's own contribution, a study of political protest in Canada between 1640 and 1840 that ended eighty years before the appearance of Major Douglas's heretical monetary doctrines in the West. Contending that there was really nothing fundamentally novel about Social Credit, Clark set his history of protest within a continental frontierist frame of reference. He argued that Canada, like the United States, had shared in a common frontier experience of successive revolts against authority. The frontier engendered an intensely localist, separatist, and anti-authoritarian spirit, and the common characteristic of all frontier peoples was their desire for autonomy and withdrawal from the infringements of outside authority. This spirit had been the driving force behind a variety of revolutionary upsurges in both the United States and Canada. But whereas these movements had been successful in the United States, leaving their imprint on the Constitution and influencing the drive to liberate adjacent territory from European control, in Canada they had been frustrated and defeated. The geography of the St Lawrence favoured centralized authority, and the very expansive revolutionary developments in the United States evoked a counter-revolutionary tradition north of the border.[13]

With a wealth of historical detail, Clark traced these democratic liberation movements from the period of the American Revolution to the War of 1812 and the Rebellion of 1837. Behind the revolt in Upper Canada, he believed, lay the revolutionary philosophy of the continental American frontier, with its faith in direct political action and democratic practice and its distrust of central authority. The 'marginal elements' in the community, who supported Mackenzie, 'sought control over economic power, and this involved destroying forms of economic endeavour such as banks and large mercantile establishments and, perhaps, most important of all, bringing to an end the intervention of governments in economic life.' Mackenzie's draft constitution presented the clear trend of the popular will. 'Responsible government', Clark wrote—and here he completely inverted Chester Martin's understanding of the matter—'developed in reaction rather than in response to the true democratic spirit of the Canadian people.'[14]

In terms of political protest the prairie west became what Upper Canada had once been. What the West revolted against in the rebellions of 1869-70 and 1885, in the Progressive party and in the Social Credit crusade, 'was being taken over or being dominated by an outside power....The West sought to be left to itself; it wished to withdraw from those allegiances which placed it in a subordinate position....'[15] It was in this sense that there were no fundamental differences between the Upper Canadian uprising and Social Credit, or for that matter between Mackenzie and Aberhart. The resemblances were further affirmed by the fact that all movements of political protest contained within their ideologies a desire to return to some simpler state of affairs in the past.[16] They were restorative and conservative, and, like the evangelical sects to which they were allied, eventually accommodated themselves to the existing metropolitan structures.

Historians' responses to Clark's work, as distinct from the Social Credit series as a whole, illuminated both their views of historical sociology and their skepticism about the frontier thesis, however it was defined. Though the ever-generous Brebner said of *Church and Sect* that it was a milestone in Canadian historiography and that there was no need to worry whether it was historical sociology or sociological history, most historians were either hostile or indifferent. They wondered about the connection—some thought it an uneasy one—between Clark's theoretical disquisitions and the new and rich documentary evidence that filled his books. Traditionalists like A. L. Burt, who once dismissed sociology as the study of fallen women, thought that Clark was too preoccupied with departures from the norms of social conduct and that he had exaggerated incidents of extremisms, in both religious and political history, to the neglect of constructive achievements. A historian of religion faulted Clark for reducing the religious impulse to an almost automatic reflex of economics, and thereby depriving it of any self-generating powers.[17]

The twin dimensions of Clark's work that were most frequently challenged were, first, the aims of sociology itself and, second, his use of the frontier thesis. Clark was above all interested in the uniformities and the cumulative patterns in social development, religious sectarianism, and political protest. He stressed the constant and repetitive regularities of human experience. The Manitoba scholar W. L. Morton probably spoke for the majority of Canadian historians in the post-war period when he said that sociology and history were incompatible. In contrast to the social scientist, he elaborated, the historian was devoted to explaining human behaviour in specific situations and at specific times and his work was guided by sensitivity for the unique and the exceptional.[18]

Historians took issue with Clark's conception of the role of the frontier in history on both specific grounds—claiming, for example, that he had overestimated the impact of backwoods' opinion in America's declaration of war in 1812—and also in more general terms...., during the later forties and throughout the fifties historians turned away from the Turner thesis and subjected it to considerable criticism. The composite, ambiguous character of the frontier as it was defined in Clark's work was one source of the difficulties, but so too was the tendency of old established disciplines to resist the encroachments of new subjects on their preserves. Clark's major works, *Church and Sect* and *Movements of Political Protest*, appeared at precisely the moment when historians were least willing to listen to his case. His historical sociology was a logical extension of Innisian social science and it was from this tradition that historians were disengaging themselves. That his books had little immediate influence on historical writing was perhaps owing as much to the shifting interests of historians and to their changing perceptions of what history was all about as to a presumed incompatibility between sociology and history.

Notes

All manuscript sources cited in the footnotes are held by the Public Archives of Canada, Ottawa, unless otherwise specified.

1 Innis, H.A. (1942). The Social Sciences: Brief Survey of Recent Literature. *Canadian Geographical Journal*, xxv, p. xi.

2 Falardeau, Jean-Charles. (1966). Léon Gérin: His Life and Work. In Laurier La Pierre (Ed.), *Four O'clock Lectures: French-Canadian Thinkers of the Nineteenth and Twentieth Centuries*, pp. 59-75, and (1994), Problems and First Experiments of Social Research in Quebec. *Canadian Journal of Economics and Political Science*, x, pp. 365-71.

3 Madge, John. (1962). *The Origins of Scientific Sociology* (Glencoe, Ill, p. 125; Dawson, C. A. (1940). Sociology as a Specialized Science. In C. W. M. Hart (Ed.), *Essays in Sociology*, pp. 19-35.

4 Bowman's Purposes were set out in *The Pioneer Fringe* (New York, 1931). His thought is discussed in Gladys M. Wrigley, Isaiah Bowman, *The Geographical Review*, xli (January 1951), pp. 7-65, which also contains a bibliography of his writings.

5 Mackintosh, W. A. (1934). *Prairie Settlement: The Geographical Setting*; Mackintosh, W.A. (1935). *Economic Problems of the Prairie Provinces*; Morton, A. S. and Martin, C. (1938). *History of Prairie Settlement and 'Dominion*

Lands' Policy; Murchie, R. W. (1936). *Agricultural Progress on the Prairie Frontier*; Lower, A. R. M. and Innis, H. A. (1936). *Settlement and the Forest and Mining Frontiers*. All were published in Toronto.

6 Clark, S.D. (1939). Sociology and Canadian History. *Canadian Journal of Economics and Political Science*, v, pp. 349-50; (1940). Review of Dawson, *Pioneering in the Prairie Provinces*, *Canadian Historical Review*, xxi, pp. 336-8.

7 University of Saskatchewan Archives, Murray Memorial Library, Saskatoon, A. S. Morton Papers, Clark to Morton, February 1,1932.

8 Clark, S.D. (1939). Sociology and Canadian History. *Canadian Journal of Economics and Political Science*, v, p. 351.

9 Clark, S.D. (1932). The United Farmers of Alberta. *Canadian Forum*, xiii, p. 78.

10 Clark, S.D. (1942). *The Social Development of Canada: An Introductory Study with Select Documents*, 1 n.; Clark, S.D. (1940). Economic Expansion and the Moral Order. *Canadian Journal of Economics and Political Science*, vi, pp. 203-25.

11 Clark, S.D. (1962, first published 1945). The Religious Sect in Canadian Politics. *The Developing Canadian Community*. pp. 131-46.

12 Morton, W. L. (1950). *The Progressive Party*; Masters, D. C. (1950). *The Winnipeg General Strike*; Thomas, L. G. (1959). *The Liberal Party in Alberta: A History of Politics in the Province of Alberta, 1905-1921*; Fowke, V. C. (1957). *The National Policy and the Wheat Economy*; Macpherson, C. B. (1953). *Democracy in Alberta*; Mallory, J. R. (1954). *Social Credit and the Federal Power in Canada*; Irving, J.A. (1959). *The Social Credit Movement in Alberta*; Burnet, J. (1951). *Next-Year Country*; Mann, W. E. (1955). *Sect, Cult, and Church in Alberta*. All were published in Toronto.

13 Clark, S.D. (1962). The Canadian Community and the American Continental System, and The Frontier in the Development of the Canadian Political Community. In *The Developing Canadian Community*, pp. 185-98, 207-20. The articles originally appeared under different titles in 1950 and 1954 respectively.

14 Clark, S.D. (1959). *Movements of Political Protest in Canada, 1640-1840*. pp. 430-34.

15 Clark, S.D. (1950). Foreword in Morton, W. L., *The Progressive Party*. p. viii.

16 Clark, S.D. *Movements of Political Protest in Canada 1640-1840*. p. 504.

17 Brebner, J.B. (1949). Review of *Church and Sect in Canada*, *Canadian Historical Review*, xxx, pp. 75-7; Spring, David. (1949). History and Sociology: A Plea for Humility. ibid., (September), pp. 211-26; Walsh, H. H. (1954). Canada and the Church: A Job for Historians. *Queen's Quarterly*, lxi, pp. 71-9.

18 Morton, review of Clark, *The Developing Canadian Community*. *Canadian Historical Review*, xliv (September 1963), pp. 235-6 and review of *Movements*

of Political Protest in Canada, *ibid*., xli (September 1960), pp. 243-5. Historians' subsequent treatments of the reformers in Upper Canada did little to confirm Clark's reading of the role of frontier radicalism, and, in the case of the Yukon during the Gold Rush era, laid greater emphasis on the successful imposition of Canadian controls. See Craig, Gerald M. (1963). *Upper Canada: The Formative Years, 1784-1841*. Chapters 10-12; Zaslow, Morris. (1971). *The Opening of the Canadian North, 1870-1914*. Chapter 5.

Chapter Six

THE LIMITS OF LIBERALISM IN CANADIAN SOCIOLOGY: SOME NOTES ON S.D. CLARK

Deborah Harrison

Abstract

This paper attempts to place S. D. Clark's contribution in a broader perspective. Distinguishing between 'the collective tradition' (metropolitanism, the staples thesis, dependency theory, and class analysis) and 'the individualist tradition' (frontierism, functionalism, continentalism and liberalism), it shows that Clark simultaneously has been the 'father of Canadian (collective) sociology' and an importer of the individualist (largely American) tradition. It concludes by using Clark's work as an examplar of the inapplicability of the individualist tradition to the Canadian society.

The importance of S. D. Clark within the development of Canadian sociology is universally recognized. Clark was the first chairman of the University of Toronto sociology department, in which, as virtually a 'head,' he recruited and hired nearly a generation of sociologists. He was a significant member of the Canadian Social Science Research Council during the 1950s and thus exercised power in determining the kind of sociological research to be done in Canada during a crucial period. Clark's publications

---

Harrison, Deborah A. The Limits of Liberalism in Canadian Sociology: Some Notes on S.D. Clark. From *The Canadian Review of Sociology and Anthropology*, 20(2). Reprinted with permission from *The Canadian Review of Sociology and Anthropology*. References have been removed from the text and replaced as endnotes.

span more than forty prolific years, with at least the first fifteen occurring when almost no other sociologists were writing in Canada; he is generally acknowledged as the father of the Canadian approach to the discipline.

Clark's empirical work has ranged over many topics. *The Canadian Manufacturers' Association* (1939) was a historical account of that organization as an interest group. *The Social Development of Canada* (1942), *Church and Sect in Canada* (1948), and *Movements of Political Protest in Canada* (1959) comprised variations on the theme of economic development and social change in the seventeenth, eighteenth, and nineteenth centuries. *The Suburban Society* (1966) and *The New Urban Poor* (1978) explored the social psychological aspects of contemporary upward mobility and poverty. So, while Clark's work can be loosely collected under the heading 'social movements,' Clark has also contributed to the fields of religion, social change, urban studies, political sociology, historical sociology, and economic development. Some of the analyses in Clark's articles and chapters, in addition, have been applicable to education, ethnic groups, and multiculturalism.

But while Clark's contributions have been recognized within many areas, only recently have we begun to assess his work as an entire corpus. Hiller (1981) has effected an interesting match between the stages of Clark's career and stages in the process through which sociology in Canada became legitimated.[1] This paper[2] will examine Clark's relationship to the development of Canadian sociology within the broader context of the influence of external (usually American) intellectual models. An examination of the intellectual roots of Canadian sociology reveals that this tradition, which reflects Canadian history, is incompatible with the tradition that has informed American sociology. But Clark's work, interestingly enough, has reflected both traditions; Clark simultaneously has been the father of Canadian sociology and a sociologist of the American variety. Through the study of Clark's work, we can more fully realize the inappropriate nature of American models for the analysis of Canadian society.

The Father of Canadian Sociology

Samuel Delbert Clark, born in 1910, grew up on a farm near Streamstown, Alberta, close to Lloydminster and the Saskatchewan border. He was nineteen when the Depression and long drought hit the Prairies, and the period undoubtedly influenced him. Anger on the Prairies at eastern indifference reached a boiling point during the 1930s, as was evidenced by the formation of the Co-operative Commonwealth Federation (CCF) party in 1933 and its determined aim to eradicate capitalism. Clark's parents were active in the United Farmers' movement and the younger Clark naturally sympathized.[3]

Clark experienced eastern indifference on a personal level in 1931 when he enrolled at the University of Toronto as a history Ph.D. student. He wanted to study the United Farmers' movement, but was denied permission on the grounds that the topic was 'too contemporary.' Clark therefore resigned from the University of Toronto program, but not before delivering a defiant seminar on 'the two million starving farmers of Western Canada' in one of his classes.[4]

It was by accident that Clark became a sociologist. By 1938, he had finally received a Ph.D. from the University of Toronto Political Science Department, after studying under Harold Innis, and was thus anticipating a political science career. But virtually the only academic vacancy in 1938 was a sociology post in the Toronto anthropology department, and Innis managed to secure it for him. Clark had learned some sociology from Everett Hughes and Carl Dawson at McGill when he had been employed by them as a research fellow between 1933 and 1935, and they had in fact granted him an M.A. in the discipline. But this episode, too, had been an accident, necessitated by the fact that Clark had had insufficient funds in 1933 to recommence his Ph.D. studies.

So Clark brought a novel perspective to Canadian sociology. He had been influenced by Hughes and Dawson (who had studied at the University of Chicago and were virtually the only sociologists teaching in Canada in those days). But he had also been Innis's Ph.D. student and, before that, A. S. Morton's history student at the University of Saskatchewan.

Clark's novel perspective was his sense of history. He had little use for American sociology, which apparently lacked this sense.[5] American sociologists, according to Clark, made precise, trivial observations about minute and insignificant current details at the expense of the deep insight attainable only through a study of history. The combination of Clark's historical and sociological training yielded a preoccupation with 'social change.' The sociologist's job was to examine society, yes, but this was always some *specific* society, with particular 'temporal and spatial boundaries.'[6] Over the years Clark has always asked the same questions about a society, whether that society has been a suburb, a rural backwater, or a pioneer farming community: What brought this society into being? How did it respond to external threats? How, ultimately, did it change?

These questions obviously reflect Clark's historical training, but they also reveal the influence of the 'ecological' perspective arising out of the Chicago sociological tradition,[7] according to which change 'of' a social system came about as a result of (usually material) changes in the system's environment. (Probably the best example of the influence of the Chicago School in Clark's work is *The Social Development of Canada*, in which the discovery of new staple resources—notably fish, fur, timber, and minerals—ultimately led to a more liberal-democratic society.)

But perhaps equally important is Clark's early experience during the Depression with the farmers' movement. This was likely the first time that Clark realized that society was a historical process, that the truly telling features of social life occurred at its turning points, when people became collectively motivated to work for social progress.

Clark has applied his perspective to the struggles of many groups in Canadian history. He has also applied it to Canada as a whole. Hence, societies in general are to be viewed in an historical perspective, according to Clark, and the Canadian society especially so. The biggest problem of the Canadian society has been survival.[8] How has Canada maintained itself, despite the looming presence of the United States? At the expense of which groups has this survival been purchased? So, unlike American functionalism, which largely comprises the relationship of individuals to ahistorically depicted social institutions, an indigenous Canadian sociology, according to Clark, is to occupy itself with the historical fates of collectivities.

This is not to imply that according to Clark there exists a 'purely Canadian sociology,' divorced from all other scholarship, or that 'Canadian' sociologists should be inward-turning and provincial. Insofar as Canada has shared historical experiences with other countries, much is to be gained from studying the sociological theories these countries have generated. But it cannot be denied that Canadian sociologists are in an especially good position to tackle issues relating to collective political and economic survival.[9]

The Collective Tradition

Clark merits the term 'father of Canadian sociology' not so much because his ideas are original as because he was the first sociologist in Canada to espouse them. Clark's perspective on the Canadian society shares many features with the perspectives of certain Canadian non-sociologists concerned with history and the survival of collectivities, all of which are hence somewhat conflict oriented. For the purposes of this paper they will be referred to as 'the collective tradition.' Within the collective tradition we can distinguish between those approaches which first depict Canada in terms of its relations with other societies and second, augment these same analyses with attention to relations between collectivities within Canada.

A prime exemplar of the first approach was the *metropolitanist* perspective. University of Toronto historian J. M. S. Careless once defined 'metropolitanism' as a version of history centred on 'the emergence of a city of outstanding size to dominate not only its surrounding countryside but other cities and their countrysides, the whole area being organized by the metropolis, through control of communications, trade, and finance, into one economic and social unit.'[10] The gist of metropolitanism was the idea that big and powerful territories tended to colonize small, defenceless ones, and these latter—the counterparts to the metropoli—were later defined by University of Alberta sociologist A. K. Davis as 'hinterlands,' i.e., 'relatively underdeveloped or colonial areas which export for the most part semi-processed extractive materials.'[11] So according to metropolitanism, the metropolis-hinterland relationship was one of unequal exchange, in which the metropolis provided protection, services, and manufactured goods to the hinterland receiving in return all the wealth of the hinterland, usually in the form of 'staples' or relatively unprocessed raw materials. Canada, for example, was originally the hinterland of France; it then became the hinterland of Britain. Now it is the hinterland of the United States.

Probably the most important exponent of metropolitanism was University of Toronto historian Donald Creighton. In his 1937 monograph, *The Commercial Empire of the St. Lawrence*,[12] Creighton took a conservative or paternalistic view of Britain's metropolis-hinterland connection with Canada and argued that Canada would have been much stronger, relative to the United States, if the lord-vassal-serf chain among British merchants, central Canadian merchants, and Canadian workers had perpetuated itself indefinitely. Had the Montreal merchants enjoyed the full co-operation of the British state, according to Creighton (which they had not), they could have used their control over both the fur trade and the St. Lawrence water route to make the Canadian state strong enough to withstand its southern neighbour's imperial designs.

Next, there is the *staples* perspective of Harold Innis. Innis, you will recall, was Clark's most important mentor at the University of Toronto. Like Creighton, Innis favoured an east-west interpretation of Canadian history. Particularly in *The Fur Trade in Canada* (1930), he stressed how essential was the traders' control over the St. Lawrence to their task of moving farther and farther inland to gather furs.[13] But unlike Creighton, who blamed the British state for the irrevocability of Canada's hinterland status, Innis emphasized the 'staple' nature of Canadian resources.

According to the staples perspective, staple exports can constitute the 'leading sector' of an economy to such an extent that an irrevocable pattern in the country's growth cycle can be established.[14] In the Canadian case, the staple products of fish, fur, lumber, and minerals were extracted by European explorers, and the ultimate effect was to stimulate European manufacturing. Once parts of Canada had become settled, it became an important outlet for Europe's newly acquired manufacturing surplus. The concentration of the Canadian economy upon staple exports inhibited the growth of domestic agriculture and manufacturing, thus setting the stage for the country's contemporary problem of foreign-owned and foreign-controlled industry.

Finally we have the *dependency* perspective of McGill economist R. T. Naylor. According to Naylor's early formulation (1972), Canada's eternal hinterland status (i.e., dependency) resulted from the 'staple' mode of its resources and from its underconcentration in industrial capitalism. If Creighton emphasized some of the political origins of Canada's dependency, and Innis concentrated on the material origins, Naylor acknowledged the material origins but was also extremely concerned with their political implications. Canada's underconcentration in industrial capitalism, according to Naylor, was a political strategy initiated by Britain (and later capitalized on by the United States), arising simultaneously from Britain's economic needs and Canada's staple strengths. In his more recent work (1975), Naylor focused with even more single-minded determination on politics by examining how the self-serving behaviour of the Canadian governing and merchant classes advanced Britain's economic designs.

University of Québec historian Stanley Ryerson further developed Naylor's political analysis by criticizing the 'personal corruption' implications of the latter's depiction of the merchants' and governors' behaviour. According to Ryerson (1976), Naylor failed to understand that the behaviour of the merchants and governors confirmed to a systematic political *pattern* of class exploitation. So, Ryerson did not simply emphasize the degree to which Canada's dependency (i.e., lack of indigenous industry) was maintained by Britain's state and merchant representatives in Canada. He suggested that the country's dependency was further increased by the internal problem of systematic labour exploitation. Ryerson, then, was an exemplar of what might be termed the *radical* or *Marxian dependency perspective*,[15] within which analyses of relations between Canada and various other societies are supplemented by analyses of relations between collectivities *within* the Canadian society.

Ryerson has not been the only one to endorse the Marxist perspective. University of Toronto political economist Mel Watkins has likewise attempted to connect class relations within Canada to demands made upon Canada's staple economy in the international sphere.[16] Can periods of labour unrest (i.e., poor working conditions), Watkins has asked, be linked with periods when the merchants were unable to find sufficient market and/or transportation outlets? McMaster sociologist Carl Cuneo has recently (1982) used Bank of Montreal archive data to illustrate his thesis that the collapse of the metropolis-hinterland economic connection between Britain and Canada during the 1840s was due to labour-capital conflicts in both countries that frustrated capitalistic aims to realize high profits.

The Individualist Tradition

So Clark's collective, historical, and conflict-oriented Canadian sociology can be located within a definite Canadian social science tradition: Creighton, Innis, and Naylor espoused a collective metropolis-hinterland perspective, albeit from differing standpoints, and Ryerson, Watkins, and Cuneo subsequently superimposed upon that paradigm a Marxist, class-oriented perspective.

But, as we noted earlier, there is an 'other half' to Clark's intellectual heritage. Consider the issue of the maintenance of harmony amongst the members of a society. Particularly the Marxist adherents to the collective tradition, whose European roots trace bark to Rousseau, tend to consign such social harmony to a utopian future to a time when current fundamental conflicts of interest amongst *groups* (e.g., classes, metropolis-hinterland connections) will have been resolved. Adherents to another intellectual tradition, however, whose European roots lie in the consensus-oriented philosophies of Burke, Saint-Simon, Comte, and Durkheim, contrastingly presuppose an identity of interests among the *individuals* in a society, and so perceive social harmony to exist already, within the *natural* evolutionary life of that society's history.[17]

Edmund Burke was among the first to liken society to a biological organism.[18] In his *Reflections on the Revolution in France*, he argued that sudden conflictual breaks with the past (such as revolutions) were as inimical to the true history of a society as they were to the natural processes of an organism. This view has continued throughout the history of the consensus tradition. By likening society to an evolving organism, the consensus tradition has precluded the possibility of social changes occurring as the result of clashes amongst groups. Because it has projected its conception of the individual organism onto its conception of society, because it has viewed society as comprised of individuals rather than interest groups, the consensus tradition will be referred to here as 'the individualist tradition.'[19] The individualist tradition encompasses (at the very least) functionalist sociology, frontierist history, continentalist (from the Canadian standpoint) economics, and liberal political ideology.

Talcott Parsons, one of the leading exponents of *functionalist sociology*, imported the consensus tradition to the United States. In beginning with the organic notion of individual equilibrium, Parsons was influenced by Durkheim and Comte, and also by the fact that he had majored in biology as an undergraduate.[20] Parsons was also influenced by Max Weber whose 'theory of social action' had as its primary analytical unit the idea of individual means-end conduct. So, like all his intellectual ancestors, Parsons worked from the individual to the society. Two people who were meaningfully oriented toward one another in a means-end manner constituted a 'relationship,' for Parsons, then, and any kind of 'stable relationship' between two or more became an 'action system.'[21] Since action systems had been erected to meet the needs of the individuals within them, what had begun at the level of individual equilibrium for Parsons had now progressed to equilibrium at the societal level.

The contrast between the individualist and collective traditions is particularly exemplified by the difference between the way social inequality is respectively handled by functionalist and Marxist sociologists. Here the

Marxist conception of 'class' clashes with the functionalist notion of 'stratification.' According to Marxist class analyses, more specifically, Marx's keynote conceptions of 'surplus value' and 'surplus labour,' inequality is a function of a social structure in which one class systematically exploits another. But for functionalists, individuals are only relevant qua individuals, unequal ('stratified') by mutual consent in the unexploitative context of a 'division of labour' in which, by virtue of 'free choice,' some individuals forego high rewards in exchange for diminished responsibilities and other individuals do the reverse.[22]

Frontierism, a direct influence on Clark's work, was largely the offspring of American pioneer historian F. J. Turner (1958), who in 1920 thought that a considerable amount of American history could be explained by the *laissez-faire* independent individualism of the early Americans, which had in turn been the product of a surplus of cheap land and the solitary nature of the privations of American pioneer life. Pioneer Americans, in other words, had discovered so bounteous a treasure in North America that they had felt able to abandon their customary obedience and loyalty to the state in favour of a new attitude of single-minded acquisitive individualism. Pioneer life was so primitive, moreover, that these individuals literally risked their lives for their properties and therefore did not feel sufficiently beholden to the state to pay taxes. Such people were products of the New World. Prior to the discovery of North America, according to Turner, no person had experienced an environment which imposed simultaneously such harsh demands and limitless opportunities. So, having been set into motion by such free and self-reliant *individuals*, the United States could not help but evolve into a '*laissez-faire* social democracy' in which serving one's private capitalist designs would be deemed inseparable from serving one's country.[23]

Continentalist economics, a contemporary extension of frontierist history, also minimizes community loyalties and, particularly from the Canadian standpoint, advocates the sacrifice of collective concerns to the imperatives of individual self-interest. The continentalists argue that with the western world so economically dominated by the United States, it seems only sensible for Canadians to forsake impractical nationalist allegiances in their more important quests for personal gain. So Canadian continentalism constitutes the political strategy of non-resistance to the continuing economic absorption of Canada into the United States with the expectation that economic subservience will advance the material interests of individual Canadians.

American or not, continentalists say, it is the corporation that creates the job.[24]

So while Turnerian frontierism was based on individual acquisitiveness, Canadian continentalism worships individual consumption.[25] According to such continentalists as Harry Johnson,[26] economic integration between Canada and the United States would encourage greater division of labour and therefore efficiency within the Canadian economy, which would in turn expand the market for 'Canadian' goods and thus increase individual Canadians' consumption power. So, unlike the metropolis-hinterland and Marxist theorists who view economic life in terms of conflicts of interest amongst specific groups, Canadian continentalists, like frontierists and functionalists, think in terms of a loose consensus amongst constituency-less individuals.

Liberal political ideology, finally, appears at first to steer a middle course between conservatism and socialism with respect to the freedom and equality of members of a society. Conservatism advocates that such matters be left to Providence, the implication being that, bad as things are, human intervention would make them only worse. Conservative societies revere tradition, law and order and, above all, the status quo. Socialism operates from the opposite premise that the task of history is precisely the one conservatives shrink from: viz, the perfection of the community in order to realize the fullest human potential. Liberalism, in the centre, shares some but not all of conservatism's antipathy toward state-level interventionism. An overactive state would indeed worsen matters, according to liberalism, but on the other hand, there exist small areas in which ameliorative reforms can be effected.

In attempting to combine the best of opposite worlds, however, liberalism overlooks an important ingredient actually shared by the extreme views. The mildly reformist nature of liberalism upholds the conservative ideal of individual freedom while rejecting that part of conservatism's preoccupation with order which retains traditional prejudices. Liberalism similarly shares socialism's wish to liberate persons, while abjuring that doctrine's overwhelmingly strong faith in the community.

But conservatism's tradition and socialism's community share a collective thrust. Irrational though it may be, tradition at least connects individuals to a sense of collective history, while the socialist community is collective in its fundamental nature, in its hopes for the future as well as in its interpretation of the past. By rejecting the collective sides of both conservatism and socialism, then, liberalism ends by exaggeratedly promoting the individual.

So the individual liberalism promotes is 'free,' but only in the sense of being released from communal and traditional loyalties and attachments. In the western world, the development of urban industrial capitalism was largely responsible for the evolution of a legal system that gave the rights of the individual pre-eminence over the obligations of community membership. Freed from the rural estates to seek work within towns, labourers needed protection within the new employment context of ephemeral and impersonal contracts. Much was made of the 'free marketplace' in which the worker was free to sell himself to whichever employer he chose. This emphasis served to obscure the workers' systematic exploitation at the hands of capitalists. It obscured the fact that however often the worker changed employers he or she would suffer the same fate and share that fate with other workers.

Contemporary corporate capitalism promotes 'the free individual' in similar terms, and also by means of a meritocracy ideology. The meritocracy ideology encourages workers to believe that the system is set up to reward the 'deserving,' and that it is only the 'deserving' who occupy positions of authority. When a worker 'fails,' then, he is encouraged to believe that he would have succeeded if, out of his own free will, he had tried harder. Workers are thus motivated to compete with one another on an individual basis and are thus often distracted from the potential collective fruits of militant unionizing.[27]

The liberal approach to science similarly postulates a freedom which is divorced from potential constituencies. Particularly, liberal sociology's fact/value distinction encourages observers to consider themselves freely separate from the phenomena they observe. Observers, according to the fact/value theorem, are supposed to 'stick to the facts' in their observations and not allow their values to contaminate these facts. The fact/value distinction, then, presupposes the possibility of separating the individual from the community in the individual's status as observer. It assumes that one can observe without morally participating, without either supporting or wanting to redirect, when in actual fact it is probably impossible to report on a phenomenon without either criticizing it or, by 'saying nothing,' lending it tacit endorsement.

Clark's Combination of the Traditions

The interesting thing about Clark's work is that it reflects the influence of both of these intellectual traditions. It reflects Clark's own prescriptive statements about what a Canadian sociology should be like (which fit in with the collective tradition), and it also reflects the influence of the individualist tradition. It therefore serves as an excellent 'test case' of the traditions' mutual incompatibility.

Let us consider some examples. Clark's first study, *The Canadian Manufacturers' Association* (1939), concerned this organization's early efforts to protect Canadian manufacturing from early annihilation at the hands of its American counterpart. The association fought its battle on two fronts; it attempted to annex other interest groups to its cause and it lobbied the state for protective tariffs.

Clark's approach to the topic was simultaneously collective and individualist. It was collective-historical in the sense that, like Naylor's much later analysis, it concerned itself with the problems of secondary industry within a staple-extracting economy. It was also collective because Clark portrayed the manufacturers as a collectivity—a collectivity that encountered many obstacles in its bid to make historical changes. (The association's behaviour had impact upon many other interest groups, as Clark's analysis pointed out, the main instance being its consistent attempts to denigrate organized labour.[28]) But Clark's approach was individualist in tone because much of his study criticized the manufacturers for inhibiting individual enterprise (i.e., disturbing 'the free operation of economic forces of equilibrium') by organizing.[29]

Clark's next two studies, *The Social Development of Canada* (1942) and *Church and Sect in Canada* (1948), concerned the impact of staple economic development upon social organization in pioneer Canada. Drawing on the 1920 thesis of Thomas and Znaniecki's *The Polish Peasant* (1958), Clark used primary sources to illustrate his idea that the new economy had a 'disorganizing' effect on social life. The exigencies of staple extracting, according to Clark, necessitated a rough, army-camp existence that manifested itself in the pioneers' failure to participate in the traditional community life imported from Europe. *Church and Sect in Canada* concentrated on the religious side of this pioneer 'separatism,' showing how the evangelical sect—a counter-community based on a highly emotional and personal form of worship—offered more of relevance to the pioneer than did the traditional church, which was directed at the tastes of the aristocracy.[30]

Here the split in Clark's approach is more obvious. The two studies were collectivist in the sense of being about social change. In economic terms, the change concerned the historical limits of an early phase of the staple economy. In social terms, a collectivity (the pioneers) took advantage of the chaos brought about by the new economy in order to 'separate' and create social institutions more responsive to its needs than those run by the dominant culture. The result indeed turned out to be a changed society, a compromise solution between pioneers and aristocracy that eliminated the pioneers' previous need for isolation. In the particular case of the church-sect conflict, completely new denominations were formed that reflected the concerns of both factions. The changed society was generally also an innovated society since the dismantling of old customs paved the way toward more efficient ways of doing things and especially toward economic development. 'Whatever course of action appeared to promise the greatest pecuniary returns was followed regardless of standards of respectability or social worth.'[31]

The studies were equally individualist, however, because the economic order advanced by the pioneers was based on an individualist ethos. According to Clark's own terminology, it was a 'frontier.' It was in the interests of the survival of the sects, admittedly, that the sectarian leaders came to use social control to transform religious revivalism into economic industriousness. But the eventual result of these undertakings was to make the sectarian followers more prosperous and hence more sympathetic to the views of the original capitalist establishment.[32] Sectarian leaders, faced with a choice between excommunicating large blocks of followers or modifying theologies, invariably allowed interests of office to sway them toward the latter.[33] So while *The Social Development of Canada* and *Church and Sect in Canada* were ostensibly concerned with grass-roots social movements, these 'movements' were in fact vehicles through which more achievement-oriented individuals co-opted themselves into an extant capitalist system.

Movements of Political Protest in Canada: 1640-1840 (1959) was about the various American efforts to annex Canada and the fact that many Canadians actually supported these efforts in protest against their own society's oppressive institutions. Here again the theme of *collective* protest was juxtaposed against Clark's view that the Canadians were protesting because the Canadian 'frontier' offered fewer opportunities than the American one for *solo* enterprise.[34]

In his final two studies, *The Suburban Society* (1966) and *The New Urban Poor* (1978), Clark used the social change theme to examine transformations between 'rural' and 'urban' societies. He did this in a positive way in *The Suburban Society*, showing how 'suburbia' was a transitory stage between the rural and urban forms.[35] *The New Urban Poor* accounted for the failure of certain areas of Canada to effect the rural-urban transition. Throughout Canada's history, according to Clark, immigrant settlers had been forced to settle on poor farmland in order to support (i.e., be exploited by) nearby industrial or staple-extracting enterprises. Over the years these settlers had provided food supplies and, eventually, a captive, cheap labour market.

These two studies were collectivist because they examined successful or failed social change. *The New Urban Poor*, in fact, even examined labour-capital relations. But, as in the preceding cases, the studies' collective orientations applied mainly to their forms. In terms of the studies' ideological contents, the suburbanites were to be congratulated for being mobility-conscious enough to want their individual homes, while the new urban poor were to be pitied for lacking the motivation and skills to individually 'better' themselves within the urban work world. The studies' ideological contents were influenced by Turner's frontier thesis, by the view that social progress results from solo enterpreneurship. As in the case of liberal ideology itself, progress in this sense emanates not from a revolutionary change *of* the system as the structural form of Clark's studies would indicate, but from the mere removal of prejudices and the opening up of the original system's opportunity structure to more persons.

This same ideological content was even more manifest in essays Clark wrote during the 1960s and 1970s. Ostensibly, these writings were also about social movements, usually in the sense of underdog groups extolling 'separatism' as a political strategy. Clark applied this model to students, women, minority ethnic groups, Quebec and, within the North American context, Canada itself.[36] But Clark almost always condemned the 'separatists' in these instances, and accused them of hypocrisy.

The movements' hypocrisy apparently operated at two levels. First, the groups claimed to be advocating social changes when they were in fact actually seeking increased recognition as *individuals*. "What...is wanted," as Clark wrote in 1975, "is not the breaking down of the establishment but its spreading out to the point where virtually everyone is made a part of it."[37] Second, and related to this, the leaders of the 'separatist' movements duped their followers in order to assure themselves of positions in the dominant culture as the partially assimilated 'separatist leaders.' By convincing their followers not to assimilate, they discouraged potential competitors from their own ranks.[38]

In contrast, Clark was especially proud of the post-war European immigrants who had integrated so well into North American society and amongst whom (in contrast to their less appreciative children) there was 'no carping...about American investment in Canada, the irrelevance of what educational institutions had to offer, the arrogance of a government establishment, or the meaninglessness of the amenities of a middle-class way of life.'[39] So Clark's ideological ideal here was the liberal variant of assimilation: the process of 'breaking out of the culturally bound social groupings...which place sharp limits upon the freedom of movement of the individual.'[40]

Even after that extremely brief overview we can see that there have been two Clarks. On the one hand, there has been a collective Clark, a 'father of Canadian sociology,' who, like other notable Canadian scholars, has emphasized historical change, conflict, and the survival and well-being of collectivities. This Clark was influenced by Innis, in his attention to the effects of a staple economy, and also by the 'ecological' side of the Chicago School, in his interest in the external factors causing a social order to change. The themes of change and collectivity membership have pervaded all of Clark's studies, as we have seen. The topics of group conflict and Canada's historical fate as a staple economy have featured in all but the second last study.

The other Clark has been individualist in the liberal sense of the individual divorced from his or her community and history. In historical terms, this has meant the person whose individualistic ambition has wrought social changes, as in the frontier thesis and the ideal hero/heroine of every one of Clark's studies. In contemporary terms, as we shall see, it has referred to the expedient continentalist Canadian abandonment of communal-historical ties in favour of the 'more progressive' order of 'greater North America.' Such individualism has been especially germane to *Movements of Political*

Protest in Canada, *The Suburban Society*, *The New Urban Poor*, and Clark's 1960s and 1970s essays. In terms of sociological theory this individualism has presupposed the universal, consensual, constituency-less order posited by (particularly the American variant of) the functionalist school.

As for the influences behind this second Clark, we can only speculate. Apart from the influence of the frontier thesis upon Clark's early studies and our doubt that self-reliant individualism has ever been entirely absent from Clark in either personal or intellectual terms, it is in Clark's analysis of post World War II events that the individualist theme has emerged most notably. It is perhaps no coincidence that much of this writing was done during the 1950s and early 1960s, since during that period Clark's endorsement of liberal-continentalism merely would have reflected the prevailing tendency to attribute the post-war economic boom to the indefatigability of capitalism. Entrepreneurship worked, so it seemed, and there appeared to be little further need for collective protest. CCF founders for example, such as Frank Underhill, now relinquished their affinities with socialism and secured the dilution of Canada's third party into the more centrist ambitions of the NDP. For Clark perhaps, as for others, collectivism became only the weak-willed sham strategy of individuals fearing healthy competition.

The American Influence

And now we come to the heart of the matter: Why are collectivism and individualism mutually incompatible in any analysis of the Canadian society, and why have they *not* been incompatible for Clark? The answer to the second question is identical to the answer to the first, and that is that *Canada is not the same society as the United States.*

Clark's ability to accept both traditions stems from his dual interpretation of the phrase 'the same.' His first interpretation has been strictly an academic one: Canada has not had the same *history* as the United States. This is the interpretation Clark has advanced when as 'the father of Canadian sociology' he has argued that Canada, unlike the United States, has had to worry about possible annihilation by a giant to its south.[41] American functionalists, according to Clark may see no need to emphasize the past or entertain the possibility of radical change because they perceive their own country as the pinnacle of world progress.[42] But if *Canadian* history comprised only consensus and integration Canada would long ago have integrated itself into the United States.[43]

Clark's second interpretation, however, has been in political-ideological terms, and herein lies the contradiction. In political-ideological terms, Canada is not the same society as the United States because as a society it is 'less advanced.' As Clark made particularly clear in *Movements of Political Protest in Canada*, his version of Canadian history is that, due largely to geography, Canadians have been less able than Americans to engage in individual business enterprise and for that reason have lived in an unprogressive system. The staple economy, according to Clark, necessitated large-scale capital investments and hence the discouragement of entrepreneurs.[44] The resulting social order was a conservative-oppressive one, dedicated to upholding extant privileges and constraining ambitious upstarts.[45] So the Canadian society has been backward, relative to the United States, because it has been able to promote less economic individualism within its ranks.

As early as 1938, Clark took for granted the view that Canada was inferior to its southern neighbour, describing its culture as 'essentially dull.'[46] Later on, in essays of the 1960s and 1970s, he argued that endeavours to base Canadian society upon any values other than the American ideology of individual enterprise had *always* represented the Canadian bourgeoisie's veiled attempts to entrench itself.[47,48]

Taking Clark's academic and ideological interpretations of Canadian-American relations together, then, we arrive at the rather interesting intellectual paradigm that while Canadian sociology must be collectivist, the political ideology within that sociology must be individualist. A Canadian sociology must exist within the collective Canadian intellectual tradition of conflict and radical change (change 'of' the system, to use Clark's terminology), but the radical changes with which it deals must always consist of liberal-individualist revolutions since these are the only revolutions Clark recognizes.

The combination, of course, is quite nonsensical. It is possible in the United States to consider the individualist idea of 'making it' simultaneously with the collective one of social change because, as Clark himself has pointed out, 'making it' has indeed been a vehicle of change in the United States.[49] 'Making it' is undoubtedly an accurate way to describe the American colonization of most of the world in the name of capitalism—the transformation of the United States from a single country into an empire. But when we turn to Canada, the 'making it' model completely collapses.

Canada cannot become more ideologically individualist, as Clark would wish, in order to become 'like' the United States. The option of becoming 'like' the United States is not open to Canada because Canada is already hopelessly *part* of the United States. Any adherence to the individualist paradigm in a Canadian sociology would imply not change but adaptation: the further integration of Canadian individuals into the American empire.[50] The Canadian individualist has never been a frontierist revolutionary, as Clark has claimed, refashioning an oppressive order into a liberal-democratic one. Canada has always been a colony within a metropolis-hinterland capitalist context, and hence individualism in Canada, unlike individualism in the United States, has meant only conformity to an extant system. The Canadian individualist has been a competitive, free-marketplace liberal; he or she has been an economic and political continentalist.

Conclusion

This paper has argued that Clark has been 'the father of Canadian sociology' and at the same time has confounded his work with models largely inapplicable to the Canadian society. But the intention has not been to minimize the enormity of Clark's contribution. For reasons of both his scholarly rigour and his articulation of a 'Canadian' sociology, Clark is the most important sociologist Canada has yet produced. Were it not for the existence of Clark's ideas concerning the nature of a Canadian sociology and of the example Clark has set in his rich historical research, sociology in Canada would be even more American than it still is in both direction and emphasis. The analysis here has presupposed Clark's pre-eminence in Canadian sociology and merely endeavoured to underscore his work's most salient points.

Because of America's supreme place in the western world, American scholars can (perhaps) afford to view social change in terms of the individualist ethos of entrepreneurship and to incorporate such swashbuckling paradigms as frontierism, continentalism, liberalism, functionalism, and even imperalism. But the Canadian approach to change must be collective because neither Canada nor any of the regions within it can politically survive as a conglomerate of self-interested entrepreneurs.

The incompatibility between collectivism and individualism is more than an academic matter. Individual opportunism versus responsibility toward one's community is a political issue that must continually be confronted by members of underdog groups. It is a particularly complicated issue in Canada, where the ethos of Canadian nationalism is confounded by the interests of class, regionalism, and the nationalism of Québec. The issue tends to be resolved in the individual instance according to whether the system external to one's constituency appears fundamentally unjust or, as the liberals would claim, developing basically in the manner that it should be.

Notes

My thanks are due to Carl Cuneo, Dan Glenday, John Jackson, Jane Synge, the two reviewers, and Professor Clark.

1 See also Hiller, Harry H. (1982). Society and Change: S.D. Clark and the Development of Canadian Sociology. Toronto: University of Toronto Press.

2 See also Harrison, Deborah. (1981). *The Limits of Liberalism: The Making of Canadian Sociology*. Montreal: Black Rose.

3 See Clark, S. D. (1932). The United Farmers of Alberta. *Canadian Forum*, 13(145), p. 7-8.

4 This and the other biographical information in this section come from personal interviews with Clark.

5 Clark, S.D. (1939). Sociology and Canadian Social History. *The Canadian Journal of Economics and Political Science*, 5(3), pp. 348-57.

6 Clark, S.D. (1968). Social Change and the Community. In *The Developing Canadian Community* (revised edition). Toronto: University of Toronto Press. pp. 295-305, p. 305.

7 Ibid. p. 296.

8 Clark, S.D. (1976). *Canadian Society in Historical Perspective*. Toronto: McGraw-Hill Ryerson, p. 5.

9 Clark, S.D. (1974). The American Takeover of Canadian Sociology: Myth or Reality? *The Dalhousie Review*, 53(2), pp. 205-18.

10 Careless, J.M.S. (1954). Frontierism, Metropolitanism, and Canadian History. *The Canadian Historical Review*, 35(1), p.17.

11 Davis, A.K. (1971). Canadian Society and History as Hinterland Versus Metropolis. In Richard Ossenberg (Ed.), *Canadian Society: Pluralism, Change and Conflict*. Scarborough: Prentice-Hall, pp. 6-32, p. 12.

12 D.G. Creighton, (1956). *The Empire of the St. Lawrence: A Study in Commerce and Politics*. Toronto: Macmillan.

13 Innis, Harold A. (revised edition 1956). *The Fur Trade in Canada*. Toronto: University of Toronto Press.

14 Watkins, Mel. (1963). A Staple Theory of Economic Growth. *The Canadian Journal of Economics and Political Science*, 29(2), pp. 141-58, p. 144.
15 See also Ryerson, Stanley. (1960). *The Founding of Canada*. Toronto: Progress; (1973). *Unequal Union*. Toronto: Progress
16 Watkins, Mel. (1977). The Staple Theory Revisited. *Journal of Canadian Studies*, 12, pp. 83-95.
17 Zeitlin, Irving M. (1981). *Ideology and the Development of Sociological Theory* (2nd ed.). Englewood Cliffs: Prentice-Hall.
18 Ibid. p. 43.
19 Such a description may seem to ignore the 'conservative branch' of the consensus tradition according to which social order is to be upheld at all costs and the individual is therefore secondary (a particular concern of Durkheimian sociology). But the truth of this dictum varies within the consensus tradition (it is less true of American functionalism than of functionalist's European roots), and much more fundamental to it is the tenet that under *no* circumstances can the larger order be suddenly ruptured by a collectivity whose members are more loyal to one another than to the larger order. They therefore belong to the larger order as individuals, not as members of constituent interest groups, and this is the reason for the consensus.
20 Wallace, Ruth A. and Wolf, Alison. (1980). *Contemporary Sociological Theory*. Englewood Cliffs: Prentice-Hall. p. 20.
21 Devereux, Edward Jr. (1961). Parsons' Sociological Theory. In Max Black (Ed.), *The Social Theories of Talcott Parsons*. Englewood Cliffs: Prentice-Hall. pp. 1-63, p. 23.
22 Davis, Kingsley and Moore, Wilbert E. (1945). Some Principles of Stratification. *The American Sociological Review*, 10(2), pp. 242-4.
23 Turner, Frederick J. (1958). *The Frontier in American History*. New York: Henry Holt. p.1.
24 Within Canada, of course, the term 'federalism' can be applied to the same phenomenon.
25 Grant, George. (1970). *Lament For a Nation: The Defeat of Canadian Nationalism*. Toronto: McClelland and Stewart. p. 90.
26 Johnson, Harry G. (1977). *The Canadian Quandary*. Toronto: McClelland and Stewart. p. 130.
27 Bowles, Samuel and Gintis, Herbert (1976). *Schooling in Capitalist America*. pp. 102-24.
28 Clark, S.D. (1937). *The Canadian Manufacturers' Association: A Political and Social Study*. Unpublished doctoral dissertation, University of Toronto. p. 65; (1938) The Canadian Manufacturers' Association: A Political Pressure Group. *The Canadian Journal of Economics and Political Science*, 4(4), p.

515; (1939). *The Canadian Manufacturers' Association: A Study in Collective Bargaining and Political Pressure*. Toronto: University of Toronto Press. pp. 43-4.

29 See especially Clark, S.D. (1939). *The Canadian Manufacturers' Association: A Study in Collective Bargaining and Political Pressure*. Toronto: University of Toronto Press. p. 62.

30 Clark, S.D. (1948). *Church and Sect in Canada*. Toronto: University of Toronto Press. p. 120.

31 Clark, S.D. (1942). *The Social Development of Canada: An Introductory Study with Select Documents*. Toronto: University of Toronto Press. p. 214-5.

32 Clark, S.D. (1946). The Religious Sect in Canadian Economic Development. *The Canadian Journal of Economics and Political Science*,12(4), pp. 439-53.

33 Clark, S.D. (1948). *Church and Sect in Canada*. Toronto: University of Toronto Press. pp. 196-7.

34 Clark, S.D. (1959). *Movements of Political Protest in Canada: 1640-1840*. Toronto: University of Toronto Press. p. 17.

35 Clark, S.D. (1966). *The Suburban Society*. Toronto: University of Toronto Press. p. 8.

36 Clark, S.D. (1964). Canada and Her Great Neighbour. *The Canadian Review of Sociology and Anthropology*, 1(4), pp. 193-201; (1965). Canada and the American Value System. In *La Dualité Canadienne à l'heure des Etats-Unis*. Quebec: Les Presses de 1'université Laval, pp. 93-102; (1970). Movements of Protest in Post-war Canadian Society. pp. 223-37 in *Transactions of the Royal Society of Canada Series*, 4(8); (1975). The Post-Second War Canadian Society. *The Canadian Review of Sociology and Anthropology*, 12(1), pp. 25-32; (1976). The Canadian Society and the Issue of Multi-culturalism. Sorokin Lecture, University of Saskatchewan; (1976). The Issue of Canadian Identity. Public address, St. Thomas University, Fredericton, N. B.

37 Clark, S.D. (1976). *Canadian Society in Historical Perspective*. Toronto: McGraw-Hill Ryerson. p. 63.

38 Clark, S.D. (1965). Canada and the American Value System. In *La Dualité Canadienne à l'heure des Etats-Unis*. Quebec: Les Presses de 1'université Laval. pp. 93-102; (1970). Movements of Protest in Post-war Canadian Society. in *Transactions of the Royal Society of Canada Series*, 4(8), pp. 223-37.

39 Clark, S.D. (1975). The Post-Second War Canadian Society. *The Canadian Review of Sociology and Anthropology*, 12(1), pp. 25-32; (1976). *Canadian Society in Historical Perspective*. Toronto: McGraw-Hill Ryerson. p. 59.

40 Clark, S.D. (1976). The Canadian Society and the Issue of Multi-culturalism. Sorokin Lecture, University of Saskatchewan.

41 Clark, S.D. (1976). *Canadian Society in Historical Perspective*. Toronto: McGraw-Hill Ryerson. p. 5.

42 Clark, S.D. (1968). History and the Sociological Method. In *The Developing Canadian Community* (revised edition). Toronto: University of Toronto Press. pp. 284-94. p. 291.
43 Clark, S.D. (1975). The Post-Second War Canadian Society. *The Canadian Review of Sociology and Anthropology*, 12(1), pp. 25-32.
44 Clark, S.D. (1968). The Limitations of Capitalist Enterprise in Canadian Society. pp. 243-52 in *The Developing Canadian Community* (revised edition). Toronto: University of Toronto Press. p. 245.
45 Ibid. pp. 248-9.
46 Clark, S.D. (1938). The Canadian Manufacturers' Association: A Political Pressure Group. *The Canadian Journal of Economics and Political Science*, 4(4), p. 245.
47 Clark, S.D. (1964). Canada and Her Great Neighbour. *The Canadian Review of Sociology and Anthropology*, 1(4), pp. 193-201; (1965). Canada and the American Value System. pp. 93-102 in *La Dualité Canadienne à l'heure des Etats-Unis*. Quebec: Les Presses de 1'université Laval; (1976b). The Issue of Canadian Identity. Public address, St. Thomas University, Fredericton, N. B.
48 As Creighton, Innis, Naylor, and Cuneo have pointed out, of course, there are many instances within Canadian history when Clark's interpretation has been utterly correct.
49 Clark, S.D. (1968a). History and the Sociological Method. *The Developing Canadian Community* (revised edition). Toronto: University of Toronto Press. p. 291.
50 Laxer, James and Laxer, Robert. (1977). *The Liberal Idea of Canada*. Toronto: Lorimer.

Bibliography

Bowles, Samuel and Gintis, Herbert
(1976). *Schooling in Capitalist America*. New York: Basic Books.

Careless, J. M. S.
(1954). Frontierism, Metropolitanism, and Canadian History. *The Canadian Historical Review*, 35(1), pp. 1-21.

Clark, S. D.
(1932). The United Farmers of Alberta. *Canadian Forum*, 13(145), pp. 7-8.
(1937). *The Canadian Manufacturers' Association: A Political and Social Study*. Unpublished doctoral dissertation, University of Toronto.
(1938). The Canadian Manufacturers' Association: A Political Pressure Group. *The Canadian Journal of Economics and Political Science*, 4(4), pp. 505-23.

(1938a). Canadian National Sentiment and Imperial Sentiment. pp. 225-48 in H. F. Angus (Ed.), *Canada and Her Great Neighbour*. Toronto: Ryerson Press.

(1939). *The Canadian Manufacturers' Association: A Study in Collective Bargaining and Political Pressure*. Toronto: University of Toronto Press.

(1939a). Sociology and Canadian Social History. *The Canadian Journal of Economics and Political Science*, 5(3), pp. 48-57.

(1942). *The Social Development of Canada: An Introductory Study with Select Documents*. Toronto: University of Toronto Press.

(1946). The Religious Sect in Canadian Economic Development. *The Canadian Journal of Economics and Political Science*, 12(4), pp. 439-53.

(1948). *Church and Sect in Canada*. Toronto: University of Toronto Press.

(1959). *Movements of Political Protest in Canada: 1640-1840*. Toronto: University of Toronto Press.

(1964). Canada and Her Great Neighbour. *The Canadian Review of Sociology and Anthropology*, 1(4), pp. 193-201.

(1965). Canada and the American Value System. pp. 93-102 in *La Dualité Canadienne à l'heure des Etats-Unis*. Quebec: Les Presses de l'université Laval

(1966). *The Suburban Society*. Toronto: University of Toronto Press.

(1968). The Limitations of Capitalist Enterprise in Canadian Society. pp. 243-52 in *The Developing Canadian Community* (revised edition). Toronto: University of Toronto Press.

(1968a). History and the Sociological Method. pp. 284-94 in *The Developing Canadian Community* (revised edition). Toronto: University of Toronto Press.

(1968b). Social Change and the Community. pp. 295-305 in *The Developing Canadian Community* (revised edition). Toronto: University of Toronto Press.

(1970). Movements of Protest in Post-war Canadian Society. pp. 223-37 in *Transactions of the Royal Society of Canada Series*, 4(8).

(1973). The American Takeover of Canadian Sociology: Myth or Reality. *The Dalhousie Review*, 53(2), pp. 205-18.

(1975). The Post-Second War Canadian Society. *The Canadian Review of Sociology and Anthropology*, 12(1), pp. 25-32.

(1976). *Canadian Society in Historical Perspective*. Toronto: McGraw-Hill Ryerson.

(1976a). The Canadian Society and the Issue of Multi-culturalism. Sorokin Lecture, University of Saskatchewan.

(1976b). The Issue of Canadian Identity. Public address, St. Thomas University, Fredericton, N.B.

(1978). *The New Urban Poor*. Toronto: McGraw-Hill Ryerson.

Creighton, D. G.

(1956). *The Empire of the St. Lawrence: A Study in Commerce and Politics*. Toronto: Macmillan.

Cuneo, Carl J.

(1982). The Politics of Surplus Labour in the Collapse of Canada's Dependence on Britain 1840-49. *Studies in Political Economy*, 7, pp. 61-87.

Davis, A. K.

(1971). Canadian Society and History as Hinterland Versus Metropolis. pp. 6-32 in Richard Ossenberg (Ed.), *Canadian Society: Pluralism, Change and Conflict*. Scarborough: Prentice-Hall.

Davis, Kingsley and Wilbert E. Moore

(1945). Some Principles of Stratification. *The American Sociological Review*, 10(2), pp. 242-9.

Devereux, Edward Jr.

(1961). Parsons' Sociological Theory. pp. 1-63 in Max Black (Ed.), *The Social Theories of Talcott Parsons*. Englewood Cliffs: Prentice-Hall.

Grant, George

(1970). *Lament For a Nation: The Defeat of Canadian Nationalism*. Toronto: McClelland and Stewart.

Harrison, Deborah

(1981). *The Limits of Liberalism: The Making of Canadian Sociology*. Montreal: Black Rose.

Hiller, Harry H.

(1981). Research Biography and Disciplinary Development: S. D. Clark and Canadian Sociology. *The Journal of the History of Sociology*, 3(1), pp. 67-86.

(1982). *Society and Change: S. D. Clark and the Development of Canadian Sociology*. Toronto: University of Toronto Press.

Innis, Harold A.

(1930, revised edition 1956). *The Fur Trade in Canada*. Toronto: University of Toronto Press.

Johnson, Harry G.

(1977). *The Canadian Quandary*. Toronto: McClelland and Stewart.

Laxer, James and Laxer, Robert

(1977). *The Liberal Idea of Canada*. Toronto: Lorimer.

Naylor, R. T.
(1972). The Rise and Fall of the Third Commercial Empire of the St. Lawrence. pp. 1-41 in Gary Teeple (Ed.), *Capitalism and the National Question in Canada*. Toronto: University of Toronto Press.
(1975). *The History of Canadian Business 1867-1914* (Vol. I and II.). Toronto: Lorimer.
Ryerson, Stanley
(1960). *The Founding of Canada*. Toronto: Progress.
(1973). *Unequal Union*. Toronto: Progress
(1976). Who's Looking After Business? *This Magazine*, 10(5 and 6), pp. 44-46.
Thomas, William and Znaniecki, Florian
(1958). *The Polish Peasant in Europe and America* (Vol. 2). New York: Dover
Turner, Frederick Jackson.
(1958). *The Frontier in American History*. New York: Henry Holt.
Wallace, Ruth A. and Wolf, Alison
(1980). *Contemporary Sociological Theory*. Englewood Cliffs: Prentice-Hall
Watkins, Mel
(1963). A Staple Theory of Economic Growth. *The Canadian Journal of Economics and Political Science*, 29(2), pp. 141-58.
(1977). The Staple Theory Revisited. *Journal of Canadian Studies*, 12, pp. 83-95.
Zeitlin Irving, M.
(1981). *Ideology and the Development of Sociological Theory* (2nd ed.). Englewood Cliffs: Prentice-Hall.

Chapter Seven

THE IMAGE OF INEQUALITY IN S.D. CLARK'S WRITINGS ON PIONEER CANADIAN SOCIETY

Richard C. Helmes-Hayes

Abstract

This paper examines S. D. Clark's views on the nature and significance of social inequality on the Canadian pioneer frontier. It suggests that Clark's theoretical-empirical "image of inequality" is both complex and paradoxical. It is complex because it contains elements of a number of theories in addition to F. J. Turner's frontier egalitarianism. It is paradoxical because Clark tries to argue on the one hand that the pioneer frontier was a theatre of equal condition and opportunity while at the same time his descriptions of life there suggest that nothing of the sort was the case. Clark's adoption of this image is tentatively explained as the result of his "idealization" of the frontier as a liberal individualist "backwoods utopia."

Introduction

The past few years have witnessed a modest but undeniable increase in the attention paid by Canadian sociologists to the history of their discipline.[1] The focus of much of this interest has been the controversial "dean"[2] of

---

Helmes-Hayes, Richard C. The Image of Inequality in S.D. Clark's Writings on Pioneer Canadian Society. From the *Canadian Journal of Sociology*, 13(3). Reprinted with permission from the *Canadian Journal of Sociology*. References have been removed from the text and replaced as endnotes.

Canadian sociology, S. D. Clark. There are two book-length discussions of Clark and his place in the history of Canadian sociology[3] as well as a number of essays addressing various aspects of his work.[4] And, without wishing to contribute to the potential overestimation of Professor Clark's relative contribution to the development of the discipline—the contributions of Carl Dawson, Everett Hughes, Leonard Marsh, and John Porter have received less attention than they deserve in this regard—it is my purpose in this paper to continue the process of examining Clark's sociological legacy. Unlike intellectual biographers Deborah Harrison and Harry Hiller, however, I shall not endeavour to do a comprehensive analysis of all of Clark's writings. The more modest purpose of this essay is to examine his interpretation of the nature and role of inequality on the pioneer Canadian frontier.[5]

The term "image" rather than "theory" has been chosen for two reasons. First the discussion outlines more than Clark's theory of inequality, it also outlines his empirical description of it. Second, the term conveys some of the nebulous, even contradictory character of Clark's views on the subject. Like other pre-*Vertical Mosaic* mainstream Canadian sociologists, Clark did not use "class" as a central theoretical concept in organizing his work.[6] In fact, his views on inequality were for the most part "hidden" in his analyses of aspects of Canadian society *other than* social inequality. Partly as a consequence of this lack of sustained explicit attention, his views on the subject were not consistent. Thus, in order to understand and assess his view of the nature and role of social inequality on the Canadian pioneer frontier, it is necessary to construct a coherent image "for him," as it were, from the pieces of empirical evidence and (often implicit) theoretical argumentation that he left scattered throughout his work.[7]

Rationale

Few scholars now appreciatively cite Clark's work in their attempts to understand current social issues. Unlike Harold Innis and John Porter, Clark founded no school of thought and inspired no intellectual disciples to follow in his footsteps.[8] As a result, the rationale for this paper must be essentially historiographic. The following considerations would seem to provide good reason to continue our assessment of the work of Clark and other Canadian sociologists whose contributions to the discipline lie for the most part in the past.

First, such studies begin to "fill in the gaps" in our knowledge of the early history of Canadian sociology; in this particular case, our understanding of the development of the sub-field of class and/or stratification studies within the discipline. Aside from the attention that has been focussed on John Porter and *The Vertical Mosaic* (1965), Canadian sociologists have generally ignored this area of the history of Canadian sociology.[9] As a consequence, they have fallen well behind their American counterparts who can draw on several studies—most notably Charles Page's *Class and American Sociology* ([1940] 1969) and Milton Gordon's *Social Class in American Sociology* (1958)—for such information.[10]

More specifically, of course, this study allows us to assess Clark's particular contribution to this field of study. Interestingly, despite the depth of their analyses of Clark's work, neither Hiller nor Harrison examine his views on inequality in any detailed way. For Hiller, Clark's major concerns were the frontier thesis, staples theory, religious sectarianism, and patterns of social change. Since, in his view, social inequalities in the form of class structure or economic and cultural dependency relations were not central variables in Clark's analysis, Hiller had relatively little to say about them. Deborah Harrison's failure to provide an in-depth discussion of Clark's theory of inequality is more puzzling, for one of the major purposes of her critique was to show the limitations supposedly built into Clark's work by his adoption of a flawed liberal sociological and ideological perspective. Given her advocacy of a Marxist alternative, we could well have expected her to have provided an outline of Clark's conception of classes and class relations, for such concerns stand at the analytic centre of the Marxist approach from which her work emanates. However, beyond noting that Clark "often treated class relations in his analyses,"[11] and making a number of scattered comments regarding the place of classes in Clark's writings, she does not provide any sort of systematic analysis of this aspect of his work.[12]

Finally, such reassessments may help us to see Clark's work and the work of other early Canadian sociological pioneers somewhat differently. In Clark's case, for example, Canadian sociologists have interpreted his work as derivative of the concerns of Harold Innis, F. J. Turner, and, to a lesser extent, the Chicago School, and they have characterized it as an attempt to understand the dynamics of the social organization and disorganization occasioned on the frontier by rapid and sporadic staples-related economic development. While this is undoubtedly one valuable way of reading Clark's work, there are others. It is my view, for example, that it is worth re-reading Clark's work using social inequality as an organizing concept since, as the analysis below shows, Clark dealt extensively with the conflicts amongst the elites, interest groups, classes, and so forth that struggled for control over Canada's various staples frontiers. In the process of analyzing these struggles he revealed both a picture of and an explanation for the structure of inequality in pioneer Canadian society. This "image of inequality" is of historical interest not only in and of itself, but also for three other reasons. First, a detailed examination of it suggests that—if Clark's work is any indication—then early Canadian sociologists were more "alive" to the study of social inequality than has generally been recognized within the discipline.[13] Second, it shows that Clark's particular approach encapsulates and exemplifies many of the liberal individualist notions that characterized mainstream history and sociology during the early and middle portions of the twentieth century and drew Porter's critical fire in *The Vertical Mosaic*. Third, an examination of the liberal individualist assumptions of Clark's approach to the study of social inequality reveals that there are a number of important underlying similar ties between his image of inequality and that of the modern "stratification" approach to the study of inequality.[14]

The basic argument

Clark draws heavily on a variant of F. J. Turner's frontier egalitarian proposition in framing his image of inequality. The analysis to follow outlines the basic elements of Clark's image and suggests that though more complex than Turner's formulation, it is no more satisfactory than the original in terms of its descriptive or explanatory adequacy. Descriptively it is inadequate because evidence, including Clark's own, suggests that pioneer frontiers were not egalitarian. Theoretically it is inadequate for two reasons: first, because of its environmentalist overemphasis on the leveling influence of geographic conditions[15] and, second, because of the limited scope and transitional nature of whatever leveling influence the frontier might impart. The paper concludes with the suggestion that Clark's use of the egalitarian proposition might be explained, at least in part, by his political views. As a scholar with a strong preference for classical liberal individualist political and economic philosophy, it may well be that he saw the frontier in somewhat idealized—if not explicitly "romantic"—terms as a sort of "backwoods liberal utopia"; a place where individual effort and merit could and would be rewarded encumbered only minimally by the economic and political constraints operative in well-established metropolitan communities.

The empirical image

Clark gives us his conception of the empirical dimensions—the structure—of inequality in two ways: (a) by making reference to the *collective characteristics* of various hierarchically ranked *groups* on the frontier (e.g., classes, elites, oligarchies),[16] and (b) by describing the *personal attributes* of specific *individuals*. I will begin by outlining Clark's view of group rankings on the frontier.

Throughout his work, Clark uses the term "class." In the discussion to follow it is argued that Clark's view of class, and his assumptions about the nature and sources of inequality more generally, are in some ways quite similar to those of the modern stratification researcher. Unlike his modern counterparts, however, Clark was not particularly careful either to define his terms precisely or to use them consistently. Without meaning in any way to patronize him—to preach to him from the advantageous vantage point provided us by more than thirty years of research in the area of class studies since Clark wrote—it is important to understand precisely what he meant when he used the term. The purpose of the discussion below, then, is to clarify his use of the term "class" and determine what the implications of this conception for his overall description and explanation of inequality on the pioneer Canadian frontier might be.

Good examples of the way Clark used the term "class" are his references in *The Developing Canadian Community* to the "agricultural class," the "well-to-do merchant class," the "local [petite] bourgeoisie," and the "official class" that made up the more prosperous elements of the population of the farming-fur trade communities of New France during the very earliest period of French domination in Canada.[17] Here, though he uses the term "class" to describe each of these groups, he very clearly links his use of the term to the "feudal" (or quasi-feudal) period of Canadian history. This suggests that at least some of them might better be seen as feudal (or quasi-feudal) *estates*. Thus, when Clark suggests that the rise of the fur traders signalled the "disintegration of the colonial *class* structure"[18] (emphasis added) based on a "feudal" form of economic and social organization, and heralded the establishment of a new hierarchy headed by the *coureurs de bois* who "came to constitute in the period 1660-1760 the aristocracy of the colonial society...[a] *class* which set...the standards for the community as a whole"[19, 20] (emphasis added), the use of the term "class" to describe the seigneurs and fur traders alike should not be interpreted as a sign that the word meant the same thing in each case. In fact, Clark's use of the term is not accurate in either instance for, if his description of the seigneurs suggests they might better be seen as an estate, his description of the fur traders—and most other collectivities in post-"feudal" Canadian society—indicates that they might better be thought of as *interest groups* (or, for a Marxist, "class fractions," perhaps). He argues, for example, that most of the social movements designed to create a new social equilibrium in New France were short-lived and specific to particular elements of the population. "Demands for changes in the system of government or in economic policy were indicative ordinarily of states of unrest which found expression in a wide variety of social movements."[21] This was a result of the fact that, according to Clark, " the break with old loyalties tended to create a disposition which discouraged stable loyalties of any sort."[22]

With relation to the fur traders, for example, Clark argues that their activities were almost entirely economic in character. Their influence became widespread, therefore, only insofar as their economic activity created social disorganization in the colony. Since the influence they gained, while considerable, was restricted to the economic realm only, then they did not constitute, in his view, more than an interest group—though he does use the term "class" to describe them.

This view of the nature of the social collectivities on the fur trade frontier was carried over to Clark's discussions of other frontier groups and populations. They were usually characterized as loose and sporadic conglomerations of individuals. He sometimes referred to them as "classes" of various types but also as "social masses"[23] or "working masses."[24] This type of usage is quite similar in a number of respects to the modern stratification researcher's use of the term class. That is, classes are portrayed as statistical aggregates and individuals are assigned to them solely on the basis of shared objective characteristics. "Consciousness-of-kind" is generally denied other than insofar as it might briefly turn atomized individuals into interest groups. In Clark's case, the only groups which he allows might possess an on-going consciousness-of-kind are those groups which occupy the topmost rungs of the social ladder. Here, though, he is careful to emphasize the separateness of their institutional bases of power and spheres of influence. Thus, it is probably more true to Clark's intentions to refer to them as elites rather than as a "ruling class."

For Clark, then, classes in the sense that a Marxist would talk about them—i.e., as groups of individuals sharing a particular relationship to the means of production (owners versus non-owners), with different, opposed interests and degrees of "in-group" feeling determined by their respective relationships to the means of production—simply did not exist on the pioneer Canadian frontier. Hiller notes on this score that "even as far back as 1938, Clark had warned about the dangers of too simplistic a view of class conflict and consequently the concept never became a dominant theme in his work."[25] It is also apparent, though, that groups of other types—elites, masses, oligarchies, etc.—*were* important actors on the pioneer frontier. Furthermore, these groups were by no means equal in terms of their resources and degrees of influence. We may safely conclude, then, that according to Clark—*and contrary to the substance of the frontier egalitarian proposition*—Canadian frontier societies were hierarchically structured from the beginning. Furthermore, this inequality was both a cause of and a reflection of a struggle amongst these groups for economic and societal dominance.

Some further sense of Clark's view of inequality can be gained from a reading of Clark's descriptions in *The Developing Canadian Community* of the individuals who populated five different "types" of frontier "societies."[26, 27] Clark's descriptions of each of these societies indicates that, in his view, a good portion of the inequality in pioneer communities stemmed from the occupational structure.[28] Even though the form of economic production and the style of life on the frontier were relatively primitive, it was characterized by a somewhat elaborate technical division of labour and a social hierarchy based on a variety of factors directly and indirectly related to the occupational structure." In the chapter "The Farming-Fur Trade Society of New France," for example, Clark makes frequent reference to twenty different occupational groupings (e.g., traders, *coureurs de bois*, skilled workers, peasants, soldiers)[29] and discusses a broad range of economic-, political-, and status-related characteristics (e.g., ownership of land, wealth, status, political influence) that differentiated them from one another and placed them at different levels of the social hierarchy. Furthermore, these discrepancies were considerable; ranging from the tremendous wealth, power, and status of the Governor, the Bishop, and the well-to-do merchants to the lack of same that led to "vagrancy," "poverty," and "social dependence" on the part of the "poor" and "destitute." Note that though these references concern conditions in New France, analysis of the articles dealing with the other four types of pioneer "societies" reveals essentially the same themes.[30]

The five articles from *The Developing Canadian Community* are not the only places where Clark discusses social inequality. His discussion of the class-related dynamics of church-sect confrontations in "Religious Organizations and the Rise of the Canadian Nation"[31] is an example of similar references elsewhere. Even here, where he was concerned with religion, references to inequality are sprinkled throughout the analysis. He notes, for instance, that there is a clear relationship between different types of economic development and patterns of religious and cultural change—including patterns of social inequality. Periods of Canadian history characterized by a large degree of Protestant sectarianism are coincident with, and caused by, the establishment of conditions of novel, individualistic entrepreneurial activity; that is, periods of sectarianism parallel periods when "open" frontier conditions obtain. Sects then change to churches when "closed" conditions are re-established with the rise of corporate forms of capitalism.[32] Furthermore, social status on the pioneer frontier is to some extent a result of the prestige attached to religious affiliation. Those in privileged positions were members of established churches, with expensive buildings,[33] while those amongst the social fringe—usually living on the geographic fringe as well—tended to belong to dissenting, sectarian groups of one sort or another.[34]

These same themes are taken up in *Church and Sect in Canada* (1948).[35] Here, as Berger describes it, Clark contends that anti-authoritarian religious sectarianism on the frontier was the church equivalent of the "political revolts against outside control" later documented by Clark in *Movements of Political Protest* (1959). The outcome in both cases was the same; "old status relations" were broken down and the importance of "individual worth and equality" were stressed.[36]

In *Movements of Political Protest*, Clark argues, for example, that the earliest movement of political protest in Canadian history, i.e., the anti-imperialist, anti-French political and economic activity engaged in by pioneer fur traders during the period of the "struggle for the St. Lawrence,"[37] revolved around the mixed success that the authorities had in their attempts to establish and maintain control over a local population rendered independent and egalitarian by their frontier existence.[38] Harrison notes in this regard that this book is an excellent example of Clark's movement beyond Innis for, if Innis "failed to examine the realm of...internal relations between classes" in early Canada,[39] Clark did not. However, while social status, economic interest, and political and military power were important features of Clark's discussion in *Movements of Political Protest*, he did not extend his analysis to describe or explain such issues in the terms that a Marxist like Harrison would use.

Summary

For Clark, inequality on the Canadian staples frontier was a very real and ubiquitous phenomenon, related both to the occupational structure and to patterns of ownership of land and capital. And, though Clark's empirical image varies somewhat by historical period, the dominant image that emerges is one very similar to that of the modern stratification researcher. He ranges people as *individuals* along a number of loosely interrelated, hierarchical continua of wealth, power, influence, status, and so forth. Sometimes, when the frontier assumed a closed form, the continua tended to run together in such a way that there was considerable overlap of membership; particularly amongst the occupants of the uppermost regions of the continua. At such times, powerful groups of individuals, variously referred to by Clark as classes, elites, oligarchies, and so forth, came not only to have some degree of in-group consciousness, but also to act as "interest groups." Occasionally, one group would form—often comprised of a set of interrelated economic, political, military, and religious elites—that was sufficiently powerful to determine the general direction of social development in these communities. At other times, the re-establishment of open frontier conditions created new sources of power, wealth, and prestige which caused a considerable degree of social breakdown. During such periods the primacy of the individual's personal characteristics were re-established as the primary basis for social worth. This in turn changed patterns of institutional organization and power-wielding and the membership of elite groups was transformed.

The theoretical image

Clark's theoretical image of inequality is derived from the "frontier thesis" developed by American historian F. J. Turner.[40] Turner argued that the putative characteristics of American society—individualism, competition, meritocracy, democracy, egalitarianism—were a personal and societal consequence of the primitive living conditions that typified the western frontier. While Clark drew heavily on this idea, his version was more than a mere reproduction of the original. It was broader and more complex, but also more vague; a reflection of the combined influence on his thought of Harold Innis, A. R. M. Lower, A. S. Morton, Carl Dawson, and Everett Hughes.[41] Berger has noted that Clark's use of the notion was neither uniform nor unconditional, a fact which rendered its meaning and place in Clark's work rather "ambiguous."[42] Despite such inconsistencies, however, there is no doubt that it was Clark's theoretical starting point. In the introduction to *Canadian Society in Historical Perspective* he argues that "focusing on frontier development represented ... an effort to seize on certain theoretically meaningful points of departure in examining the character of change of the Canadian society."[43, 44]

The "Innisian" slant to Clark's interpretation of the frontier thesis is apparent in his decision to study the *social* developments that accompanied economically induced movement into new areas of *staple* exploitation.[45] At the same time, his interest in the kinds of changed behaviour originating in the new location and not "just" transferred from Europe "distinguished him from Innis and gave his work a decidedly frontierist…emphasis."[46] In adopting this perspective, Clark demonstrated the influence on his thought of A. S. Morton and A. R. M. Lower, for it is partly from them that that he developed an interest in extending Innis' concern with the frontier as an area of economic expansion to an interest in it as a venue of important socio-political developments.[47] For our purposes here the most important of these influences is Lower's concern with the "leveling" influence of frontier conditions for this is the source of the proposition of *frontier egalitarianism*, the "corollary" to the frontier thesis, that is the centrepiece of Clark's theoretical conception of social inequality.

Clark's version of frontier egalitarianism may be stated as follows: the movement of a population into a hitherto unsettled geographical area (usually, but not always) for the purpose of exploiting a staple, has a *democratizing* and *levelling* effect on the population. For Clark, the frontier was a place characterized by "simplicity and cooperative spirit"[48] where there developed a "strong spirit of independence, impatience of authority, local autonomy, democracy and egalitarianism"[49] that was intolerant of entrenched class privilege. There was neither a class structure nor a formally and legally entrenched aristocracy on the frontier. In addition, there was only a very small gap between the top and bottom of the social hierarchy. As a result, the pioneer frontier was a theatre of equal opportunity, a place where positions could be made rapidly because, more than anywhere else, it was a venue where the enterprise, talent, and competitiveness of the *individual* determined his social standing.[50] The frontier created not only considerable equality of condition and opportunity, however. It also generated a general adherence to individualistic, liberal egalitarian values.

> Canada shared with the United States in the great democratic movement, with its almost fanatical emphasis upon the principle that all men are equal. This frontier provided unfavorable ground on which to build an elaborate structure of social classes, which broke down under the influence of the common experience of frontier life. The social worth of the individual was measured in terms of accomplishment rather than in terms of family background.[51]

While the critical assessment below suggests a number of reasons that the frontier egalitarian proposition is problematic, an obvious one worthy of mention here is Clark's own "evidence" (outlined above) regarding the existence on *all* pioneer frontiers of considerable social inequality. This presents a puzzling contradiction in need of an explanation. Why would Clark on the one hand insist that the pioneer frontier was an egalitarian place where "distinctions of social class found little recognition"[52] and, on the other, make frequent reference not only to inequalities of condition and opportunity but also to "conservative" political, ideological, religious, economic, and military forces at work there that "greatly moderated [the] spirit of equalitarianism generated within the frontier situation"?[53] Part of the answer may be found by examining other elements of Clark's eclectic theoretical worldview.

Like all analysts of the human condition, Clark adopts a number of assumptions. One of the most important of them for our purposes here is his adoption of the classical liberal's theory of human nature as competitive and self-seeking,[54] for it explains two things. First, it explains Clark's preference for the open frontier. On the open frontier the social constraints on egoistic economic activity are minimal. Thus, the social order allows the freest possible "realization" of innate human nature. That is, people are free to establish a liberal individualist and entrepreneurial capitalist society. As Harrison describes it:

> [The] frontier thesis was an epistemological and moral paradigm of personal freedom. In its most rudimentary form, it connected the "natural" state of liberty with the natural state of the physical frontier.[55]

Second, it explains Clark's use of "personality" as a causal variable. For, if it is true that people are innately aggressive, competitive, and self-seeking, and if it is true that on the open frontier these proclivities are given free rein, then it is the personality (industriousness and competitiveness) and the merit (intelligence) of the individual that determines his place in the social hierarchy. While Clark was never clear as to whether it was something about the frontier that caused persons living there to have independent, individualistic personalities or whether it was that the frontier that drew to it persons of such a type,[56] he was certain that either way the "frontier was the habitat of the impatient and the restless, and its very character implied an emancipation from social controls and a reliance upon individual effort and will."[57, 58] This view of human nature had other implications as well; for it directly influenced his view of the character and significance of collective, group activity on the frontier.

For Clark, it is the individual's characteristics as an *individual*—rather than as a member of a group—that are most important in determining his or her fate. Thus it follows that Clark has little use for classes as "actors" (in the sense that a Marxist would use the term) when he is describing empirical reality. Similarly, insofar as we can say he has a theoretical conception of class, it is by no means the same sort of conception that would be used by a Marxist like Harrison. For him, individuals naturally tend to engage in ethically egoistic behaviour.[59] If it happens that a number of them come to engage in common types of action, then it might turn out that they have some influence as a group on the workings of society, but such activity is almost always a result of common individual responses to a particular situation rather than the consequence of any collective, orchestrated, class-conscious action determined by that group's relationship to the means of production.[60]

Another aspect of Clark's theoretical image that might be labelled an "assumption" is his implicitly functionalist view of the nature and legitimacy of constituted authority. In fact, I would argue that despite Clark's professed disagreement with Parsons' perspective, he adopted much of the structural functionalist framework or, at least, had many ideas which paralleled Parsons' closely.[61] Clark's consensualist view of "leadership" as a relation of authority rather than power, and his view of social inequality as both necessary and functional are good examples. The discussion below of the inequality and power structure of Maritime villages settled by New Englanders captures the sentiment of both arguments precisely.

> Many of the vestiges of the proprietary system persisted in the village organization of these settlements. The proprietors provided the nucleus of an upper social class. As substantial farmers and tradespeople or persons of superior education, they gained a position of influence in the local villages...The "Esquires" and "Gentlemen"...enjoyed a standard of life somewhat above that of ordinary inhabitants, but in return they provided the leadership so necessary in pioneer settlements.[62]

Summary

If we consider Clark's views on human nature, personality, individualism, group membership, and power as a whole, it is obvious that his conception of "egalitarianism" is that of the classical liberal. Thus, he is not at all critical of inequalities of power, wealth, and status amongst pioneer Canadians as long as they are not based on the "wrong" kinds of social forces; i.e., tradition and class privilege rather than individual merit and industriousness. He favours "equality," then, only in the sense of equality of opportunity. This is only partly a result of the fact that, as a liberal, he views the distribution of rewards according to ascriptive criteria rather than individual merit as unjust. Equally importantly, he regards it as *irrational*. Clark complains that Canadians—who otherwise would, in his view, be competitive, striving, individualistic entrepreneurs like Americans—were historically prevented from becoming so by the existence north of the 49th parallel of a closed frontier.[63] This closure was, to him, *doubly irrational*, because it both *denied human nature at the level of the individual* and because it *prevented the realization of a suitable liberal form of social rationality*. "Canada has suffered throughout her history by the comparison of her rate of progress with that of the United States."[64] "The American society grew and prospered in giving expression to the free enterprise interests of the middle class."[65]

Critical assessment

There is a strong sense of ambivalence, if not confusion, in Clark's treatment of the theme of inequality. His empirical "image" or *description* vacillates between the statement that the frontier was a theatre of equal condition and opportunity to a "documentation" of the fact that nothing of the sort was the case. This confusion is further compounded by his attempt to use the frontier egalitarian proposition as an *explanatory* tool; while the explanatory logic of the egalitarian proposition stresses the levelling influence of the frontier, Clark's descriptions of life there suggest that structures of condition and opportunity have almost always been inegalitarian on both counts. In fact, a basic feature of pioneer life to which Clark himself frequently refers was the absence of truly open and therefore egalitarian frontier conditions.

> *The Canadian frontier has never been*, like the American frontier, *an area of unrestricted economic development*. Rather, it has developed under what might be described as conditions of monopoly control.[66]

> The claims to the interior of [Canada] were staked not by advancing frontiersmen, acting on their own, but by advancing armies and police forces, large corporate economic enterprises and ecclesiastical organizations supported by the state.[67]

In fact, Canada's numerous frontiers have been examined by many historians and social scientists. These investigations have clearly indicated that the frontier was egalitarian neither in terms of living conditions nor in terms of life chances. The wheat-farming frontier of the prairies, perhaps Canada's archetypal frontier—and in some areas one that persisted into the

1930s—is an example. Though free or cheap land was available to homesteaders as late as the end of the nineteenth century, most of the best and most valuable land was owned by land companies and the railroad.[68] Many of those who were able to obtain a plot of land had to borrow passage money from one of the trading companies and/or seed grain money from the government. The result was that many of them could never "get ahead" of their debts and decades later they would still owe as much or more as when they first came to the West.[69] Not all pioneers were this poor, however. For example, Carl Dawson's investigations of life on the Canadian prairies in the 1930s (as part of the Canadian Frontiers of Settlement series) revealed that pioneers of different religious and ethnic backgrounds brought widely different amounts of money, livestock, equipment and so forth with them to the Canadian West.[70, 71] Dawson is not the only person to have discussed the relative degrees of power and wealth wielded by groups and individuals who opened up Canada's various frontiers, however.

The chapter on "Socio-Economic Forces, Instructions and Elites in Canada's Development" in Wallace Clement's *The Canadian Corporate Elite*,[72] for example, outlines in broad strokes the national and international trade, political, and military relations that created the context within which the benefits and opportunities that accompanied Canadian economic development after 1600 were distributed. Like H. Clare Pentland ([1961] 1981) and Gustavus Myers ([1914] 1975) before him, Clement argues that the centralist, monopolistic character of Canadian economic development placed very narrow limitations on the possibilities for equal opportunity in Canadian society right from the beginning.[73] The introductory essay by editor Michael Cross in *The Workingman in the Nineteenth Century*[74] gives a sense of the class differences that characterized Canadian society during this period, while excerpts in the book clearly reveal the different lifestyles and life chances experienced by the wide variety of people that populated Canada's frontiers. The same may be said of Alfred Dubuc's essay, "Problems in the Study of the Stratification of the Canadian Society from 1760 to 1840"[75] and other of the contributions to *Studies in Canadian Social History* edited by Michiel Horn and Ronald Sabourin.

Taken together, these studies—along with a growing body of research in the area of labour and working-class history—contradict any claim that structures of condition and opportunity were open in pioneer Canada. At the same time, however, there is a point made by Professor Clark on the subject that merits consideration. In an interview,[76] Professor Clark, having read a draft of this manuscript, challenged my analysis and stood by his claim that the frontier was an egalitarian place. On a *true frontier*, he said, one on the very fringes of civilization, the levelling influence of Nature was both undeniable and irresistible. At the same time, however, he granted that there was an obvious "tension" or lack of fit between his use of frontier egalitarianism as a descriptive framework and his clear depiction of obvious and thoroughgoing inequality in all of the frontier societies he had examined. He even went so far as to agree that this constituted a "contradiction" in his work; though one not so "blatant" as I had intimated. In fact, during our discussion of the issue[77] he made an important "qualification" to his original position as I had outlined it, suggesting that the contradiction was caused by his failure to adequately specify what he referred to as the "boundaries" of the frontier. He indicated that, in retrospect, he would now be more circumspect about stressing the general levelling effects of the frontier while he would maintain the descriptive and explanatory usefulness of the egalitarian proposition on the "real"—the furthest—frontiers of settlement.

While this is an important qualification—for by geographically circumscribing the levelling impact of the frontier to areas of brand new settlement he seems to rescue a more limited version of the frontier thesis—even this less general version of the proposition is problematic. Though Professor Clark is to be given credit for noting the important fact that some degree of levelling occurs at the fringes of "civilization," it is essential to remember that such equalization is unlikely to be any more than superficial and/or limited in nature and transitory in character. At the superficial level of face-to-face daily interaction amongst neighbours, and between bosses and workers, some "levelling" might well occur. Even here, though, the *descriptive adequacy* of the proposition is strained to its limit. Certainly, as I noted above, people who came to the frontier were very unequal in terms of the material resources (land, cash, implements, livestock) they owned. Thus they may have been made superficially more equal, but whatever degree of levelling occurred, it certainly did not make up on any grand scale for the differences in resources—tangible and otherwise—that differentiated, for example, wealthy United Empire Loyalists from impoverished Irish peasants or British army officers from *coureurs de bois*. Overall, in fact, as Innis (1956) and Watkins (1963), among others, noted as long as thirty years ago, the early, staple-extracting period of Canadian history described by Clark in his essays on pioneer Canada was a period during which large existing disparities of wealth and power between classes changed little.[78]

If the features of Canadian pioneer societies described by Clark and the others call the descriptive adequacy of the egalitarian proposition into doubt, its adequacy from an explanatory point of view seems little better. In the first place, the strict environmental determinist interpretation of the frontier thesis is clearly faulty. If it were true that the actual physical characteristics of the frontier could cause the development of certain kinds of institutions, then all geographically similar frontiers should generate similar institutions. As Stanley (1940) has pointed out, however, this has not been the case in Canada: the frontiers of New France and Upper Canada spawned very different social institutions despite their geographical similarities. The same holds true, as Clark himself suggested (see quotation above) for respective developments on the Canadian and American prairie frontiers. Cultural differences amongst pioneers had a tremendous impact on pioneer frontier social structures. Both Stanley and Dawson have pointed out that differences in the ethnic, economic and political backgrounds of the successive generations of immigrants that peopled the Canadian prairies produced quite different sets of economic and political institutions.[79]

This latter point suggests a second limitation of the explanatory utility of the frontier egalitarian proposition. That is, aside from the fact that pioneers were not equal in terms of their material resources, all of them certainly would have possessed a knowledge of the culturally specific standards of "social worth" characteristic of the societies from which they had come.[80] Since many of them came to Canada to escape poverty in their home countries, their choice of life venues bespoke a desire not for equality but for self-"betterment." Even more importantly, it must be remembered that—aside from the possible exception of subsistence farming—frontier economic activity was not isolated from the broader patterns of political and economic activity which went on beyond the frontier. The exploitation of the frontier was carried out either on the direct behalf of mercantile capitalists or, at least, within the constraints of political battles and market forces which had their nerve centres far beyond the geographical boundaries of the pioneer frontier. Staples were generally procured not for local use but for sale to interests operating within the protective confines of huge mercantile capitalist trade networks. Furthermore, right from the outset the state made a concerted attempt to establish some sort of *inegalitarianism*; setting up political, social, and economic elites on the frontier, access to which was for all intents and purposes quite closed. This closure was a function of the purpose the frontier was to serve; i.e., it was not developed "just" for economic purposes but for political and military purposes as well. Frontiers constituted "important outposts of Empire or nation."[81] This meant the necessary existence within the social structure not only of those with greater economic resources than others, but also those with different degrees of "administrative" influence; functionaries with positions in the Church, business, government and the military.[82] The existence of trading and military-political links between those in the hinterland and those in the colonial and imperial metropoles, then, prevented the development of any kind of real, long-lasting equality on the frontier.

Conclusion

The foregoing discussion suggests that social inequality was an important variable in Clark's analysis of the variety of pioneer frontier societies with which he dealt in his research. It also suggests that it is possible to construct from Clark's writings a comprehensive empirical and theoretical image of inequality. Insofar as a coherent image of inequality emerges, we may say that it is based on a liberal individualist model of social structure, in this case a variant of the frontier egalitarian proposition made popular by Frederick J. Turner. It would seem relatively easy to explain why Clark would not employ a form of sociological analysis which had the concept of class—again in the sense that a Marxist would use it—as an important part of its "working equipment." Canadian historians, who were Clark's most important reference group—at least until the 1960s—and Harold Innis, Clark's most influential mentor, were not persuaded that this sort of class analysis was appropriate for the study of Canadian society.[83]

It is not so easy to explain Clark's use of the frontier egalitarian proposition, however. The evidence above clearly indicates that frontier egalitarianism is adequate neither as a description nor as an explanation of the nature of social relations on the Canadian pioneer frontier. How do we then account for Clark's use of it? Certainly, it cannot be explained as a function of its general stature within the disciplines of history or sociology at the time for, as Careless's essay "Frontierism, Metropolitanism, and Canadian History" (1954) points out, Turner's frontier thesis was by the 1940s clearly into a phase of declining popularity within the discipline.

One explanation is that Clark, in arguing that the frontier was egalitarian, did not mean to suggest that it was a venue of "absolute" equality. Rather, he was implicitly comparing it to the *relatively* more rigid structures of inequality of condition and opportunity in metropolitan areas. There is, no doubt, some merit in this interpretation, for it accounts for his remark in the interview (cited above) that on the *real* frontier, the one furthest from established settlement, a considerable degree of levelling occurred as a consequence of the impact of the primitive living conditions there. That this is in fact what Clark intended is by no means clear, however, for as with A. R. M. Lower and other historians of the period, there is a strong hint in his work that the equalizing impact of the frontier *was* quite thorough—people *really were* made equal by the frontier. Recall on this point that in my interview with him Clark defended the idea that the frontier had a levelling impact. He modified the geographical boundaries within which it had an impact, but he maintained that within these more narrow boundaries it had a very strong levelling influence.

A second, somewhat related interpretation[84] is that we might think of Clark's concepts of the "frontier" and the "metropole" as *ideal types* at opposite ends of a continuum measuring degrees of equality of opportunity and condition. Clark could then be regarded as performing a sort of primitive multivariate analysis based on two "variables" (the two "ideal types") and his conclusions could be stated as follows. The effect of the frontier, *other things equal*, is to force people to rely on their individual resources and talents. The effect of the metropole, *other things equal*, is to structure people's relationships; most significantly along social class lines. As other things were *not* equal, however, this created problems for the typology. According to such an interpretation what appears as inconsistency on Clark's part was simply his attempt to trace through the conflicting effects of these two variables. This is a much more persuasive explanation, and it dovetails quite nicely with written comments made to me by Professor Clark in response to an early draft of this paper:

> I have been pondering further your criticism of the way I contradict myself in dealing with the problem of inequality. I do not really think there is a contradiction here. Running through all my writing is the elaboration of the theme of the play of opposing forces in the development of the Canadian

> society. *Sect and Church* [*sic*] represents the fullest elaboration of this theme.... The play of forces of order and disorder, the opposing forces of centralization and decentralization represent a further elaboration of the same theme. There were at work in the Canadian society forces making for increased social equality and forces in the very opposite direction.[85]

But this interpretation, too, has a drawback. While it may well be that the frontier had a tendency to force people to rely on their own individual resources and talents, this in no way meant that they would therefore be made particularly equal for, as I noted above, the evidence—including Clark's own—clearly indicates that people came to the frontier with highly unequal resources.

While each of the foregoing explanations undoubtedly contains some part of the explanation for Clark's adoption of the frontier thesis, it is my view that there is more to his stress on the levelling impact of the pioneer frontier than either of these interpretations would allow. It cannot simply be that he was convinced by the evidence that the frontier was an equal place, because his own evidence suggested that it wasn't equal. Nonetheless, it is true that he does seem to have been genuinely convinced that the frontier was an equal place and, in this regard, insofar as it can be argued that he believed in frontier egalitarianism, we can safely say he erred by overemphasizing its levelling impact. To account for this error in judgement, I think we would do well to consider Professor Clark's political views. For a classical liberal like Clark, the *idea* of the egalitarian frontier would have tremendous ideological appeal. Since he has noted more than once that he is morally disposed to accept the "rightness" for Canada of a liberal democratic, capitalist social order,[86] we might then surmise that this view had some impact on his sociological analysis of the frontier; specifically, that his description of life there came, in some measure, to take on the character of a *celebration* rather than "just" a *documentation*. If this is the case, it suggests, in turn, that at least part of the real message of the frontier egalitarian proposition in Clark's writings is *ideological*.[87] It might be viewed, that is, as an idealized version of what Clark would have *liked* to have been the case. It is my view that when looked at in this way, Clark's confusing decision to adopt the frontier egalitarian proposition becomes less so, since its use on grounds of descriptive and/or explanatory adequacy simply cannot be accounted for—even on the basis of his own evidence. To conclude, then, it is my view that Professor Clark's political preferences intruded into his analysis sufficiently that he tended to overemphasize the levelling impact of the frontier and to idealize—if not romanticize[88]—it as a place which epitomized the best periods of Canada's development. The prominence of liberal individualist themes in the rest of his work indicates that these values served him throughout his career as a model or a vision of the individualistic and entrepreneurial form that Canadian society should take.

Notes

This is a revised version of a paper presented at the Annual Meetings of the Canadian Sociology and Anthropology Association at the University of British Columbia, Vancouver, June, 1983. Please address all correspondence and offprint requests to Professor Richard Helmes-Hayes, Department of Sociology, University of Waterloo, Waterloo, Ontario, N2L 3G1.

1 This paper is based on chapter 6 of my unpublished Ph.D. dissertation, *Images of Inequality in Early Canadian Sociology, 1922-1965* (University of Toronto, 1985). Details of many of the points made here may be found in the dissertation. I would like to thank Professor S. D. Clark who not only read three early drafts of this manuscript, but also graciously granted two interviews to discuss his work. I would also like to thank Bernd Baldus, Robert Brym, William Carroll, Jim Curtis, David Niece, Michael Ornstein, Lorne Tepperman, Dennis William Magill and five anonymous reviewers from the *Canadian Journal of Sociology* for their thought-provoking and helpful comments. Finally, I would like to express my thanks to the Social Sciences and Humanities Research Council of Canada for the doctoral and post-doctoral fellowship funding that allowed me to carry out this work.

2 Hiller, Harry. (1982). *Society and Change: S. D. Clark and the Development of Canadian Sociology*. Toronto: University of Toronto Press. p. 41.

3 Harrison, Deborah. (1981). *The Limits of Liberalism: The Making of Canadian Sociology*. Montreal, Black Rose; Hiller, Harry, (1982). *Society and Change: S. D. Clark and the Development of Canadian Sociology*. Toronto: University of Toronto Press.

4 Other studies of Clark's work include Nock (1983; 1986), Campbell (1983) and Wilcox-Magill (1983). The present study seeks to examine Clark's views on inequality in much the same way that Hiller (1976-7) examines his views on religion.

5 The decision not to discuss Clark's view of inequality in modern Canadian society was made on the basis of space constraints. There is considerable continuity between his portrayal of the two periods, however (Helmes-Hayes, 1985, pp. 522-36, 562-8).

6 Leonard Marsh is an example of someone who did make inequality an explicit focus of extended analysis; most particularly in *Canadians In and Out of Work* (1940). See Horn (1986, p. 68), Helmes-Hayes (1986).

7 This sort of exercise is always problematic and there will be those who will disagree with my characterization of Clark's views. Readers may wish to know on this count that Professor Clark did not in any of our discussions quarrel with my summary of his position. He did, however, take exception to some of the elements of my critique (see my account of our interview below). For a discussion of technical and other problems associated with "constructing" Clark's image, see Helmes-Hayes (1985, pp. 501-5, 580-95).

8 Hiller (1982, p. 159) lists a number of people that might have been in some measure influenced by Clark, but says that none of them could be considered disciples.

9 In fact, it is a part of the "folk wisdom" of Canadian sociology that prior to the publication of *The Vertical Mosaic* in 1965 Canadian sociologists had basically ignored the study of social inequality (see, e.g., Vallee and Whyte, 1968; Jones, 1977).

10 American sociologists seem generally to have spent much more time examining the history of their discipline than Canadian sociologists have spent examining theirs. The extensive critical literature on the now-passé human ecology perspective of Robert Park and the Chicago School is an example. Other research (besides Page and Gordon) which has examined the history of the study of stratification in American sociology includes Hinkle and Boskoff (1957), MacRae (1953), and Pfautz (1953).

11 Harrison, Deborah. (1981). *The Limits of Liberalism: The Making of Canadian Sociology*. Montreal: Black Rose. p. 59.

12 In the same vein, Marsden (1983) has noted that Harrison did not provide an in-depth or accurate portrayal of what she meant by liberalism and/or do a very good job of outlining the specifically liberal elements of Clark's thought.

13 Helmes-Hayes, Richard. (1985). *Images of Inequality in Early Canadian Sociology, 1922-1965*. Unpublished Ph.D. dissertation, University of Toronto; (1986) Images of Inequality in pre-Porter Canadian Sociology. A paper presented at the annual meetings of the Ontario Anthropology and Sociology Association. Wilfrid Laurier University, Waterloo (October).

14 On the two latter points, see Helmes-Hayes (1985, pp. 730-53).

15 See Careless, (1954). Frontierism, Metropolitanism and Canadian History. *Canadian Historical Review*, 35(1), pp. 1-21.

16 One feature which differentiates Clark's analysis of frontier society from more recent studies of the period is his limited discussion of the role and status of women in these societies (see Helmes-Hayes, 1985, pp. 762-7).

17 Clark, S.D. (1968). *The Developing Canadian Community*. Toronto: University of Toronto Press. pp. 32-3.

18 Ibid. p. 35.

19 Loc. Cit.

20 Other examples of a similar type of usage of the term class may be found throughout Clark's work. For a summary in tabular form of the frequency and range of the groups to which Clark applied the term "class," see Helmes-Hayes (1985, pp. 508-12, Tables VI: 1-VI: 5).

21 Clark, S.D. (1968). *The Developing Canadian Community*. Toronto: University of Toronto Press. p. 19.

22 Ibid. p. 17.

23 Ibid. pp. 121,125.

24 Ibid. p. 165; see Helmes-Hayes, (1985). *Images of Inequality in Early Canadian Sociology, 1922-1965*. Unpublished Ph.D. dissertation, University of Toronto. pp. 508-12, Tables, V:1-V:5

25 Hiller, Harry. (1982). *Society and Change: S. D. Clark and the Development of Canadian Sociology*. Toronto: University of Toronto Press. p. 156.

26 Clark, S.D. (1968). *The Developing Canadian Community*. Toronto: University of Toronto Press. p. 20-112.

27 These five societies are: "The Farming-Fur Trade Society of New France" (20-40), "The Rural Village Society of the Maritimes" (41-62), "The Backwoods Society of Upper Canada" (63-80), "The Gold Rush Society of British Columbia and the Yukon" (81-98), and "The Prairie Wheat-Farming Frontier and the New Industrial City" (99-112). These articles were scrutinized by a simple form of "content analysis"; i.e., by going through each article and noting the number of times a particular "occupation" or "attribute of inequality" was mentioned (see Helmes-Hayes, 1985, pp. 505-12, 597 n.7, 8).

28 The centrality of *occupation* to the entire fabric of frontier society is emphasized by Clark elsewhere. "The distinctiveness of these frontier communities [Canadian and American] was related more to their economic activity than to their national location. 'What emerged were not two cultures—an American and a Canadian culture—but several cultures which could be described by the basic occupation of the population'"(Hiller, 1982, p. 96, citing Clark, 1944, p. 133).

29 Clark, S.D. (1968). *The Developing Canadian Community*. Toronto: University of Toronto Press. pp. 20-40.

30 Helmes-Hayes, Richard. (1985). *Images of Inequality in early Canadian Sociology, 1922-1965*. Unpublished Ph.D. dissertation, University of Toronto, pp. 505-12.
31 Clark, S.D. (1968). *The Developing Canadian Community*. Toronto: University of Toronto Press. pp. 115-30.
32 Ibid. pp. 148-49.
33 Ibid. pp. 149-50.
34 See, e.g., Clark, S.D. (1968). *The Developing Canadian Community*. Toronto: University of Toronto Press. pp. 120-1; see also Berger, C. (1976). *The Writing of Canadian History: Aspects of English-Canadian Historical Writing: 1900 to 1970*. Toronto: Oxford University Press. p. 165; Hiller, Harry. (1982). *Society and Change: S. D. Clark and the Development of Canadian Sociology*. Toronto: University of Toronto Press. pp. 79-80.
35 Hiller notes on this account that *Church and Sect* was an early analysis of "the effects of social mobility or social class on the movement from sect to church or the relationship between sectarianism and status improvement on conditions of social organization" (1982, p. 85).
36 Clark, S.D. (1976). *Canadian Society in Historical Perspective*. Toronto: McGraw-Hill Ryerson. p.165.
37 Clark, S.D. (1959). *Movement of Political Protest in Canada, 1640-1840*. Toronto: University of Toronto Press, pp. 13-30.
38 See Harrison, Deborah. (1981). *The Limits of Liberalism: The Making of Canadian Sociology*. Montreal: Black Rose. pp. 78, 113.
39 Ibid. p. 59.
40 Turner's article was first published in the American Historical Association *Annual Report for 1893* (Washington, 1894, pp. 199-227).
41 The influence of Innis, Morton, Lower, Dawson, and Hughes is noted in Clark (1976: 16-7, 133- 44 *passim*).
42 Berger, Carl. (1976). *The Writing of Canadian History: Aspects of English-Canadian Historical Writing: 1900 to 1970*. Toronto: Oxford University Press. p.164.
43 Ibid. p. 6.
44 Clark has argued that he did not use a frontier determinist sort of argument and that, if anything, he tended to stress the impact of metropolitan forces in his analyses. This view is certainly open to debate with relation to his overall perspective. As the analysis below points out, however, there can be little doubt that a strong measure of frontier determinism characterized his explanation of social inequality (1976, pp. 6, 54).
45 See Hiller, Harry. (1982). *Society and Change: S. D. Clark and the Development of Canadian Sociology*. Toronto: University of Toronto Press. p. 67; Magill,

Dennis William. (1983). Paradigms and Social Science in English Canada. In J. P. Grayson, (Ed.), *Introduction to Sociology: An Alternate Approach*, pp. 1-34. Toronto: Gage. p. 29.

46 Hiller, Harry. (1982). *Society and Change: S. D. Clark and the Development of Canadian Sociology*. Toronto: University of Toronto Press. p. 70.

47 Clark's debt to both Turner and Lower on this score is obvious. Berger summarizes Turner's position (1976, p. 118). Clark's conception of the frontier as more than just a "place" is rooted in Turner's own understanding of the term.

48 Clark, S.D. (1968). *The Developing Canadian Community*. Toronto: University of Toronto Press. p. 78.

49 Clark, S.D. (1976). *Canadian Society in Historical Perspective*. Toronto: McGraw-Hill Ryerson. p. 56.

50 His position *vis-à-vis* modern Canadian society is based on a similar sort of logic. According to Clark, the expansion of industry sparked by American investment in the Canadian economy created a much larger opportunity structure than had existed prior to World War II. This, then, was a new "frontier." The traditional barriers to the achievement of middle-class status were broken down and the establishment of a more open educational system, particularly at the university level, created the basis for a new meritocratic and technocratic power structure (1968, pp. 253-66; also 1976, pp. 35-51).

51 Clark, S.D. (1968). *The Developing Canadian Community*. Toronto: University of Toronto Press. p. 193.

52 Ibid. p. 65.

53 Ibid. p. 193; see also Hiller, Harry. (1982). p. 96.

54 Nock (1983) suggests that we should not be too quick to see Clark as a lifelong adherent to the values of classical liberalism. He argues that Clark's earliest works were strongly influenced by socialist principles.

55 Harrison, Deborah. (1981). *The Limits of Liberalism: The Making of Canadian Sociology*. Montreal: Black Rose, p. 48.

56 Clark's statements on this score are not always clear cut. Compare his remarks (1968: 152-3) with (1968: 8).

57 Clark, S.D. (1968). *The Developing Canadian Community*. Toronto: University of Toronto Press. p. 65.

58 Clark uses the same explanatory mechanism to account for certain developments in modern "frontier" areas. Part of his "culture of poverty" explanation for persistent rural poverty (and the phenomenon of the "new urban poor" relies on personality-type variables—complacency, lack of initiative, etc. (Clark, 1978).

59 On "ethical egoism" and other aspects of individualism, see Lukes (1973).

60 Clark, S.D. (1968). *The Developing Canadian Community*. Toronto: University of Toronto Press, p. 11.

61 Despite his protestations to the contrary, Clark's view of society is very similar to Parsons'. His essays in the concluding section of *The Developing Canadian Community* (1968, pp. 269-313) and the introduction to *Canadian Society in Historical Perspective* (1976, pp. 1-19) make this clear. Hiller, too, has noted the "affinities" between the work of Parsons and Clark (1982, pp. 72-3).

62 Clark, S.D. (1968). *The Developing Canadian Community*. Toronto: University of Toronto Press. p. 48.

63 Ibid. p. 226; see Harrison, Deborah. (1981). *The Limits of Liberalism: The Making of Canadian Sociology*. Montreal: Black Rose. p. 77.

64 Clark, S.D. (1968). *The Developing Canadian Community*. Toronto: University of Toronto Press. p. 167.

65 Ibid: 227; see Harrison, Deborah. (1981). *The Limits of Liberalism: The Making of Canadian Sociology*. Montreal: Black Rose. p. 101.

66 Clark, S.D. (1968). *The Developing Canadian Community*. Toronto: University of Toronto Press. p. 172.

67 Ibid: 214; cf. 163.

68 Chodos, R. (1973). *The CPR: A Century of Corporate Welfare*. Toronto: Lorimer. p.1-26; Myers, (1975). *A History of Canadian Wealth*. Vol. 1. Toronto: Lorimer. pp. 150-300 *passim.*

69 Rodwell, L. (1974). Settling in the West. In M. Cross, (Ed.) *The Workingman in the Nineteenth Century*, pp. 37-43. Toronto: Oxford.

70 Dawson, Carl (1934). *The Settlement of the Peace River Country: A Study of a Pioneer Area*. Toronto: Macmillan.; (1936). *Group Settlement: Ethnic Communities in Western Canada*. Toronto: Macmillan.; Dawson, Carl and Younge, E.R. (1940). *Pioneering in the Prairie Provinces: The Social Side of the Settlement Process*. Toronto: Macmillan.

71 For a discussion of Dawson's work that focuses on his treatment of themes of inequality, see Helmes-Hayes (1985, pp. 290-413).

72 Clement, Wallace. (1975). *The Canadian Corporate Elite: An Analysis of Economic Power*. Toronto: McClelland and Stewart. pp. 44-96.

73 Ibid. pp. 44-71.

74 Cross, Michael. (1973). *The Workingman in the Nineteenth Century*. Toronto: University of Toronto Press, pp. 1-7.

75 Dubuc, Alfred. (1974) Problems in the study of social stratification of the Canadian society from 1760 to 1840. In M. Horn and R. Sabourin, (Eds.), *Studies in Canadian Social History*, pp. 123-39. Toronto: McClelland and Stewart.

76 The interview was held in Professor Clark's office on November 27, 1984.

77 The issue was also mentioned in two brief notes written to me by Professor Clark in late March and early April of 1985.

78 See Harrison, Deborah. (1981). *The Limits of Liberalism: The Making of Canadian Sociology*. Montreal: Black Rose. p. 72.

79 Stanley, G. (1940). Western Canada and the frontier thesis. *Canadian Historical Association Report*, pp. 105-14; Dawson, Carl. (1936). *Group Settlement: Ethnic Communities in Western Canada*. Toronto: Macmillan; Dawson and Younge. (1940). *Pioneering in the Prairie Provinces: The Social Side of the Settlement Process*. Toronto: Macmillan.

80 See e.g. Cross, Michael. (1973). *The Workingman in the Nineteenth Century*. Toronto: University of Toronto Press. pp. 1-11.

81 Clark, S.D. (1968). *The Developing Canadian Community*. Toronto: University of Toronto Press. p. 189.

82 Ibid. p. 66.

83 For a discussion of the general attitude of early Canadian historians toward class analysis, see Mealing's essay, The concept of social class and the interpretation of Canadian history (1965, *Canadian Historical Review* 46(3): 201-18.). S. B. Ryerson, among others, has noted Innis's disaffection, until very late in his career at least, with Marx's variety of class analysis (1975. "Introduction." In *A History of Canadian Wealth* Vol. 1 by Gustavus Myers. Toronto, Lorimer, pp. viii). Clark notes in this regard that "Innis never felt called upon to prove Marx right or wrong" (1976 *Canadian Society in Historical Perspective*. Toronto: McGraw-Hill Ryerson, p. 144).

84 I would like to thank one of the *Canadian Journal of Sociology's* anonymous reviewers for this interpretation.

85 This is from Professor Clark's note to me dated 11 April 1985.

86 Clark explicitly mentions his liberal philosophical preferences in the essay "The development of the social sciences in Canada and the issue of national autonomy" (1980, p. 12). When I asked Professor Clark in our interview (27 November 1984) whether it was fair to characterize him as a classical rather than welfare-state liberal, he said that it was.

87 The tendency to interpret historical developments in a way which celebrates particular values is portrayed nicely in Careless's 1954 article where he argues that Canadian historiography has passed through several phases, each of which reflected and celebrated a particular ideological view of Canadian historical development.

88 Clark's tendency to "romanticize" the frontier is not entirely uniform. While he portrayed the frontier — particularly the *open* frontier — as a source of economic progress and democratization, he also saw it as in some measure both culturally backward and as a venue where questionable social and economic behaviour took place. "In a cultural sense," he argued, "the frontier was not a rich and progressive but a poor and retarded society" (1968: 218). Furthermore, because of the crass materialism of the capitalist frontier, it "tended to become a society of social and economic misfits" (1968: 153).

Bibliography

Berger, C.

(1976). *The Writing of Canadian History: Aspects of English-Canadian Historical Writing: 1900 to 1970*. Toronto: Oxford.

Burt, A. L.

(1940). The Frontier in the History of New France. *Canadian Historical Association Report*, pp. 93-9.

Campbell, D.

(1983). S. D. Clark: The dean of Canadian sociology. In D. Campbell, (Ed.), *Beginnings: Essays on the History of Canadian Sociology*. pp. 98-138. Port Credit: The Scribbler's Press.

Careless. J. M. S.

(1954). Frontierism, metropolitanism and Canadian history. *Canadian Historical Review*, 35(1), pp. 1-21.

Chodos, R.

(1973). *The CPR: A Century of Corporate Welfare*. Toronto: Lorimer.

Clement, W.

(1975). *The Canadian Corporate Elite: An Analysis of Economic Power*. Toronto: McClelland and Stewart.

Clark, S. D.

(1939). *The Canadian Manufacturers' Association: A Study in Collective Bargaining and Political Pressure*. Toronto: University of Toronto Press.

(1942). *The Social Development of Canada*. Toronto: University of Toronto Press.

(1944). The social development of Canada and the American continental system. *Culture*, 5, pp. 132-3.

(1948). *Church and Sect in Canada*. Toronto: University of Toronto Press.

(1959). *Movements of Political Protest in Canada, 1640-1840*. Toronto: University of Toronto Press.

(1966). *The Suburban Society*. Toronto: University of Toronto Press.

(1968). *The Developing Canadian Community*. Toronto: University of Toronto Press.

(1976). *Canadian Society in Historical Perspective*. Toronto: McGraw-Hill Ryerson.

(1978). *The New Urban Poor*. Toronto: McGraw-Hill Ryerson.

(1979). The changing image of sociology in English-speaking Canada. *Canadian Journal of Sociology*, 4(4), pp. 393-403.

(1980). Development of social sciences in Canada and the issue of national autonomy. Annual Inaugural Lecture No. 5. The University of

Edinburgh Centre of Canadian Studies. University of Edinburgh, Scotland.

(1984). Personal interview with Richard C. Helmes-Hayes. November 27.

(1985). Personal correspondence of the author with S. D. Clark. n.d. (late March): Personal correspondence of the author with S. D. Clark, April 11.

Cross, M., Ed.

(1973). *The Workingman in the Nineteenth Century*. Toronto: University of Toronto Press.

Dawson, C. A.

(1934). *The Settlement of the Peace River Country: A Study of a Pioneer Area*. Toronto: Macmillan.

(1936). *Group Settlement: Ethnic Communities in Western Canada*. Toronto: Macmillan.

Dawson, C. and E. R. Younge

(1940). *Pioneering in the Prairie Provinces: The Social Side of the Settlement Process*. Toronto: Macmillan.

Dubuc, A.

(1974). Problems in the study of social stratification of the Canadian society from 1760 to 1840. In M. Horn and R. Sabourin (Eds.), *Studies in Canadian Social History*. Toronto: McClelland and Stewart. pp. 123-39.

Gagan, D. and H. Mays

(1974). Historical demography and Canadian social history: Families and land in Peel County, Ontario. In M. Horn and R. Sabourin (Eds.), *Studies in Canadian Social History*. Toronto: McClelland and Stewart. pp. 96-115.

Gordon, M.

(1958). *Social Class in American Sociology*. Durham: Duke University Press.

Harrison, D.

(1981). *The Limits of Liberalism: The Making of Canadian Sociology*. Montreal: Black Rose.

(1983). The limits of Liberalism in Canadian sociology: Some notes on S. D. Clark. *Canadian Review of Sociology and Anthropology* 20(2), pp. 150-66.

Helmes-Hayes, R.

(1985). *Images of Inequality in Early Canadian Sociology, 1922-1965*. Unpublished Ph.D. dissertation, University of Toronto.

(1986). Images of inequality in pre-Porter Canadian sociology. A paper presented at the annual meetings of the Ontario Anthropology and Sociology Association. Wilfrid Laurier University, Waterloo (October).

Hiller, H.

(1976-77). The contribution of S. D. Clark to the sociology of Canadian religion. *Studies in Religion*, 6(4), pp. 415-27.

(1980). Paradigmatic shifts, indigenization and the development of sociology in Canada. *Journal of the History of the Behavioural Sciences*, 16, pp. 263-74.

(1980-1). Research biography and disciplinary development: S. D. Clark and Canadian sociology. *Journal of the History of Sociology*, 3(1), pp. 67-86.

(1982). *Society and Change: S. D. Clark and the Development of Canadian Sociology*. Toronto: University of Toronto Press.

Hinkle, R. and A. Boskoff

(1957). Social stratification in perspective. In H. Becker and A. Boskoff, Eds., *Modern Sociological Theory: In Continuity and Change*. New York: Holt, Rinehart and Winston. pp. 368-95.

Horn, M.

(1986). Leonard Marsh and his ideas. 1967-1982: Some personal recollections. *Journal of Canadian Studies*, 21(2), pp. 67-76.

Horn, M. and R. Sabourin, Eds.

(1974). *Studies in Canadian Social History*. Toronto: McClelland and Stewart.

Innis. H.

(1956). *The Fur Trade in Canada: An Introduction to Canadian Economic History*. Toronto: University of Toronto Press.

Jones. F. E.

(1977). Current sociological research in Canada: Views of a journal editor. *Journal of the History of the Behavioural Sciences*, 13, pp. 160-72.

Lower. A. R. M.

(1930). The origins of democracy in Canada. *Canadian Historical Association Report*, pp. 65-70.

(1946). *Colony to Nation: A History of Canada*. Toronto: Longmans, Green.

Lukes, S.

(1973). *Individualism*. Oxford: Basil Blackwell.

MacRae. D. G.

(1953-4). Social stratification: A trend report. *Current Sociology* 2(1), pp. 7-33.

Magill, Wilcox D.

(1983). Paradigms and social science in English Canada. In J. P. Grayson, (Ed.), *Introduction to Sociology: An Alternate Approach*. Toronto: Gage. pp. 1-34.

Marsden, L.
(1983). The importance of S. D. Clark. *Canadian Forum*, 63, pp. 26-9.

Marsh, L.
(1940). *Canadians In and Out of Work: A Survey of Economic Classes and Their Relation to the Labour Market*. Montreal: Oxford.

Mealing, S.
(1965). The concept of social class and the interpretation of Canadian history. *Canadian Historical Review*, 46(3), pp. 201-18.

Moodie, S.
(1974). The leveling principle. In M. Cross, Ed., *The Workingman in the Nineteenth Century*. Toronto: Oxford. pp. 138-41.

Morton. A. S.
(1930). *History of Prairie Settlement*. Toronto: Macmillan.

Myers. G.
(1975). *A History of Canadian Wealth*. Vol. 1. Toronto: Lorimer.

Nock, D.
(1983). S. D. Clark in the context of Canadian sociology. *Canadian Journal of Sociology*, 8(1), pp. 79-97.
(1986). 'Crushing the power of finance': The socialist prairie roots of S. D. Clark. *British Journal of Canadian Studies*, 1(1), pp. 86-108.

Page, C.
(1969). *Class and American Sociology: From Ward to Ross*. New York: Schocken.

Pentland, H.C.
(1981). *Labour and Capital in Canada 1650-1850*. P. Phillips (Ed.), Toronto: Lorimer.

Pfautz. H. P.
(1953). The current literature on social stratification: Critique and bibliography. *American Journal of Sociology*, 57, pp. 391-418.

Porter, J.
(1965). *The Vertical Mosaic: An Analysis of Class and Power in Canada*. Toronto: University of Toronto Press.

Rodwell, L
(1974). Settling in the West. In M. Cross (Ed.), *The Workingman in the Nineteenth Century*. Toronto: Oxford. pp. 37-43.

Ryerson. S. B.
(1975). Introduction. In *A History of Canadian Wealth* Vol. 1 (by Gustavus Myers), pp. viii-xxx. Toronto: Lorimer.

Sage, W. N.
(1928). Some aspects of the frontier in Canadian history. *Canadian Historical Association Report,* pp. 62-7.

Shore, M.
(1987). *The Science of Social Redemption: McGill, the Chicago School and the Origins of Social Research in Canada.* Toronto: University of Toronto Press.

Stanley, G.
(1940). Western Canada and the frontier thesis. *Canadian Historical Association Report*, pp. 105-14.

Turner, J.
(1961). The significance of the frontier in American history. In R. A. Billington. (Ed.), *Frontier and Section: Selected Essays of Frederick Jackson Turner*. Englewood Cliffs. New Jersey: Prentice-Hall. pp. 37-62.

Vallee, F. and D. Whyte
(1968). Canadian society: Trends and perspectives. In B. Blishen, F. Jones, K. Naegele, J. Porter, (Eds.), *Canadian Society: Sociological Perspectives*, 3rd edition. Toronto: Macmillan. pp. 849-52.

Zaslow. M.
(1948). The frontier hypothesis in recent historiography. *Canadian Historical Review*, 29(2), pp. 153-67.

Chapter Eight

THE STUDY OF CANADIAN SOCIETY

S.D. Clark

When I undertook in 1938 to offer a course on Canadian society I had a very simple idea in mind: that the student of sociology should know something about the society in which he lived, as it had developed in the past as well as what it was presently like. The major concern in sociology as it had developed in the United States had been to demonstrate that society could be studied scientifically. The emphasis as a consequence had been upon the examination of small units as they existed in the present. Before 1938 the major theoretical framework guiding work in sociology had been human ecology. After 1938, under the lead of Talcott Parsons, functional theory took over as the dominant theoretical perspective of sociology.

In the effort to reach back into an examination of the Canadian society of the past, there appeared initially to be involved no crucial break with prevailing sociological theory, particularly that of structural-functionalism. The rural society of New France, the village society of Nova Scotia, the backwoods society of Upper Canada, the gold-mining society of the Klondike, and the city of the past or present could be examined in structural-functional terms. Indeed, it was just such an examination of the Klondike gold-mining society that was undertaken by my fourth-year honour students as a term

---

Clark, S.D. (1979). Originally printed as Introduction: The Study of Canadian Society. From *Canadian Society in Historical Perspective*. Toronto: McGraw-Hill Ryerson. pp. 1-19. Reprinted with permission from the author.

assignment in 1938-39, however little they thought of it in structural-functional terms. One could talk about such a society as a "boundary-maintaining social system".

What quickly became apparent, however, even in the examination of such a time-limited and boundary-limited society as that of the Klondike, was that the society at one point was a very different society from what it was at another point in time. The gold rush to the Klondike began in 1897. It reached its peak in 1898. By 1900 there had come a "settling down" of the society. What was evident was that very great changes had taken place in these three short years. Descriptions of Dawson City or of life out on the creeks contained in books written by travelers or in reports of the Mounted Police differed markedly as between the winter of 1898-99 and that of 1899-1900. People were really not talking about the same society in 1898 and 1900.

If that divergence was true of the Klondike gold-mining society, it was even more true of a society like that of the backwoods of Upper Canada. Like the Klondike gold-mining society, the backwoods society of Upper Canada could be analyzed in structural-functional terms. There did exist in Upper Canada in the early nineteenth century a society with a distinctive character which could be given the title of backwoods. However, one could not proceed very far in the analysis of this society without becoming aware of the great changes which had taken place in it over the years. How the society was described depended very much upon what particular areas were being looked at and at what time. There was a vast difference between the rural Upper-Canadian society of, say, 1812 and 1845; the character of these differences and how they came about appeared as important to understand as the way in which the society was structured in functional terms.

The further one probed into the Canadian society of the past, therefore, the more one was compelled to look at this society in terms not of how it was structured, but of how it was undergoing change. Concepts like boundary-maintenance, equilibrium, consensus, and integration (upon which structural-functional theory depended so heavily) appeared to have no meaning when society was thus viewed in relation to the problem of change. The backwoods society of Upper Canada in 1820, for instance, could be described as a boundary-maintaining social system in a state of equilibrium, but so it could in 1840 or in any year between 1820 and 1840. Functional theory appeared useful only where the interest was in describing the structure of a particular society without regard to how it had changed over time. Where the interest was in how it had changed, what seemed to be required was a very different framework of analysis.

In the effort to look at Canadian society in terms of how it had changed over the years, the temptation was strong to fall back upon a nineteenth century philosophy of history approach seeking outside of society whether in the dictates of governments, the demands of a geographical environment, or the dialectic of a class war developing out of an economic mode of production a single "law" or force which determined the changing structure of a society. Much, indeed, that had happened to Canadian society over the years, it seemed, could be accounted for in Griffith Taylor style by the demands made upon the Canadian people by the changing geographical environment they encountered in their march across the continent. Even more convincing appeared the explanation of the changing structure of the society in terms of the demands made upon it by a profit-motivated capitalist system of production.

Yet clearly a resort to an explanation of social change in terms of any such determining law or force involved a step backwards in sociological analysis. The great move forward which came with the development of sociology in this century had been the establishment of the autonomy of the social universe and thus the freeing of the discipline from a dead-end deterministic position. The sociologist could come now to speak of "laws", but they were in Pareto fashion social laws, discoverable only within society itself. They had about them no determining quality.

Human ecology, as developed by the so-called Chicago school of sociology, failed to wholly rid itself of a deterministic theoretical framework. Human ecologists talked about "natural" history, "natural" areas, and in many of their writings there was the strong suggestion that the ecological order determined the social order.

It was the accomplishment of functional theory to very largely rid sociology of a reliance upon a single outside determining force as an explanation of what happened within a society. Functional theory sought to explain society by an examination of those processes of social organization at work within it: how for instance, a people's religious beliefs could only be understood in relation to their economic behaviour or their form of family life, or how something happening outside the society became related to what was happening within the society. Charges that the theory was merely descriptive of society have come very largely from those sociologists still not prepared to give up the simplistic notion that somewhere out beyond society was to be found the law, force, or determining agent which offered the explanation for all which happened within it. Such has been the stance of the Marxist sociologist. Any effort to explain society by the examination of forces operating within the society has assumed, in the view of such critics, a descriptive rather than explanatory character.

Functional theory does offer an explanation of society. As it has been elaborated and employed, however, the explanation that is offered for the most part is one of a society in a state of order rather than in a state of change. Here, of course, is the place to start. One cannot understand how a structure of social relationships changes without first examining how it is ordered and held together. The failing of functional theory has come from its not being developed as a theory of change as well as of order. By the heavy stress upon order, by talk of equilibrium, consensus, integration, the theory has appeared to offer a defence for things as they are, to enshroud itself in a philosophy of conservatism.

The bias of functional theory develops out of its historical origin. It began as a theory of social anthropology. The major task of the social anthropologist was to make sense out of primitive society. Viewed from the perspective of modern western society, much that went on in primitive society, in forms of economic behaviour, religious practices, and rules of family conduct appeared to lie beyond the reach of rational explanation. It was only when what went on came to be viewed from within the primitive society itself, in terms of the society as a system of interdependent relationships, that it became explainable.

The primitive society lent itself readily to analysis in functional terms. Primitive society had no history, in the sense that it had no accumulation of historical records. The social anthropologist, therefore, had no urge to engage in an enquiry about the past development of the society, except only what could be learned from archeological remains or the tales of village elders. Nor did he find himself tripping over facets of the society that could only be understood by viewing it simply as part of a larger society. Primitive society not only had no past, it had few connections with the outside world. Because of its seemingly unchanging character and its very isolation, it could be conceived as a boundary-maintaining social system.

One other factor relating to the primitive society lent support to functional theory and was instrumental in hardening its conservative bias. The invasion of the primitive society by the Western World had been headed up by the colonial administrator, the missionary, and various do-gooders. In the effort to modernize the society, to Christianize, or in other ways to change the people, much damage was done to the culture by the failure to take account of the fact that no part of a society could be changed without the change affecting the whole society. Functional theory offered itself as a powerful tool in arguing the case for non-interference in the way of life of primitive peoples. In putting forward such a case, social anthropology was forced almost inevitably into a position of defending the status quo. Change came almost to be a dirty word in the language of the social anthropologist.

It may appear strange that a theory directed to an emphasis upon order and non-change should have become so widely accepted by sociology in a country which for long had been thought of as one undergoing rapid change. In an important respect, however, American society, like primitive society, lent itself to analysis in functional terms. The American social scientist, whether an economist, political scientist, or sociologist, at least up until the 1960s could take the existence of his society for granted. The task of explaining how it had come into being could be left to the historian. The major concern of the social scientist was with how it worked. In the effort to examine the society as a working social, economic, and political system, whether in macro or in micro terms, what appeared to require analysis were the functional relationships of the various parts of the system to the whole.

Transposed to Canada with its non-historical approach, however, functional theory failed to guide sociology to the study of what were the most urgent problems of the Canadian society.

The Canadian social scientist cannot take the existence of his society for granted. There is nothing about the society that can be fully understood except in relation to how the society developed, how its very survival as a society, flanked as it was by the powerful republic to the south, remained problematic at least until very recent times. In a word, Canadian society can be understood only if viewed within an historical perspective.

It was within such an historical perspective that the late H. A. Innis sought to explain the economic structure of the country. Whatever the limits of his "staples approach", what Innis succeeded in doing was to pull Canadian economics away from a functional, non-historical theoretical perspective which had grown out of the concerns of developed economies, such as those of Britain and the United States.

It was an effort to look at the Canadian society within a similar historical perspective which guided my first attempts to study it. A theoretical framework was required to organize the facts about the development of the society; otherwise, one would have been forced to fall back upon a simple social historical approach, organizing facts in terms of the beginning of things, such as the first family to become established in New France, the first Congregational church in Liverpool, Nova Scotia, the first mental hospital in Toronto, the first farmers' organization in Alberta. It was in the search for a theoretically meaningful way of organizing the facts in the analysis of the Canadian society that led to my focussing on "frontier" developments.

What seemed apparent, in looking at the Canadian society over the whole course of its development, were the long intervals when nothing much of importance happened and then there occurred a sudden, widespread upsetting of the established order and a new, different course of development. It was what was happening to the Canadian society in such areas of disturbance and rapid change that commanded my attention in the early efforts to examine its development in the past: the rural society of New France with the breakdown of the monopoly control of the fur trade and the opening of the interior to individual traders from the colony, the village society of Nova Scotia with the American War of Independence and the settlement of Loyalist refugees in the colony, Upper Canada with overseas immigration and the pushing of settlement into the backwoods, British Columbia and the Klondike during the times of the gold rushes, the city of central Canada with the opening of the western market for manufactured products and the concentration of industry in large urban centres, the western Prairies during the period of rapid settlement, the suburbs of the 1950s with the mass movement of population out of the city into the surrounding countryside.

The examination of developments in such areas of disturbance and rapid change emphasized the way in which established forms of social organization and patterns of behaviour and thought broke down and new forms and patterns took their place. It also, however, emphasized the way in which powerful vested interests of the established order (the Government, Church, the social class system, forms of clan organization, and such) succeeded in arresting certain kinds of changes and maintaining the status quo. Thus was introduced the distinction between the "open" and "closed" frontier. Examination of developments in the Canadian society in such terms made possible not only the contrast between areas where outside restraining forces remained strong as opposed to areas where they did not (the sect type of farm settlement, for instance, in contrast with the farm settlement established by individual families acting on their own), but also made possible the contrast between developments in the Canadian and American societies where, in the development of the Canadian society, the frontier had less of an open character.

Unfortunately, the use of the term "frontier" as a way of depicting the character of these forces or happenings which triggered or set off new or different courses of development in the Canadian society led to the charge that I was a frontier determinist, particularly by those social scientists and historians wedded to their own favoured brand of determinism. There was no implication in the use of the term that the frontier determined anything that happened to the society. The focussing on frontier development represented only an effort to seize on certain theoretically meaningful points of departure in examining the character of change of the Canadian society.

Without such points of departure no analysis of change is possible unless one is prepared to settle for a concept of change as ubiquitous, all things changing at all times. Thus, for instance, in the analysis of the society of a small town it is evident that every time a new by-law is passed by the town council, a new street opened up, or even a new family settles in the community, the town changes. But how to distinguish between such changes and those which bring about a complete transformation of the town, it being made, for instance, into an industrial city or so abandoned by its residents that it comes to assume a ghost character?

The distinction between one kind of change and another is not something that is given. It is the problem set for analysis which determines what changes are considered significant and what not. Thus, for instance, in Simmel fashion one might fasten on the consequences for the society of a small town of the settlement in it of a new family or, to move in completely the opposite direction, one might in S. M. Lipset fashion fasten on the manner in which the society of the town did not change even when it became transformed into an industrial city.

In theoretical terms, there can be no quarrel with Lipset's *First New Nation* where the interest was in showing how certain values of the American society had persisted from the time of the War of Independence to the present. Viewed in such a perspective, American society had not changed. If viewed in a still broader perspective, however, neither had human society changed from the day of the cave man or tree dweller to the day of modern man. Continuity is a fact of human society and the Parsonian model of a social system, where the emphasis is upon the persistence of certain values described as basic, makes possible its examination. Here what is talked about is change within the system, change that can be described in terms of stresses and strains, the disturbance of equilibrium, the vested interests of the social system and the re-assertion of its basic values, and, finally, the restoration of equilibrium.

Where, however, the interest shifts from an examination of the way in which a society persists over time to the way in which it changes and becomes a different kind of society, one can no longer talk about change within the system. What now comes to be talked about is change of the system; otherwise, there are no means of distinguishing between those changes which bring about the establishment of a different kind of society from those changes which do not. In a word, one has to begin to work now with more than one model of the social system or society.

What particular models are employed depends upon what changes in the society are undergoing examination. Thus, if the interest was in the way the society of New France had changed in the period 1650-1700, one would begin with an examination of this society as it had become established before 1650, then proceed to examine the changes that brought about the establishment of a very different kind of society in 1700. If, however, the interest was in the way the society of French Canada had become transformed in the years since the Second World War—"the quiet revolution"—then all that had happened in the society before that time, reaching back even beyond 1700, would be examined in relationship to the type of society which had become established by the time of the war—"the old order" of French Canada—and it would be changes which have taken place in the society since that time that would demand attention.

An examination of change, thus, involves beginning with a model or picture of the society as it was before the changes being examined occurred. What becomes constructed initially is a Parsonian type of model of a society or social system described as being in a state of equilibrium. Here the interest is in showing what the society was like before it was made into a different kind of society. Any change that had occurred within the society as such is looked at in relationship to the way in which the society had become structured or ordered. Thus, in the example of the small town, the passing of a new by-law by the town council or the opening up of a new street would not be considered as having altered the basic character of the society as that of a small town, nor would the delinquent behaviour of a gang of teenagers across the tracks, nor some shady dealing in real estate on the part of the town councillors. Changes or forms of deviant behaviour of such a sort would be considered "normal" to a small town society.

In the employment of such a model of a society one could talk about boundary maintenance, integration, basic values, consensus, vested interests, indeed even of a basic personality type. It would be those features of the society giving to it a distinctive character which would be seized upon in the determination of its boundaries, whether the society was that of a small town or a larger geographical unit such as the backwoods of Upper Canada, say in 1820, or of French Canada, say in 1939. Thus, one could describe the society so boundary-limited in terms of its economic order, its ecological structure, its social stratification system, its institutional order, its primary group structure, its system of values.

What becomes important to recognize in the employment of any such model as this is that talk about basic values, or basic anything, has meaning only in relationship to the way the society was defined. It is the effort to find within a social system a determining agent that has led to much of the confusion in the development of a theoretical framework for the analysis of social change. Thus, in using the adjective "basic" in speaking of those values considered vital for the survival of the society, Parsons has given to such values a determining quality. One can speak of basic values if by that is meant those values which are considered an essential characteristic of the particular society undergoing examination—for instance, that of a small town or of French Canada before 1939. Equally as basic, however, would be the institutions of the society, or its stratification or ecological structure. A small town would not be a small town if the predominant values of the population were those of a big city population; nor would it be a small town if the population and institutions of the society were ordered in the manner of a big city or of a mining camp. What are seized upon in the construction of a model of a society are those characteristics in the way of values, institutions, ecological structure, and such which are considered distinctive of the society. To those characteristics, for purposes of analysis, can be applied the adjective "basic."

The distinction between what is considered basic and what is not allows for the examination of those changes within a social system which are considered not to lead to a change of the system. One might take the case of the Ontario small town of the 1920s where the interest was in showing not how the society had changed but how it had remained basically the same. Much happened to the Ontario small town during that decade. The automobile became widely adopted and radio was introduced. Women began to smoke in public and to bob their hair and wear short skirts. Labour, in those small industries characteristic of the small town, made its first moves towards unionization. Old people with limited incomes began now to receive a government pension cheque in the mail and young people no longer thought to the same extent of grade eight, or fourth form, as marking the end of a full education. The town remained, however, still a small town.

In such an examination of the small town, developments like the mass production and marketing of the automobile, the "liberation" of women which came with the First World War, the growth in the larger society of the need for people of education, and such come to be viewed as happenings outside which extended into the small town society and disturbed the existing state of things. The small town changed but, as it had been defined, not in ways that altered its basic character as a small town. It is at this point in the analysis of a society considered not to have altered its fundamental character that one can speak of the vested interests of the social system. Those people had a stake in the society of the small town whose way of life would have been adversely affected had it become a different kind of society. By the process of socialization and by means of repression, forms of conduct considered damaging to the society were held in check or accommodated in a manner which did not threaten the society's basic character. Thus, if the town's clergymen may have sought to bring down on all those women who smoked in public the charge of sinful conduct, the accommodation of such conduct within the town's social class structure meant in the end that it no longer was considered to pose a threat to the way of life of the small town; women could smoke as ladies or, if not as ladies, in a manner which reinforced the small town social class structure.

There may appear to be only a thin line—indeed, no line at all—between what here has been talked about as change within the social system and change of the system; in fact, only in analytical terms can such a line be drawn. How the line is drawn, how the distinction is made between a society considered to be one maintaining its basic structure and one undergoing change in a way that makes it a very different society, depends simply upon what problem of change is commanding attention. To revert to the example of the Ontario small town, the interest could have been not in showing how it retained the character of a small town in face of what happened to it in the 1920s, but in how over this period of time it became a different society. Now one would begin with a picture or model of the small town society of 1920 and what happened to it after 1920 would now be viewed in terms of those changes occurring which made it into a different society by the end of the 1920s.

In the examination of change of the society, therefore, one moves from talking about equilibrium, integration, consensus, and the vested interests of the system to talking about disequilibrium, disintegration, dissensus, and the vested interests of change. What happened outside the society to lead to disturbance within the society comes now to be examined in relation to the effect in bringing about the change of the society. In such manner would proceed the analysis of how a small town became transformed into an industrial city or how the old order of French Canada gave way to that society which was a product of the quiet revolution. For such an analysis, what becomes necessary is the construction of a model not only of the society that was but also of the society coming into being.

In an analysis of change of the social system or society, the starting point would be that happening or series of happenings outside the society so consequential in their impact on the society, that the changes engendered resulted in the establishment of a society very different from the one that was, in terms of the model employed. What happened outside could be anything. There is no search here for a single determining agent or "cause" of change. What happened could have been the building of a four-lane expressway out to an isolated village bringing it within easy commuting distance of a large city; or it could have been the discovery of oil in an area of the country long given to farming. Or it could have been an earthquake. The interest here is not in reaching back to determine what caused the four-lane expressway to be built, the oil to be discovered, or the earthquake to occur. The interest rather is in examining the consequences of such "happenings" for the society being analyzed. Happenings of this sort were in the character of disturbances which in the model employed led to the breakdown or disintegration of the established order—the society that was—and the establishment or integration of a new order—the society coming into being.

In such an analysis of change of a society, one begins with an examination of the process of disintegration of the society that was: the breaking down of old established habits of thought and behaviour and of established institutional forms, the development of types of deviance which no longer could be considered "normal" to the society, the growth of new social movements at war with the society, the strengthening efforts of segments of the population to separate from the society and form a little social world of their own. In such manner could be examined the disintegration of the small town society, in the example of the small town being transformed into an industrial city, or of the old order of French Canada now giving way to the society of the quiet revolution.

But social phenomena, thus examined as representing the process of disintegration of the society, represent as well the process of integration of the society coming into being. Disintegration is not something which occurs in time before integration. Rather, they are one and the same process looked at in two different ways. As the analysis shifts from the breaking down of an established social order to the emergence of a new social order, social phenomena come to be examined in terms of the process of integration rather than in terms of the process of disintegration: the development of new habits of behaviour and thought; new institutional forms; types of deviance, while "abnormal" to the society that was, can be considered "normal" to the society coming into being; social movements which point the direction in the establishment of the new society; and, finally, efforts of the population to separate from the society that was in building the society coming into being. Clearly, in such an analysis of the processes of disintegration and integration, no element of time or chronology enters into the analysis. Established habits of thought and behaviour cannot break down without new habits of thought and behaviour taking their place. Nor can there be a breaking down or disintegration of established institutional forms or of social values without there emerging new institutional forms and social values. Integration and disintegration, consensus and dissensus, equilibrium and disequilibrium, conformity and deviance are simply different ways of looking at society, depending upon whether the interest is in social order or social change.

It is not social processes but events or happenings which take place in time, and events or happenings are the stuff with which the sociologist has to work. Once, however, events or happenings are looked at in terms of their sociological meaning they lose their chronological character and become built into an analytical process, of order or change. Thus, returning to the example of the small town being transformed into an industrial city, there might have occurred at a particular time a mass meeting of the congregation of the local Protestant church at which the minister, now considered by the town's changing population old-fashioned, was fired and a new, modern minister hired to take his place. Here, in such a "happening" might be offered a hint of the kinds of changes taking place in the town leading to its transformation to an industrial city: the way in which the old established order of the town was breaking down and the way in which a new social order was coming into being.

If the interest was in the way a small town was being transformed into an industrial city, no great sociological significance, of course, would be attached to any one event, such as, in the example above, the mass meeting in the town of the local Protestant congregation. It is when, in a particular context, a great number of events of a certain kind occur that they begin to take on a significance sociologically. The determination of the meaning of events is the task of sociological analysis. Events take on sociological meaning only in relation to the problem of social change (or of social order) being analyzed. Thus, the firing of the old-fashioned minister in the example of the small town and other events of a similar sort only gained significance because the problem undergoing analysis was how the small town became transformed into an industrial city. Had the interest been in the way the Canadian society has undergone change and become a different kind of society in the years since the Second World War, little attention would have been paid to such an event. Attention rather would have become focussed upon such "happenings" as the separatist movement in Quebec, the increased numbers of women in the labour force, student unrest in the universities, the large-scale movement of population out of rural areas to the cities, mass immigration from Europe, the development of new types of economic enterprise, the increasingly strident demands of the native population.

Thus, to return to the major concern of this introductory essay, the study of Canadian society, what is involved is a focussing upon those events or happenings which have sociological significance in relation to the problem being examined. It is not claimed here that there is only one way to go about the analysis of the Canadian society. It is only claimed that, if the society is to be examined as it has changed over time in all its dimensions, the examination necessarily involves working with more than one analytical model of the society. It is simply not possible to talk about Canadian society (or American society, as Talcott Parsons is wont to do) as if, for all purposes at hand, there were only one society. How one conceives the society depends upon the problem of change undergoing analysis. The historian or sociologist concerned with the process of nation building can quite properly treat the federal union of Canada after 1867, and for that matter the British colonies of North America before that time, as a political, economic, and social unit, and engage in an examination of those forces at work which furthered or retarded the creation of a Canadian nation. In such an analysis, the inclusion of Prince Edward Island, the Western provinces, and ultimately Newfoundland in the federal union would be viewed as involving an adjustment of the boundaries of the society, but not in a way that brought about a change of the society; nor would the growth of industrialism, the shift of population from rural areas to urban, the official recognition of the French language or the adoption of a Canadian flag be considered as involving a fundamental change of the society. Stresses and strains in the society would be evident in such developments as the growth of the separatist movement in Quebec, the increasing militancy of labour and other disadvantaged groups, the rise in the rate of crime, the demands of the native peoples, and the strengthening demands of provincial governments, but such stresses and strains, it could be shown in terms of the model of the society employed, were contained by the vested interests of the social system—that is, by all those people and institutions with a stake in the maintenance of Canada as a nation.

Such an analysis of the process of nation building would tell us much about the Canadian society. However, there would be much that it would not tell, or tell only very inadequately. What would not be told was how, at different times or in different areas of the country, the society that was in existence—the urban society of central Canada of the 1890s, for instance, or the rural society of French Canada of the 1930s—underwent change and became a different kind of society. The reason would be the bias built into the model employed. By adhering to the conception of Canadian society as *the society*, the emphasis necessarily comes to be placed upon those forces securing the formation and survival of the society. What gets played down, so to speak, if not wholly ignored, are those forces of disruption in the society which brought about the disintegration of established forms of organization and the emergence of new forms. For such an analysis of change of the society, the sociologist must work with more than one model of the society, both in spatial and temporal terms.

Thus, he may want to talk about the Canadian society of, say, 1870, 1939, or 1960, or he may want to talk about the society of French Canada in 1939 or of the rural community of 1950 and show how this society underwent change and became a different kind of society. Or, indeed, he may want to talk about the society of the Canadian town of 1950, here with an interest in showing how rapid urban growth and the mass push of population out of large urban centres resulted during the 1950s in transforming its character. All the time the interest may remain in the larger problem of what is happening to the Canadian society. But only by this shifting from macro to micro types of analysis in time and space can the full dimensions of the Canadian society be brought under review.

It is this way of looking at Canadian society that has characterized my efforts to analyze it. Caught up in such efforts, it should be admitted, has been a bias of my own. I have wanted to look at what is wrong about society as well as what is right; to look at the way old established structures of a society broke down as well as the way new structures came into being. In a word, the interest has been in the problem of change rather than in the problem of order.

Such an interest was clearly apparent in my early study, *The Social Development of Canada*, where what secured emphasis were the kinds of problems of organization thrown up by the pushing of the Canadian population into new areas of development, but scarcely less evident was such an interest in *Church and Sect in Canada* and *Movements of Political Protest in Canada* where the major concern was with how old established forms of organization, religious in the one case and political in the other, broke down and gave way to new forms. In *The Suburban Society*, as well, what secured emphasis was not how the suburban society was structured, the "suburbia" that had received so much sociological and journalistic attention, but rather how urban forms of organization and patterns of behaviour broke down with the mass push of population out of the city into the surrounding countryside and how a new society in the suburbs came into being.

Developing out of this interest has been another which, the more the Canadian society was viewed within the context of the larger North American continental system, came to receive in creasing emphasis. The society of Canada, like that of the United States, has been caught up over the years in forces of growth associated with the peopling of the continent and the development of new forms of economic enterprise and community structures. Whereas in the United States, these forces of growth contributed to the political strengthening of the nation—the realization of the manifest destiny of the American people—in Canada their effect was to threaten the separate political existence of the Canadian nation or, before 1867, of the British North American colonies. Thus, in Canada the "breakdown" of forms of social organization and patterns of behaviour which resulted from the mass movement of population into new areas of development was allowed to proceed only so far. "Rebellions in the backlands" offered a means to the American society of ridding the continent of rival political jurisdictions, whether represented by the empires of France, Britain, or Spain, or by the claims of native people. In Canada, such rebellions constituted a threat to the very survival of the society.

Thus, running through *Church and Sect in Canada* and even more *Movements of Political Protest in Canada* was the theme of revolution and counter-revolution where developed the argument that forms of religious and political organization in Canada were a product largely of counter-revolutionary forces in the society. The implications for the society as a whole of this play of revolutionary and counter-revolutionary forces became explored more generally in essays appearing in *The Developing Canadian Community*, particularly in Part IV.

It is now thirty years since the end of the Second World War. Much has happened to the Canadian society in these thirty years. No longer is it the Canadian society that is threatened by the expansive forces of the American society. Rather, it is the American society which has become threatened by the expansive forces of new growing political powers in the world. One indeed might argue the reversal of the revolution and counter-revolution theme. Now the American society has become caught up in forces of counter-revolution, whereas the Canadian society has become caught up in forces of a revolutionary character.

Whatever, there can be no questioning that far-reaching changes have been taking place in the Canadian society since the Second World War. How to assess the character of those changes becomes now one of the major tasks of the student of Canadian society. Assessments will differ, depending upon the particular interests and biases of the sociologist undertaking the assessment.

It would be for me an impossible task to indicate all the various sources of ideas which have gone into my work over the past thirty-five or more years. One source is very evident, and it probably explains some of the weaknesses as well as the strengths of this work. Much of my thinking has come out of the research on which I have been engaged. Whether in the study of church and sect, suburban society, or whatever, I have never known precisely where I was going until much of the research was completed and a good part of the writing undertaken. Those who argue that research interferes with teaching have little appreciation of how ideas become generated, whether in the physical science laboratory or the social scientist's study. It is upon research that I have relied primarily in the development of a theoretical framework for the analysis of Canadian society.

That is not to deny, however, my very heavy debt to a large number of scholars, in Canada and beyond. Though I would hesitate to include any of his writings in a bibliography on Canadian society, I owe much to one of my very early university teachers, Arthur S. Morton. His work on the history of Western Canada prompted my early interest in the development of the frontier. I owe much as well to C. A. Dawson. One could not be a student of his without being caught up, at least to some degree, in the human ecological approach to the study of society. His *Group Settlement: Ethnic Communities in Western Canada* deserves to be on any reading list relating to Canadian society. So as well does E. C. Hughes' *French Canada in Transition*, though his greatest influence on my thinking, as on that of so many other scholars, was not through his writings but through discussions of various sorts. He remains today a great teacher, as he was back in the 1930s when I had the privilege of being one of his students.

No one familiar with my work would fail to note my very heavy indebtedness to H. A. Innis. It is difficult to get students in sociology to read Innis. For a full appreciation of his contribution to an understanding of Canadian society there is no shortcut past *The Fur Trade in Canada* and *The Cod Fisheries*, yet the best one can do is assign to students some of his essays or *Settlement and the Forest and Mining Frontier* which he did in collaboration with A. R. M. Lower.

Lower's work makes less difficult reading, and his *From Colony to Nation* and *Canadians in the Making* provide a good historical background for the study of Canadian society, as do M. L. Hansen and J. B. Brebner, *The Mingling of Canadian and American Peoples*, J. B. Brebner, *The Neutral Yankees of Nova Scotia*, George Stanley, *The Birth of Western Canada*, Fred Landon, *Western Ontario and the American Frontier*, G. deP. Glazebrook, *Life in Ontario* and *The Story of Toronto*, and Mason Wade, *The French Canadians, 1760-1967*. The geographer has contributed much as well to an understanding of the Canadian society. Particularly worthy of note are Donald Kerr, *The Changing Face of Toronto*, J. J. Spelt, *The Urban Development in South-Central Ontario*, and William C. Wonders, *Canada's Changing North*.

Perhaps, on the whole, less significant for the student of Canadian society has been the work of the political scientist, but certainly, whether counted a political scientist or sociologist, no bibliography on this society would be complete without including at least some of the writings of Mildred Schwartz, in particular *Public Opinion and Canadian Identity*, though her work departs far from my interests. Of a different character but of equal sociological interest is J. A. Irving's *The Social Credit Movement in Alberta*.

Any selection of the sociological literature relating to Canadian society must necessarily reflect a bias on my part. Such older studies as J. R. Burnet, *Next-Year Country*, E. K. Francis, *In Search of Utopia: The Mennonites of Manitoba*, John Kosa, *Land of Choice: The Hungarians in Canada*, W. E. Mann, *Sect, Cult and Church in Alberta* and Horace Miner, S*t. Denis: A French Canadian Parish* certainly deserve a place, along with the work of Dawson and Hughes, on any reading list on Canadian society. So, also, do J. C. Falardeau, *Essais Sur le Québec Contemporain*, M. Rioux and Y. Martin, *French Canadian Society* Vol. I, and Mason Wade and J. C. Falardeau, *Canadian Dualism*.

Published later than any of these studies and marking the beginning of a great move forward in sociological work in Canada is John Porter's *The Vertical Mosaic*. In less historical terms, Porter's analysis of Canadian society at many points agrees very much with mine.

Of more recent sociological literature, one can do little more than list names of books. I would single out for special mention R. A. Lucas, *Minetown, Milltown, Railtown*, but on any reading list on Canadian society one or more of the many Readers which have recently appeared would have to be included. In my view, none of them presents a satisfactory theoretical framework for the analysis of Canadian society, but they do bring together a great number of significant papers relating to the society. Of the various Readers, none has surpassed B. R. Blishen et al., *Canadian Society*, in the quality of its selections and its comprehensiveness.

One would have to be up on recent publishers' lists to attempt to provide a full covering of very recent books on Canadian society. The most I can do is indicate the names of some of those with which I am familiar: D. G. Clairmont and D. W. Magill, *Africville: The Life and Death of a Canadian Black Community*; Wallace Clement, *The Canadian Corporate Elite*; Dennis Forcese, *The Canadian Class Structure*; Patricia M. Marchak, *Ideological Perspectives on Canada*; and Lorne Tepperman, *Social Mobility in Canada*. Among other books that perhaps should secure mention are Gerald L. Gold and Marc-Adelard Tremblay, *Communities and Culture in French Canada*, George A. Nader, *Cities of Canada* Vol. I, Robert Pike and Elia Zureik (Ed.), *Socialization and Values in Canadian Society*, and Robert A. Silverman and James J. Teevan, *Crime in Canadian Society*.

Any adequate covering of recent work on Canadian society would have to include writings by various historians, economic historians, and political scientists, as well as by sociologists, but such an undertaking lies beyond the scope of this essay. All that can be noted is that the interest of a number of younger Canadian scholars in a Marxist type of analysis of Canadian society has led to efforts to bring back into the fold of political economy work developing out of the various social science disciplines. L. A. Johnson's *History of the County of Ontario, 1650-1875* perhaps deserves mention as representative of this new, "critical" approach to the study of Canadian society.

Any reading list on Canadian society would scarcely be complete if it did not include some of those major theoretical works which provide the basis for an understanding of any society, but it seems pointless to begin listing here the writings of such sociologists as Max Weber, Emile Durkheim, Vilfredo Pareto, Georg Simmel, and Robert K. Merton. Nor can more than mention be made of the work of Robert E. Park, Talcott Parsons, Neil Smelser, S. M. Lipset, E. C. Hughes, and Reinhard Bendix, though the reader of this essay cannot be unaware of my indebtedness to these and many other scholars, however much I may quarrel with the theoretical orientations of some of them, Canada has yet to produce a sociological theorist of note, but the growing interest in problems inherent to the Canadian society offers the promise of a strengthening theoretical basis for work going forward in Canada.

Chapter Nine

THE CHANGING IMAGE OF SOCIOLOGY IN ENGLISH-SPEAKING CANADA

S.D. Clark

This paper proposes to examine the changing image of sociology over the past half century within the English-speaking Canadian academic community and the society at large. A consideration of how sociology has been regarded tells much about the history of the discipline. What I have to say develops very much out of my personal experience, and inevitably as a consequence reflects my biases and, as well perhaps, my ignorance respecting certain developments. I make no attempt to detail all the various facets of sociological work that have gone on. Rather, it is my impressions of how sociology in a general way has been regarded that I shall attempt to set out.

I go back a little more than fifty years. I have often pondered the question of why I never heard of the discipline of sociology in the years I was a student at the University of Saskatchewan. Outside the university, in political circles, the term sociology was frequently tossed about. William Irvine, one of the U.F.A. members of Parliament, could well have been described as a student of sociology, and I was early familiar with his writings. It had no place, however, in the program of studies offered by the university, and among my teachers in history, political science, and economics no mention was ever made of it in my hearing.

Clark, S.D. The Changing Image of Sociology in English-speaking Canada. From the *Canadian Journal of Sociology* 4(4). Reprinted with permission from the *Canadian Journal of Sociology*.

Nor did it have any place in the program of studies offered by the University of Toronto where I moved on to graduate study. Though I was to learn later that MacMillan in Victoria College had once offered courses in this discipline, and that R. M. MacIver, who had been head of the Department of Political Science before leaving for Columbia University, had supervised two Ph.D. theses in the subject, about the closest I got to any literature that might be considered in any way sociological was that of the writings of such as F. J. Teggart, Sir Henry Maine, Charles and Mary Beard, Frederick Jackson Turner, Karl Marx, and Gustavus Myers.

It was only at the London School of Economics that I came to know something about the discipline as such, and what I learned was certainly not flattering to it. Morris Ginsberg was there, but I did no work with him. It was from Harold Laski that I heard much about sociology, a discipline he associated with one of the worst features of American university education. To him, sociologists were people running around ringing doorbells and asking people silly questions. The stereotype thus cultivated persisted for a long time in British academic circles, and in Canadian academic circles as well where the British influence was strong.

With such an introduction to the discipline I could develop no great interest in it. Yet when the lack of alternative opportunities to pursue graduate work led me to adopt a fellowship in sociology at McGill University I discovered I was more of a sociologist than I had realized. They were two good years at McGill, with Dawson and Hughes as my teachers. It was perhaps, however, something more than the scathing remarks about the discipline made by Harold Laski that led me to be highly sensitive about how it was regarded. I did not come into sociology with the feeling that this was the discipline that had all the answers. I had nothing of Dawson's commitment to the subject. Thus I remained in my two years at McGill highly conscious of the low regard in which sociology was held in other departments of the university and even more within the larger Canadian academic community.

One certainly had the impression that the Department of Sociology was off in a little corner by itself and that within the larger Canadian academic community the McGill sociology group was largely isolated. When the Canadian Political Science Association met at McGill University in 1934, if my memory serves me right, I was the only one out of the department who showed up at the sessions. Innis, Mackintosh, the senior Keirstead, Brady, McQueen, among other Canadian social scientists were there, but these were scholars scarcely known within McGill sociological circles. I speak of the years 1933-35; Dawson with Gettys had produced his textbook, but no other publication called attention at the time to the work going on in the department. Within the department itself, the faculty and graduate students were heavily involved in three major projects financed by American foundations, but, in circles outside, the research activity that attracted attention served only to reinforce views of the discipline not unlike those held by Laski.

It was during the 1940s that sociology, even if in only a very small way, began to win the favorable regard of other Canadian social scientists. Already, by the mid-1930s, an honors program in sociology had been established at Toronto under the direction of a committee chaired by E. J. Urwick who at the time was not only head of what was then known as the Department of Political Science, but acting director of the School of Social Work, then known as the Department of Social Science. No one could have given to sociology a more respectable image. A gentleman and scholar of the old school, a social philosopher, Urwick brought to the program he established a breadth and depth which made it one of the finest honor programs within the faculty of Arts and Sciences.

In my view however, it was Harold Innis who played the key role in pulling sociology out of its isolated position within the Canadian academic community. Appointed head, in 1937, of what now became known as the Department of Political Economy, Innis immediately came to have a strong interest in the development of sociology, though it remained yet under the direction of a committee headed by Urwick. At the time its only teacher was C. W. M. Hart, brought over from anthropology on a part-time basis. When, in 1938, a full-time appointment was to be made, the head of the Department of Psychology pushed hard for a graduate of his department who had gone on to do a Ph.D. in sociology at the University of Chicago; I was favored by Urwick, who had all of the English scholar's aversion to American sociology, and by Innis. My appointment thus might be described as the culmination of a power struggle revolving around the issue of the type of sociology to be introduced in Toronto. When, a year later, sociology became attached to the Department of Political Economy, the issue appeared to be firmly settled in a way favorable to Innis's view.

Innis's endorsement of sociology did much to strengthen the regard in which it was held not only at Toronto but as well as McGill. Important for the position of sociology at McGill was Innis's growing respect for the work of Carl Dawson with the publication of his Peace River and ethnic communities studies. It was Innis who was responsible for involving Dawson in the establishment of the Canadian Social Science Research Council and I suspect he had more than a little to do with his election as a Fellow of the Royal Society of Canada. Something in the way of bridges were being built between sociology and the other social sciences and between Toronto and McGill sociology. Visits to Toronto during the years 1940-45 of such American sociologists as Robert E. Park, Talcott Parsons, Robert Merton, and, as well, Dawson, did much to enhance its standing in the Toronto academic community.

Yet there remained nothing in the way of a community of sociologists in Canada. Topping in the University of British Columbia, Jones in the University of Manitoba, Prince in Dalhousie University were scarcely known either at McGill or Toronto. More unfortunate still was the lack of feelings of good will between Toronto and McGill. While Innis had done much to further Dawson's standing in the Canadian academic community, Dawson, on the other hand, refused to recognize that there was any such thing as sociology at Toronto. In his view, I had deserted sociology in my unwillingness on his urgings to do my Ph.D. at Chicago, while Hart, a disciple of Radcliffe Brown, brought to sociology a rigorous functionalist approach sharply at variance with the sociology taught by Dawson.

It was not only the division between sociology at Toronto and McGill which retarded its acceptance. Within the University of Toronto, the type of sociology expounded by Hart aroused in academic circles strong antagonisms. Hart had much of the character of a charismatic teacher who, in Durkheimian positivist fashion, challenged the cherished religious and moral beliefs of his students and some of the most basic assumptions of the discipline of philosophy. There developed a running battle in the teaching of second and third year students between Hart and those members of the faculty in other departments involved with the same students. So strong were feelings that the Registrar of Victoria College came close to forbidding students in that college to take sociology. Sociology, with Hart as a teacher, did not suffer from being ignored; it came rather to be viewed as a threat. Increasingly uncomfortable relations between Innis and Hart did little to strengthen the claims of the discipline within the university. In the community at large, irate parents made known to such as the Registrar of Victoria their feelings about what their sons and daughters were learning in their classes in sociology, but beyond such parents little was known about the discipline.

The truth was that in the early 1940s the University of Toronto, let alone the public at large, was not yet prepared to accept a Durkheimian analysis of human relations. Hart was a great teacher, who built about himself a number of devoted students, but unfortunately his difficulty in getting along with people led many persons in the university to associate their feelings toward him with their attitude to sociology. He was not one to tread softly in advancing the claims of the discipline.

By the mid-forties, Hart had departed and Toronto sociology entered quieter days. Devereux, Lipset, Chinoy, and others who joined the sociology staff for shorter or longer stays did much to forge links with American sociology, but in ways that did not upset personal relationships with scholars in other disciplines. Still the subject continued to remain highly suspect in the view of historians, philosophers, and, as well, within the department headed by Innis, by economists and political scientists. It received its strongest endorsement from Vincent Bladen who had become director of the Institute of Industrial Relations and involved in the activities of the Society for Applied Anthropology. If, well before this time, Innis had come to regard with favor the work of C.A. Dawson, Bladen's work of directing the Institute of Industrial Relations established close links with E. C. Hughes, now at the University of Chicago.

Yet the stereotype of American sociology as a discipline concerned only with the gathering of useless facts persisted throughout the Canadian academic community, in Toronto as elsewhere. When, back in the late 1930s, I heard that Hughes might leave McGill, Hart and I proposed his appointment at Toronto, but the proposal attracted no interest. Innis never did view with favor what he regarded as American sociology. When, in the later years of his life, sociology figured in his graduate seminar in economic history, it was the sociology of such European scholars as Weber, Hobhouse, Pareto, and Mosca. If he had developed considerable respect for Carl Dawson, it was the work of Helen Hughes not Everett Hughes which began to attract his attention, as his interest in the area of communications grew. Though Park had visited Toronto, to my knowledge there was no contact between he and Innis over the years, however much they were alike as scholars.

Innis never had any very clear view of what sociology was all about, yet it was his favorable regard for it which led to its increasing acceptance within the University of Toronto and in a number of other Canadian universities. In Toronto, in such departments as that of history, the only sociology that was known was that represented by my work, and, if it was not viewed wholly favorably, I nevertheless commanded a certain regard since, after all, I had once been a graduate student in the history department. Outside Toronto, to the extent that sociology met with favor at all, it was the sociology at Toronto endorsed by Innis. In universities such as Saskatchewan, Manitoba, Western, and New Brunswick, the sociology associated with the University of Chicago and represented in Canada by McGill remained still suspect in the eyes of deans and heads of economic departments responsible for sociology appointments. If graduates from Toronto were not available, such universities tended to turn to Harvard, as did Saskatchewan and Manitoba. Apart from Jean Burnet, who wrote her Ph.D. dissertation as much under my direction as Hughes, I can think of no Chicago trained sociologist who received an appointment at a Canadian university, outside McGill, before the 1950s.

However, by the early 1950s, marked changes had taken place in the sociology of McGill University. Graduates of the department now went off to pursue their studies at Harvard, Columbia, and other distinguished graduate schools as well as at Chicago. No longer was a Chicago Ph.D. required to secure an appointment at McGill. Carleton, McMaster, British Columbia, among other Canadian universities, recruited people who had come out of McGill and received their graduate training in the United States. By the 1950s, I think it can be said, the lead in the development of sociology in Canada was taken by McGill, not Toronto. One reason perhaps lay in the fact that sociology students at McGill received a more rigorous training in the discipline. More important still, however, was the fact that sociology at Toronto, still a part of the department of Political Economy, was very largely associated with me. More than Dawson harbored doubts about whether I was a sociologist. There was at the time little appreciation of the extent to which sociology was an autonomous unit within the department and of the extent to which catholicity had determined the character of development of the discipline within the Toronto setting.

Before the decade of the 1950s came to an end, however, something of a community of sociologists was beginning to emerge in Canada, and sociology was coming close to establishing itself as a respectable discipline within the Canadian academic community. By the year 1958-59, the Canadian

Political Science Association had had its second sociologist as a president and, even earlier, the Royal Society of Canada its second sociologist as a Fellow. The move of Oswald Hall from McGill to Toronto, the appointment of John Porter at Carleton, and the strengthening of sociological offerings at most of the other Canadian universities clearly established the discipline within university programs of study. Only in Queens, at the end of the decade, had sociology failed to secure a foothold.

There was still in Canadian academic circles nevertheless a good deal of uneasiness about this upstart. McGill remained, at the beginning of the 1960s, the only university with an autonomous department of sociology. Elsewhere, apart from British Columbia, it became linked with economics; in British Columbia, it was taken under the wing of anthropology. In most universities it succeeded in establishing distinctive programs of study, and attracting a sizeable body of students. It was, however, so to speak, kept under wraps; grudgingly recognized, because of its appeal to students, by university administrators and by the chairmen of those departments in which it was situated.

Outside the university, it attracted somewhat the same sort of mixed reaction. The public at large had no comprehension of what the subject was all about, and, if any notice was taken of it, it was only when some of those more zealous students, calling in simple-minded fashion upon what they had learnt from their sociology instructors, engaged their parents in debate about such matters as sex or religion. In governmental circles there was evident a growing interest in what sociology had to offer. The term "sociological" entered frequently in the vocabulary of politicians and even more of public servants. Yet, unlike the case of economics, or for that matter political science and history, there was on the part of government bodies no significant drawing upon the resources of the discipline from Canadian universities. Sociology graduates, assured, on being recruited by the public service, that the work they would be called upon to do would be within their area of training, soon found themselves engaged in bureaucratic tasks of a non-sociological character. While there was a good deal of talk among people in government circles about the importance of sociology, much of it revealed little understanding of the subject.

On the other hand, it has to be said, much of the work going forward in sociology within the Canadian universities had little to contribute to public policy. The concern to dissociate the discipline from anything having to do with social welfare or social reform had the effect, in my view, of discouraging kinds of research which involved grappling with some of the most serious problems of the society about. When sociologists did undertake studies commissioned by public bodies only too often what was offered in return for the financial support received did little to enhance the reputation of the discipline.

Such was the state of the discipline as the decade of the 1950s gave way to that of the 1960s. In the quarter century leading up to 1960 no spectacular developments had occurred which, so to speak, put sociology on the map. On the other hand, nothing had happened to do damage to the discipline's image within the Canadian academic community. In my view, the most significant move forward resulted from the gradual breaking down of the stereotype of American sociology as a discipline concerned only with the gathering of useless facts. In some academic circles, such as in Queen's, the old unfounded prejudices against the discipline persisted, but with sociology faculties across the country now made up of persons recruited from a great number of American graduate schools (and from Britain) there developed a greater appreciation of the breadth and depth of the discipline.

It was, however, the decade of the 1960s which marked the great move forward in the establishment of sociology as an accepted discipline within the Canadian academic community and beyond. The creation in a number of universities, including Toronto, of autonomous departments, and the establishment of the Canadian Sociology and Anthropology Association, with its *Review*, represented something of a formal recognition of its importance. As well, by the 1960s, a modest body of Canadian sociological literature was making its appearance. Though the Royal Commission on Bilingualism and Biculturalism did not do for sociology what, thirty years earlier, the Royal Commission on Dominion-Provincial Relations had done for economics, the sociological contribution to the work of this commission was nevertheless by no means insignificant. Canadian sociologists were beginning to demonstrate that they had something to say about public issues.

Equally important, in my view, to the acceptance of sociology in the Canadian academic community and beyond was the increasing involvement of sociology faculty in the life of the university. Many of those teaching in the mid-1960s had developed close personal associations with economists and political scientists, having been situated within the same department, and belonged to the same learned society. Such associations tended to persist after sociology went off on its own. Moreover, Canadians very largely made up sociology faculties across the country, and more particularly in central and eastern Canada. These were scholars who had done their undergraduate if not graduate work in a Canadian university, and who could meet in academic halls with historians, political scientists, economists, and join in discussions about Canadian politics, the state of the Canadian economy, or about matters relating to Canada's past. In my view, it is scarcely possible to exaggerate the importance of these personal links forged by sociologists within Canadian universities in the decade of the 1960s. If sociology as a discipline did not yet meet with whole-hearted favor in Canadian academic circles, sociologists like Kaspar Naegele in British Columbia, Aileen Ross in McGill, Frank Jones in McMaster, Oswald Hall in Toronto, John Porter in Carleton, to mention only a few, came to command the respect of their fellow scholars. So fully, indeed, had Kaspar Naegele won that respect in British Columbia that he was appointed, not long before his tragic death, dean of his faculty.

Between sociologists and scholars in other disciplines there was a very full sharing in the traditions of the Canadian university. Though I can think of no sociologist of that time who could be described as a Progressive Conservative, neither can I of any political scientist and only two economists of that political persuasion come to mind. Sociologists were no more conservative nor radical than their fellow social scientists. If the Great Depression of the 1930s had produced in Canada intellectual socialists like Frank Underhill, King Gordon, and Frank Scott, in none of the Canadian social sciences was there a tradition of militant political radicalism such as that in the United States associated with the City College of New York, nor was there during the cold war years of the 1950s the development of that kind of unreasoning fear of communism which came to influence the thinking of a number of American sociologists, particularly those who earlier had been caught up in political radicalism. Marx, to the Canadian social scientist, never came to be looked upon as the prophet of a new and glorious age, nor as a false prophet responsible for misleading the unwary and ill-informed.

I speak of the years leading up to 1968. Though Harold Innis was long dead, and sociologists trained in American graduate schools had come to introduce the many specialisms characteristic of the discipline across the border, Canadian sociology nevertheless continued to remain largely faithful to the liberal tradition it had inherited from Innis, and from Carl Dawson. It had little interest in proving Karl Marx right or wrong. If John Porter's work had departed little from the Fabianism of Frank Underhill, Oswald Hall's remained faithful to the catholicity of Robert Park and Everett Hughes. There were few ramparts a C. Wright Mills could be called upon to breach in Canadian sociology.

As a discipline, it perhaps has to be said, sociology remained weak in Canada. As late as 1965 there were no great number of sociology teachers in the country, and no great body of sociological literature. There was thus no "school" of sociology to wage war upon. If J. J. Loubser in Toronto, Frank Jones in McMaster, and the late Howard Roseborough in McGill exposed students to the structural-functional theory of Talcott Parsons, in none of these departments did the Parsonian approach determine the character of the program of studies offered. Nor did a quantitative type of sociology, with its heavy dependence upon the computer, come to dominate offerings in any of the Canadian universities.

It was only with the great expansion of Canadian sociology staffs after 1965 that the discipline became caught up in a large way in conflicts between faculty members representing different specializations and espousing opposing ideological positions. We began in a big way to import American sociology and American sociologists. As I have argued elsewhere, the heavy dependence upon recruitment of staff in sociology from the United States was inevitable during these years. We owe much to those American scholars taking up posts in Canadian universities.

The effect of this large infusion of teachers from across the border, however, was to greatly alter the position of sociology within the Canadian academic community. On the positive side, there was evident a very considerable acceleration of research activity in sociology departments across the country, and a marked strengthening of graduate teaching. American scholars brought to the Canadian university that spirit of drive and hard work which had characterized the faculty of many of the larger American graduate schools. Sociology was put on the map in a way that it had never been before.

In terms of sociology's image however, the effect of this sudden infusion of teachers from outside the country would have to be considered not wholly for the good. Whatever their ideological leanings, most of these new recruits to sociology staffs had one thing in common: highly professional in outlook, they had only a limited interest in the affairs of the university at large, and they had little knowledge or interest in matters relating to Canadian politics, the Canadian economy, or Canada's past. The contacts they sought to cultivate were with fellow professionals back in the United States. The result was a strengthening of that tendency, early evident on the part of sociology faculties, to isolate themselves in their own little university corners, to avoid such common university meeting places as faculty clubs or faculty councils. At best, the effect was to create a situation where only a few sociologists were known to other members of the university.

Time might have been expected to bring a change, but the vast increase after 1968 in the size of university faculties and the fact that sociology staffs tended to be of a younger age group than the staffs of other departments of the university had the effect of hardening forms of behavior leading to the continued isolation of sociologists on university campuses. In a university like Carleton the strong Canadian contingent within the sociology staff resulted in maintaining those personal links long established by people like Porter; in Toronto, the small Canadian contingent which maintained such links was given such names as "the faculty club clique" or, where it appeared appropriate, "the establishment."

It was partly out of an ignorance on the part of university faculties of who sociologists were and what they were up to which led in the late 1960s to the stereotyping of sociology departments as centres of discord and disruption. In my first year at Dalhousie University, I was the only member of the sociology staff who regularly frequented the faculty club. There I continuously found myself correcting the false or exaggerated views of the Department of Sociology held by faculty in other departments. What became public knowledge were the distorted stories appearing in the student newspaper. Given the difficulties within the department associated with one member of the staff, it was not easy to convince people that the department as a whole was not riddled by factional strife or given up to the cause of political radicalism.

There remained throughout those troublous years 1968-73 serious sociological work going on in Canadian universities, and the pity only was that such work was largely lost sight of in the face of the noisy clamorings of those sociologists, faculty members and students, who had convinced themselves that their mission was to bring down the capitalist order of society, whatever the cost. The turmoil of those years extended beyond sociology departments, but it was within these departments that the drive to make over the university, and the society at large, was particularly concentrated. In one university after another, what was going on in the sociology department became in faculty circles a major topic of discussion, to the discredit of the discipline.

It will take a time yet before sociology in Canadian universities will regain that favorable regard which it enjoyed in the early 1960s. If there is no longer any effort on the part of sociology teachers and students to raise the banner of revolution, it is nevertheless not so long ago that a session of the Sociology and Anthropology Association in its annual meeting was broken up because it was devoted to a discussion of the government's Green Paper on Immigration. The spirit of free enquiry finds little favor among those who believe they alone hold the truth. A Marxist type approach to the study of social phenomena is not something new to the social sciences, and more than those who in doctrinaire fashion subscribe to such an approach can find much value in it. What is new is the intense intolerance of many of those who today think of themselves as Marxists.

I speak of those sociologists who have taken up Marxism as a cause with all the fanaticism of the newly converted. The hold of Marxism upon sociological thinking, however, extends much further than as an emotional commitment. It has become, in many sociological quarters, the accepted theoretical framework for the analysis of social phenomena. Critical sociology has set itself up in antithesis to structural-functionalism. To give a sense of Canadian legitimacy in such an exercise, the name of Harold Innis has been seized upon on the presumption that Marxist type analyses of society represent an extension of lines of thought developed by him. Critical sociology is coming now to be made into critical political economy.

Looking back, it is not too difficult to agree with such critics of sociology as C. Wright Mills that a good deal of the work going forward in the discipline in his time contributed little to an understanding of the world in which people lived. If psychology had gone far in removing man from its area of concern, sociology was on the way to removing social beings. As the United States moved into the troubled 1960s with its race riots, widespread urban poverty, increasing violence and, before the decade was out, a calamitous war in Vietnam, there did, indeed, appear much that was irrelevant in an American sociology which talked about integration, consensus, pattern variables, and avoided mention of such processes in society as class conflict and social disruption. For the more disillusioned of this generation of sociology students, "dropping out" offered itself as seemingly the only possible means of rejecting a sociology that to them had come to be meaningless. For a good many of the disaffected, however, C. Wright Mills, now dead but made to appear alive, pointed the way to what was conceived as a more relevant sociology. Thus was revived that radical thrust in American sociology reaching back to the 1930s and associated with the names of such sociologists as Robert Lynd.

Within the Canadian context, the rejection of the sociology of the 1960s became specifically a rejection of American sociology. Nationalistic sentiments combined with an ideological thrust to generate a demand for a sociology more meaningful in the Canadian setting. It would be impossible within the limits of this paper to unravel all the various influences which came to give force to the drive to make over sociology as a discipline more truly Canadian. In its simplest form, the "Canadianization" movement developed in protest against the heavy concentration of Americans in Canadian sociology faculties. It took on, however, a more ideological cast as an increasing emphasis came to be placed upon the much wider dependency relationship of Canada as a nation to the United States, and upon the evils of American imperialism. Some of those who became the most ardent Canadian "nationalists" were Americans now teaching in Canadian universities. Thus became joined together the ideology of critical sociology and that of the movement to make sociology more Canadian.

It would be presumptuous on my part to attempt to assess in any sort of definitive fashion the effect of the developments which have occurred in sociology in Canada in the 1970s upon its image. Certainly, any such attempt would reveal my biases as well as my lack of knowledge of occurrences in a number of Canadian universities. I cannot help but think, however, that a good deal of sociology in Canada has moved too far in what might be described as a leftist direction. Perhaps nowhere is this more apparent than in the programs, and even more the business meeting agendas, of the Canadian Association of Sociology and Anthropology. The politicization of the Association has very much diminished its standing as a force of scholarship in the country. As well, the concentration within a narrow Marxist framework of a considerable body of sociological work going forward has led, in my view, to a near total abandonment, where such a concentration has occurred, of a concern for many of the most critical problems of our society. Sociologists adhering to a Marxist approach have become hung up on the broad general problem of Canada's dependency relationship as a nation to the United States. While the power structure of an imperialist-capitalist system will explain much about our society, there is much that such a power structure cannot explain.

Yet some shaking up of sociology as it had become established in Canada in the early 1970s was called for, and some shaking up perhaps is still needed.

If a narrowness of concern with the problems of society has characterized critical sociology, it has characterized no less that sociology which has become so dependent upon quantitative methods of analysis that what lies beyond the reach of such methods comes to be viewed as no part of the sociological exercise. It would be revealing of the generation of sociologists to which I belong for me to suggest that sociology in Canada would gain much by a return to that liberal-philosophical tradition of the discipline associated with such names as those of Robert E. Park and Robert Redfield, but certainly, it seems to me, the effect of developments of the past decade has led to a much too great fracturing of the discipline, whether the fracturing has resulted from the taking up of opposing ideological positions or from adhering to differing, and often highly narrow, methodologies.

In the end, perhaps from more than anything else, sociology in Canada today is suffering from that phenomenal growth it experienced in the late 1960s and early 1970s. Compared with American universities, the rate of growth and the present size of sociology departments in Canadian universities are staggering. There appeared no end to the growing body of students pouring into sociology programs, and the more off-beat were the course offerings the more attractive to students became the discipline. Out of the urge of students back in the early seventies to "do their own thing" sociology prospered. No discipline was more ready than sociology to offer students "the thing" they thought they wanted. Thus developed that proliferation of course offerings, and squandering of resources, which has characterized the development of the discipline in recent years.

Those days are gone. It is a tough labor market that students graduating in sociology are now facing. And it is a society become skeptical about what has been going on in sociology in which now the discipline has to make its way. There is much very good work being done in sociology in Canadian universities; more good work, indeed, than has ever been done in the past. In time, it can be hoped, such work will become recognized to the point where sociology will again take its place as one of the accepted and well regarded disciplines within the Canadian university community and beyond. It is not possible, however, to conclude this paper on an unqualified positive note. Much damage over past years has been done to the image of the discipline and not all of that damage has yet been repaired.

Appendix

BIBLIOGRAPHY OF S.D. CLARK'S WORK

H.J. Hiller

Books and Monographs

1939 *The Canadian Manufacturers' Association: A Study in Collective Bargaining and Political Pressure*. Toronto: University of Toronto Press.

1942 *The Social Development of Canada*. Toronto: University of Toronto Press.

1948 *Church and Sect in Canada*. Toronto: University of Toronto Press.

1959 *Movements of Political Protest in Canada, 1640-1840*. Toronto: University of Toronto Press.

1959 *The Employability of the Older Worker*. Ottawa: Department of Labour.

1961 *Urbanism and the Changing Canadian Society*. (Ed.). Toronto: University of Toronto Press.

1962 *The Developing Canadian Community*. Toronto: University of Toronto Press. The 1968 revised edition contains 6 additional chapters.

1966 *The Suburban Society*. Toronto: University of Toronto Press.

Compiled by Hiller, Harry H. (1982) From *Society and Change: S.D. Clark and the Development of Canadian Sociology*. Toronto: University of Toronto Press. pp. 165-167. Reprinted with permission from the publisher.

1975 *Proceedings of the Symposium on Problems of Development in Atlantic Canada*. Ottawa: Royal Society of Canada. (Edited with P.G. Clark).

1976 *Canadian Society in Historical Perspective*. Toronto: McGraw-Hill Ryerson.

1976 *The Canadian Society and the Issue of Multi-culturalism*. Saskatoon: University of Saskatchewan Sorokin Publications.

1978 *The New Urban Poor*. Toronto: McGraw-Hill Ryerson.

Articles

1932 The United Farmers of Alberta. *Canadian Forum*, 13, pp. 7-8.

1938 The Canadian Manufacturers Association: Its Economic and Social Implications. In H.A. Innis (Ed.), *Essays in Political Economy* (pp. 75-84). Toronto: University of Toronto Press.

1938 Economic Organization; Canadian National Settlement and Imperial Settlement; Opinions and Attitudes in English-speaking Quebec. In H.A. Innis (Ed.), *Canada and Her Great Neighbor* (chapters 9, 10, 17). Toronto: Ryerson Press.

1938 The Canadian Manufacturers' Association and the Tariff: A political Pressure Group. *Canadian Journal of Economics and Political Science*, 4, pp. 505-23.

1939 The Canadian Manufacturers' Association and the Tariff. *Canadian Journal of Economics and Political Science*, 5, pp. 19-39.

1939 Sociology and Canadian Social History. *Canadian Journal of Economics and Political Science*, 5, pp. 348-57.

1940 Economic Expansion and the Moral Order. *Canadian Journal of Economics and Political Science*, 6, pp. 203-25.

1944 Religious Organization and the Rise of the Canadian Nation. *Report of the Canadian Historical Association*, pp. 89-97.

1944 The social development of Canada and the American Continental System. *Culture*, 5, pp. 132-43.

1945 The Religious Sect in Canadian Politics. *American Journal of Sociology*, 51, pp. 207-16.

1946 The Religious Sect in Canadian Economic Development. *Canadian Journal of Economics and Political Science*, 12, pp. 439-53.

1947 The Religious Factor in Canadian Economic Development. *Tasks of Economic History* (supplement to the *Journal of Economic History*), 7, pp. 89-103.

1950 The Canadian Community. In G.W. Brown (Ed.), *Canada*. Berkeley: University of California Press. pp. 375-98.

1951 Religion and Economic Backward areas. *American Economic Review: Papers and Proceedings of the American Economic Association*, 41, pp. 258-65.

1951 Social Sciences. In *Royal Commission Studies: A Selection of Essays Prepared for the Royal Commission on National Development in the Arts, Letters and Sciences*. Ottawa: King's Printer (with B.S. Kierstead).

1954 The Frontier and Democratic Theory. *Transactions of the Royal Society of Canada*, series 3, 48, pp. 65-75.

1956 Education and Social Change in Canada. *Transactions of the Third World Congress of Sociology*, 5, pp. 64-70.

1958 The Support of Social Science Research in Canada. *Canadian Journal of Economics and Political Science*, 21, 141-51.

1959 Sociology, History and the Problem of Social Change. *Canadian Journal of Economics and Political Science*, 25, pp. 389-400.

1963 The Society of Suburbia. In William Peterson and David Matza (Eds.), *Social Controversy*. Belmont: Wadsworth. pp. 304-15.

1963 Group Interests in Canadian Politics. In J.H. Aitchison, (Ed.), *The Political Process in Canada*. Toronto: University of Toronto Press. pp. 64-78.

1964 Canada and Her Great Neighbour. *Canadian Review of Sociology and Anthropology*, 1, pp. 93-201.

1965 Canada and the American Value System. In *La Dualité canadienne a l'heure des Etats Unis*. Quebec: Les Presses de L'université Laval. pp. 93-102.

1967 Higher Education and the New Men of Power in Society. *Journal of Education Thought*, 1, pp. 77-87.

1970 Movements of Protest in Post-War Canadian Society. *Transactions of the Royal Society of Canada*, series 4, 8, pp. 223-37.

1971 The Position of the French-speaking population in the Northern Industrial Community. In Richard J. Ossenberg (Ed.), *Canadian*

Society: Pluralism, Change, and Conflict. Scarborough: Prentice-Hall. pp. 62-85.

1972 Rural Migration and Patterns of Urban Growth. In Edward B. Harvey (Ed.), *Perspectives on Modernization*. Toronto: University of Toronto Press. pp. 96-105.

1973 The American Takeover of Canadian Sociology: Myth or Reality. *Dalhousie Review*, 53, pp. 205-18.

1975 Sociology in Canada: an Historical Overview. *Canadian Journal of Sociology*, 1, pp. 225-34.

1975 The Post Second World War Canadian Society. *Canadian Review of Sociology and Anthropology*, 12, pp. 25-32.

1976 The Attack on the Authority Structure of Canadian Society. *Transactions of the Royal Society of Canada*, series 4, 14, pp. 3-15.

1979 The Changing Image of Sociology in English-speaking Canada. *Canadian Journal of Sociology*, 4, pp. 393-403.

Social Credit in Alberta: its background and development.

A series of Studies directed and edited by S.D. Clark and published by the University of Toronto Press. Forewords to each volume were written by Clark.

1950	W. L. Morton	*The Progressive Party in Canada*
1950	D. C. Masters	*The Winnipeg Strike*
1951	Jean Burnet	*Next-Year Country*
1953	C. B. MacPherson	*Democracy in Alberta*
1954	J. R. Mallory	*Social Credit and the Federal Power in Canada*
1955	W. E. Mann	*Sect, Cult and Church in Alberta*
1957	V. E. Fowke	*The National Policy and the Wheat Economy*
1959	L. G. Thomas	*The Liberal Party in Alberta*
1959	John A. Irving	*The Social Credit Movement in Alberta*
1959	S. D. Clark	*Movements of Political Protest in Canada*